The Eighteen-Seventies

The Eighteen-Seventies

Essays by Fellows of the Royal Society of Literature

Edited by

HARLEY GRANVILLE-BARKER

Cambridge

at the University Press

1929

CAMBRIDGE UNIVERSITY PRESS
Cambridge, New York, Melbourne, Madrid, Cape Town,
Singapore, São Paulo, Delhi, Mexico City

Cambridge University Press
The Edinburgh Building, Cambridge CB2 8RU, UK

Published in the United States of America by Cambridge University Press, New York

www.cambridge.org
Information on this title: www.cambridge.org/9781107618152

First published 1929
First paperback edition 2013

A catalogue record for this publication is available from the British Library

ISBN 978-1-107-61815-2 Paperback

Contents

Preface

THESE papers upon the Eighteen-seventies were written for—and mostly read to—the Royal Society of Literature. With the fixing of the subject and the parcelling of its field collaboration ended. There has been little trespassing; and if, now and then, the temptation to stray has been stronger, neither life nor letters, as Dr Macan reminds us, will 'arrange themselves in neat packets of ten years for our convenience'.

Our immediate concern, of course, is with letters, less directly with life; but the time is close at hand when the life of the Eighteen-seventies will be found in its letters and nowhere else at all. So, if anyone should ask 'Why the Eighteen-seventies?' here is one answer: it is a period that is just about to become historical. It is, indeed, entering the orbit of the romantic. Those of us who were born in it found our elders still clothing their romance in powder and patches and brocade. We were soon for the bucks and buckskins of the Regency, high waists and sandals. Books of Beauty, John Leech and his crinolines, whiskers and peg-top trousers, looked the height of the absurd. We have lived to see them grow in grace again; a little more, and the crinolette and that 'sort of tongs' of Mr de la Mare's recollection (and mine) 'which were worn dangling from the hips to keep the train from out of the dust' will take their place, re-created by the poet and romancer, among the glamorous beauties of the past. At this moment, then, the Eighteen-seventies are a period 'just remote and just retrievable enough to be singularly beguiling'. I quote Mr de la Mare again; it is an editor's privilege to pillage his contributors for phrases. In literary reputation, moreover, they are

decidedly down on their luck. It seemed worth while
before they became subject to the more absolute inquisition
of history to take a casual, friendly glance at them.

It is no better than a glance, in no sense a digest. There
is no passing of judgment. But by good luck and de-
serving—more precisely perhaps, by the generous sense
of duty of some of its Fellows, stealing time and energy
from their own literary affairs—the Society has had
at command what is rather a full battery of glances,
fired from varying points of vantage. One main difference
of position will be noted. Some of us write out of recollection: to some the Eighteen-seventies are but history
already. If there is a hint of attack and defence, if
a slight deflection of the firing would make our area a
battleground—well, the book will not be the less instructive
or entertaining for that.

There is better reason for leading off with a paper on
Lord Houghton than the fact—though in academic
courtesy this would be reason enough—that in it the
Society's president writes of his father. For, as Lord
Crewe tells us, 'the tale of his friendly acquaintance
among men of letters up to 1870 would be little more
than an exhaustive catalogue of the workers in that field'.
It is surprising indeed that he was never president himself.
He so typified the relation between Letters and Affairs
which is England's nearest practical approach to the
recognition of literature as a public service. Now, whether
this is a satisfactory one is a large question, far too large
for present discussion. That it is better than none will
hardly be disputed; though Lord Houghton himself—
if ever a little chafed by that 'alarming reputation for
benevolence to aspiring writers'—might excusably have
protested that a human link is, after all, only human.
He was a patron of letters, and sympathetic and dis-
cerning as perhaps only one who was also a man of letters

could be. In this he inherited a tradition, under which, from the time of the Tudors and yet more remotely, English literature had subsisted—if it had sometimes starved. A tradition changed and dying in his day: it may almost be said to have died with him. 'Patronage' has a less pleasing sound to modern ears: we relegate it to charity concerts and country bazaars. But condescension is still the dictionary's last gloss upon the word, and by the authentic thing itself much good work in the past has been, in a proper sense, protected and supported. There was, we may be sure, no condescension, nothing of the Chesterfield in Houghton, nor did Nineteenth-century authorship depend upon dedication and subscription. What he did, beside his many acts of personal kindness, was to help form public opinion. That was a thing worth doing. Sir Edmund Gosse cites instance after instance of such watchful interest in Swinburne. He did not, be it noted, set out to make his young poet a best-seller; the sales of *Poems and Ballads* to date would probably, for that matter, leave a best-selling publisher of today bewailing. But he could see to it—and he did—that educated public opinion recognised and acknowledged the significance of the new thing. Swinburne's books might sell or not sell, be praised or abused; but, with Houghton for sponsor, he could not be neglected.

An easier task no doubt—a more grateful one certainly —so to dominate on occasion the Victorian forum, than single-handed to set about inoculating the mob-mind of to-day. How that has to be done is a study for the curious cynic, though a part of the process is visible enough in the costly columns of advertisement which support (in more than one sense) a newspaper's 'literary' pages and leaves mere criticism to show like chinks of faint light in between. Good work, as well as bad, it may be owned, can be planted on the public in this costermonger fashion.

It very often is; and it will be for as long—just as long—as
the business proposition pays. But for how long will that
be? If good and bad alike must be brought into such competition and given the same currency—or *none*—it may
well be that a Gresham's Law for literature will begin to
function, and the bad money drive out the good. It is
soon to say. The method of the literary world, in which
Lord Houghton was ascendant, had changed but slowly
till, our pre-war yesterday past, it took on of a sudden its
present hectic complexion. The business man himself
cannot yet have counted the final business cost. What
the cost to our more sober-sided literature may be, that
which is, after all, the staple of our intellectual credit, it
well becomes a Royal Society of Literature to ask. The
patron of letters was humanly partial, no doubt, and
made his mistakes of omission and commission alike; but
at his best he did discriminatingly and disinterestedly do
something for literature which cut-throat business competition and its less overt accompaniments can hardly be
trusted to do. If we have now finally lost him, what is
to take his place?

Yet, spite of all changes, the relation to Affairs which
gives, for good or ill—in the main, surely, for good, since
it is of the English nature of things—its peculiar prag-
matic tinge to our maturer literature, does essentially
endure; is here exemplified indeed, in Lord Crewe himself
and his presidency. And one would suppose it a unique
scope of family experience: a Robert Milnes who in 1809
refuses a seat in the Cabinet as Chancellor of the Exchequer, an office which is not then (Oh, happy England!)
'of quite the first rank'; his son elected to Queen Victoria's
first parliament; his grandson, a Liberal statesman in 1929.
The son's political career was, we are told, 'disappointing
to himself'. But he was, without doubt, one of the chief
architects of English Liberalism, his share in the work the

cultivating of an attitude of mind, more tolerant and more sensitive, perhaps, than party politics could then easily accommodate. And one imagines him generously satisfied to see—could he have seen—in conditions he had helped to create, his ambitions fulfilled by *his* son.

The editor of this sort of book is supposed to do no more than pay passing—and quite superfluous—compliments to the contributors. The difficult thing is to avoid that intolerable gesture of the pat on the back; the more intolerable, if, as in instances here, one must stand upon tiptoe to administer it. I venture, then, no more than a most modest Thank you to Dr Saintsbury for his tribute to Andrew Lang, that writer from a full mind, written for us from a mind as full. But I cull from it a summing up of Lang's style which any young aspirant might do well to pin for a motto over his desk ' ... pervasive, but not obtrusive; varied but not superficial; facile to a wonderful degree, but never trivial or trumpery'. And again, one feels the praise come boomeranging back to its author.

Of Sir Arthur Pinero, I will only say that I am tempted, behind his back, to alter the title of his paper to 'The Theatre as I found it'. He does needed justice to T. W. Robertson. And if the truth of his saying that 'in dealing with the stage you must judge an author's work in relation to the age in which he wrote', is, it may be claimed, as applicable to other arts, no one who has never been tangled in its machinery can know *how* true it is of the Theatre! Therefore, when we consider what, spite of generous excuses, the theatre really was in those 'seventies my temptation is to prepare the way for a companion paper, should this series extend, say, to the Nineties, to be written by a younger dramatist (there are many who could gratefully write it) with the title 'The Theatre that Arthur Pinero did most to make'. For it

would be a far more inspiriting picture. My own paper
by the way, the present companion to his, could as well
be called 'The Theatre of the 'seventies as it might have
been'.

Mr Walpole and Mr de la Mare have an easier time
with the novelists, one notices, than do Miss Sackville-
West and Mr Drinkwater with their poets. Mr Walpole's
generalisation that in the extreme *Englishness* of the
English novel lay its primitive store of strength which
sophistication must sap (for a time, will he let us interject?)
and his sympathetic view of the 'seventies as a period of
mediocre achievement, truly, but of the struggle towards
a lost honesty in the picturing of life—this surely is a
far-reaching truth, and other things than novel-writing
come under its searchlight. But English life, as lived
beyond the borders of Bloomsbury, and the English
character have changed less than some modern novels
(though not Mr Walpole's own) would lead us to suppose.
I fancy that Mr James Payn's hero with his 'I am none
of your dreamy ones, thank God! It is eleven o'clock.
There are one, two, three good hours of fishing before me;
and then, ah, then, for my sweet Mildred!' is still a fairly
common object of the countryside, though he may not
phrase his feelings quite so elegantly (he would if he
could, however); and his sweet Mildred, truly, is apt,
nowadays, to have gone fishing too.

Mr Walpole and Mr Drinkwater have a fortuitous and
stimulating difference of opinion upon the possibility of
discussing literature by periods; but it turns out, as so
often happens, not to be a real difference after all.
Miss Sackville-West and Mr de la Mare come to an equally
fortuitous agreement upon the sound principle that self-
consciousness is fatal to creative art, and that this
weighed heavily and sometimes disastrously upon the
women writers of the 'seventies. The two papers do indeed

complement each other very admirably. I thank Miss Sackville-West for that phrase 'the high Victorian standard of bashfulness' and Mr Drinkwater for his test of the minor poet; one found just destitute of saving original grace, his best hardly ever failing to remind us of the men that have done better. And for all that their field looked barren, they do find some flowers in it. One knew that in many ways the 'seventies must prove a barren field. It was stubble time and seed time. But one of our tasks was to search for the flowers, however few.

Mr de la Mare's field on the other hand, proved to be a perfect jungle, and his paper set me thinking about all the other papers we might have had; upon Punch in the 'seventies; upon the songs of the Seventies (if he pursues his investigations I commend to his notice the works, in this kind, of Virginia Gabriel, particularly 'Weary, so weary of waiting, longing to lie down and die!' with, for an antidote, the comic drawing-room ballad—an extinct species—'There were three old maids of Lee'); the domestic culture of the 'seventies, and what not! He does most usefully point out to the future social historian that there will be no authority upon the then appearance of the homes of England, stately and other, to compare with the woman novelist. In such matters men are not to be trusted.

Dr Boas seems to have had the most straightforward task; though an admirably ordered result is no sure sign of it. But he finds his 'seventies undoubtedly robust in critical, whatever they may have been in creative power. It is to be remarked that he lays stress—and with good reason, surely—upon Pater's influence, which Dr Macan, in his re-integrating of Pater's university, can dismiss in a sentence; an instance of our fruitful diversity of outlook.

With the two authentic pictures of the Oxford and
Cambridge of the decade we end—end with them because
they make the spring board for the decades to come, the
five of them, now nearly past. These are perhaps, then,
if we examine them closely, the most significant pictures
of all. For out of that Oxford, looking 'mild and
modest and mid-Victorian beside the Oxford of today,
but...alive and moving', out of that Cambridge, which
saw the making of Newnham and Girton, most that still
steadies, if it with ever greater difficulty dominates, the
immediate intellectual life of England has come. Mild
they may have looked, both of them; but from Dr
Macan's and Mr Heitland's mellow pages come echoes of
conflict enough. It was a time (for all kindliness of
reminiscence) of hard struggle, that is clear, for men
there, whose eyes were, as they should have been, on the
future rather than the past; '...a period', says Dr Macan,
'of disappointment, unsatisfied demands, apparent reaction, yet with a touch of Spring in the air'. Thanks
then, to the men, in the persons of these honoured
survivors of them, who endured the disappointments,
refused to be satisfied, withstood the reaction, and had
the faith that could discern the 'touch of Spring in
the air'.

There will never be a time when Oxford and Cambridge
and England have not need of their like. By a wider
view than we can take from the top of the pile—though
it makes a high enough pile, heaven knows!—of imaginative
and sometimes unimaginative literature, the Englands of
the Eighteen-seventies and Nineteen-twenties may have
more in common than the change in the noise of their
life lets us suppose. And, to pillage Mr de la Mare once
more, 'The very years we now so actively occupy will
soon be packed up in an old satchel....' But, no! There
are limits to an editor's privilege.   H. G-B.

Lord Houghton and his Circle

By The Marquess of Crewe

RICHARD MONCKTON MILNES was born in the year 1809, distinguished by the entry into this troublesome world of the more famous figures of Gladstone, Tennyson, and Lincoln. He received his first name from a custom which had obtained in his family for several generations of using it alternately with Robert for the eldest son. The second name was that of his mother's family, she being the daughter of the fourth Viscount Galway. The family was prosperous, owning landed properties in Yorkshire and elsewhere, some by direct descent, others through fortunate marriages; and they also enjoyed wealth made in more than one business. So that when Richard Milnes was born, his father, Robert Milnes, might have seemed one of the spoilt children of fortune. He had left Cambridge with a reputation for extraordinary ability, as is clear from the allusions to him in the letters of his younger contemporary, Lord Byron, and from other sources; and, having succeeded his father just as he came of age, he entered Parliament a year later. In 1807 he created a sensation of a moment by his speech in defence of the Portland administration, in its struggles with the disastrous events of that spring in the theatre of war. Two years later, Spencer Perceval offered him a seat in the Cabinet, either as Chancellor of the Exchequer or as Secretary at War. Neither of these offices was then of quite the first rank, but the compliment to a man of twenty-five was no slight one. His wife noted in her journal that he immediately said: 'Oh, no, I will not accept either; with my temperament, I should be dead in a year'. This prompt refusal remained a puzzle to everybody. Robert Milnes was a close follower of Canning, and in general sympathy with the Government. He was a scholar, and a man of very wide reading, besides enjoying cheerful society and being a brilliant horseman and shot, so that neither diffidence nor health could have been the real obstacle, and it can only be surmised that he was deterred by the restrictions of office, and by the dread of having to give up country life for the greater part of the year. When he died, just fifty years later, Lord Palmerston wrote to remind his son that it was Robert Milnes's refusal of office which had first opened the political gateway to himself in the post of Secretary at War.

Accordingly, Richard Milnes grew up as the son of a country gentleman, not of a Minister, though his father remained in Parliament for a number of years. An illness prevented his being educated at Harrow, and he spent his time with a tutor, mainly in the country, but with a little travel to Scotland and elsewhere, until he went to Cambridge in 1827. It is never easy to estimate the importance of intellectual groups as they flourish at different periods, and the Cambridge set of that day grew up into the mid-Victorians, whose aims and achievements it is now the fashion to belittle; but, to us of the generation who succeeded them, it certainly seems that a University at which Whewell and Thirlwall were College tutors, and where Charles Buller, John Sterling, R. C. Trench, Julius Hare, Cavendish (the seventh Duke of Devonshire), and Stafford O'Brien were undergraduates, shortly followed by the three Tennyson brothers, Thackeray, Ralph Bernal Osborne, G. S. Venables, the Lushington brothers, James Spedding, Arthur Hallam, and W. H. Thompson, presents such a constellation of names as it would be difficult to equal. Most of these were at Trinity, and it would be possible to mention a good many others who made their mark in one direction or another. I have heard my father say that Arthur Hallam stood easily first of them all. With one or two exceptions, all those of whom he, in later life, delighted to speak as his 'playfellows' are to be found in this list. He thoroughly enjoyed Cambridge, and he worked hard, though on too wide a field to admit of distinction in a tripos, even if his life-long aversion from mathematics had not tended to bar that particular door. But he won some prizes, took part in the theatricals which were then becoming popular, spoke at the Union (though expressing doubts whether this might not be in reality damaging to the correct parliamentary manner), and entertained his friends largely. He headed, with Arthur Hallam and that most brilliant of failures, Thomas Sunderland, the famous expedition to the Oxford Union, in which Cambridge argued the claims of Shelley against Oxford's championship of Byron. In his letter to his mother, describing the Oxford hosts, of whom Manning was one, he said: 'The man that *took* me most was the youngest Gladstone of Liverpool, I am sure a very superior person'. The last phrase was used, one may be certain, without the ironical suggestion that later attached to it at Oxford.

Richard Milnes was no athlete, and in those days organised games and sports only attracted real devotees; but his nerve was good, and he distinguished himself by the then uncommon feat of a balloon ascent, from which he landed miles off at Castle Ashby. His *exeat* was couched in the form 'Ascendat R. Milnes'.

It is clear from the correspondence of that period that he had expected to pass straight from the University into Parliament. But for the time being these hopes were dashed to the ground by a crisis in the family affairs. His father, though at one time he spent lavishly, was too shrewd to get into difficulties, but his uncle, Rodes Milnes, was of another type. Better endowed than most younger sons, and enjoying a post which was little more than a sinecure, he was an inveterate gambler, and a supporter of the famous racing-stable of John Scott. After a long course of varying successes and failures, the latter, as usually happens, began to predominate, and brought about a financial crash. The elder Mrs Milnes, who had been a considerable heiress, was still alive, and she and Robert Milnes came to the rescue. He, for his part, to sustain the honour of the family, paid large sums for which he was in no way responsible. Everything was shut up for a time, and the family went to live abroad before 1830, so that the expectation which Richard Milnes had entertained of standing for Pontefract in that year could not be gratified, though possibly less for financial reasons than from his father's doubts at the moment of his aptitude for political life.

For some years, therefore, he spent a great part of his time abroad. His family lived chiefly at Milan and Venice. But he also was in London from time to time, and visited Ireland and Scotland. In 1832 he made a five months' tour in Greece, which in those days meant roughing it considerably, and the eventual outcome was his first volume of poetry, the *Memorials of a Tour in Greece*, published in 1834.

In 1835 his family resumed life in England, their affairs being tolerably re-established, though on a somewhat reduced scale. And two years later Richard Milnes entered the House of Commons for Pontefract. He sat as a Conservative, though in some ways but loosely attached to the party. Through the earlier years of the century his father had been in favour of Emancipation, and of a moderate measure of Reform giving representation to the larger towns. But his real devotion was to the landed interest, and conceiving this to be imperilled by the measure of 1832, he described himself as belonging to the Tory party; and his son, who had always disliked Parliamentary Reform, did the same. The conservatism of each was of a quite different type. The father, though of an age when his powers might have been at their fullest maturity, was in fact a belated survival of the eighteenth century. He had sat in the House of Commons with Pitt and with Fox, and he had seen the statesmen but a decade older than himself, such as Canning, Castlereagh, and Liverpool, rise to eminence and pass away one by one. He and his son were united by real affection, and by admiration for each other's gifts, but two more incompatible people could scarcely have been found, and though there was never any breach between them, there was very little genuine understanding.

The son, as it happened, through the circumstances of his life, had never had to undergo any course of discipline. He had not been at a public school, University life was in the main untrammelled, and during the years spent abroad, he had been very much his own master. And criticism, however pointed, does not take the place of discipline. It says much for the inherent sweetness of Richard Milnes's nature that he did not resent the cynical attitude sometimes taken by his father, but his entry into London life would have been easier, and he might have avoided some mistakes if he had had to spend, so to speak, more hours on the drill ground and fewer in the orderly room.

This paper is not a biography, and I cannot attempt to sketch, except in the briefest outline, my father's political career up to the 'seventies. He was in the main a follower of Sir Robert Peel, and supported his fiscal policy in 1846.

But here, for the first time in public, he found himself in friendly opposition to his father, who emerged from his retirement in order to head in Yorkshire the Protectionist opposition to Peel. Before this crisis my father had carried on a political flirtation with 'Young England', though he was never actually a member of that remarkable forerunner of the Fourth Party of later days. After the fall of Sir Robert Peel, he did not join the brilliant little band of Peelites, but declared himself a Liberal and left the Carlton Club, though remaining a man of the Centre rather than of the Left. Later he regarded himself as a follower of Lord Palmerston rather than of any other leader, though I remember hearing him say that the statesman with whom he found himself in the fullest sympathy was Lord Aberdeen. Of the two great figures who dominated in Parliament the later years of his life I will say a word in a moment, but it is necessary to mention the two fields in which he principally exercised himself—that of foreign politics, and that of penal reform at home. On the first ground he was extremely well equipped by his knowledge of foreign countries, and by the ease with which he penetrated into political circles abroad. He had close personal friends in France, especially Tocqueville, Guizot, and Montalembert; his principal tie with Germany was his close friendship with the family of Baron von Bunsen; curiously enough, with all his knowledge of Italy, he had fewer friends and correspondents in the Italian political world. He wrote frequently, in the monthly *Reviews* and elsewhere, on foreign affairs, and in 1849 he published, in the form of an open letter to Lord Lansdowne, a remarkable pamphlet on *The Events of* 1848. This created some sensation, which was not diminished by the appearance, in the *Morning Chronicle,* of an article not merely assailing the opinions expressed in the pamphlet, but filled with coarse

personal abuse of the writer. This was the work of George
Smythe, one of the heroes of 'Young England', and the
original of Coningsby. He had been Peel's Under-
Secretary for Foreign Affairs in 1845, and was the person
my father most disliked, on various grounds. He therefore—rather surprisingly in view of the date—challenged
George Smythe to a duel. The affair was patched up,
though the parties never spoke again; and my father
always said that his second and great friend, the brilliant
writer Eliot Warburton, could not quite conceal his disappointment at the tame ending of the business—as
might have been expected from a loyal son of Co. Galway.
Two years later George Smythe had to fight a duel over
an election squabble, the last, I believe, that was fought
in England. And, almost at the same time, Eliot Warburton met a heroic death on the deck of the burning ship
Amazon.

Robert Milnes died in 1858. He had, some years before,
refused a peerage offered him through Lord Palmerston,
and the honour was conferred on his son in 1863. The
latter took kindly to the atmosphere of the House of
Lords, and intervened in the debates from time to time.
He spoke out stoutly on the Federal side in the American
Civil War, partly from holding a real conviction on the
rights of the dispute, and partly from being more and
more closely attracted to those elements in English public
life which were conspicuous in sympathy for the Northern
cause. But both before and after he went to the House of
Lords, his interest in foreign affairs was at least equalled
by his keen desire to help in reforming the treatment of
criminals at home. The great social reforms associated
with the name of Lord Shaftesbury had his full sympathy,
though he was never specially prominent in advocating
them. But he was the first to force through Parliament a measure establishing reformatories for youthful

offenders, and he became President of the original institution at Redhill. I can testify from my own recollection that, in the midst of his thousand occupations, the question of the treatment of young criminals was the one nearest to his heart. He was also active in the movement for abolishing public executions. In Thackeray's account of his expedition to watch the crowd at the execution of Courvoisier in 1840, X., the friend who drove him to the scene, was my father.

He was never attached to the Court in any capacity, but received much consideration from the Prince Consort. And his early knowledge of the German character enabled him to discern the fine and sympathetic qualities which underlay the rigid crust of education and caste, below which contemporary British society was quite unable to penetrate. It was, perhaps, more surprising that my father should have been something of a favourite with the Duke of Wellington. The great man, as we know, once wrote that he had 'been much exposed to authors', and he regarded them with a terror never inspired by the batteries of the enemy. But he appreciated the good temper, the varied knowledge, and the many-sided humour of the younger man, who should here receive as much credit, though of an entirely different kind, as he does for securing the approbation of Thomas Carlyle. He held in the highest esteem the abilities of his contemporary, the second Duke of Wellington, saying, 'He would have been one of the greatest men in England if he had not been so completely overshadowed by his father'.

The twenty-six years of Richard Milnes's membership of the House of Commons, and the twenty-two during which he sat in the House of Lords, were crowded with occasions of interest, though it would not be true to regard him as an important figure in either House. It was certainly a disappointment to him that in the 'forties he was never offered office. He considered, surely not without reason, that he was well equipped for the Under-Secretaryship at the Foreign Office in particular. He had at that time a reputation for eccentricity which was a little puzzling to those who only knew him in later life, though it is true that the passage of years sometimes makes mellow personal idiosyncrasies which are startling in a younger man. His great friend, Charles Buller, once said to him: 'I often think how puzzled your Maker must be to account for your conduct'; and political leaders may have thought it dangerous to entrust a responsible post to him with the uneasy feeling of never quite knowing what he would do next. His sub-conscious knowledge of this perhaps reacted unfortunately in one direction. As his friend Venables observed in his affectionate obituary notice, 'He failed as a Parliamentary orator through the adoption of a formal and almost pompous manner which was wholly foreign to his genius and disposition. One of the most humorous of companions, he reserved for the House of Commons a curiously artificial gravity'. In 1855 he was offered a Lordship of the Treasury, but felt that it was too late to make a beginning.

Richard Milnes was closely intimate throughout his life with the two great political rivals who were his contemporaries. He first knew Disraeli well in the cheerful Bohemian atmosphere of Gore House, and was sitting beside him at the moment of the famous maiden speech that ended with the phrase, 'The time will come when you will hear me'—'Yes, old fellow, it will', said his friend. And the intimacy continued over years, with possibly a slight tinge of jealousy on each side—though Disraeli paid many visits to Fryston and Bawtry, the two Milnes houses in Yorkshire, and developed a special cult for his friend's father, whom he apparently regarded as the ideal country squire. Later on a breach occurred which has never been completely explained. Milnes criticised most of the novels in quarterly *Reviews*, not disparagingly, though not always with unmixed admiration. In the Corn Law controversy they took different sides, but never came specially into collision. Disraeli's attachment to George Smythe might be taken to account for a quarrel, but Smythe and Disraeli had themselves parted company when the former joined Peel's Government. In *Tancred* Disraeli had drawn his amusing portrait of Mr Vavasour, which was certainly not ill-natured, though a shade patronising; in 1852, when Disraeli perpetrated his famous *gaffe* of borrowing from an old address of M. Thiers for his speech on the Duke of Wellington, my father put matters right with *The Times*, and Disraeli wrote thanking him—'I really think you have the best disposition in the world'. It was a surprise, therefore, to find in Lord Beaconsfield's *Life* that in the 'sixties, among various memoranda describing his acquaintance, he wrote one about Richard Milnes which can only be described as venomous. I am sure that my father never realised the extent of his former friend's distaste, and so far as it troubled him at all, accounted for it by the critical tone of his own review of *Lothair*. When they met, as I once or twice remember their doing, their relations were apparently quite friendly, though in no way cordial.

With Mr Gladstone it was quite another story. Here there was real personal attachment, though I do not think that my father as a rule shared Gladstone's political enthusiasms, or sympathised with the vigour with which conviction made him drive home any argument in support of his case at a given moment. 'Gladstone's method of impartiality', he once said, 'is being furiously earnest on both sides of a question.' But his admiration for that wonderful genius and that lofty character was, in fact, unbounded. He enjoyed from time to time writing critical notes to his friend on some issue of policy, and he always received at once reasoned replies, with the detailed arguments needed in support of the particular case. My father's visits to Hawarden always gave him keen pleasure, which, I believe, his hosts entirely shared.

Such, in brief outline, is the history of my father's activities in public life. Disappointing to himself, as I very well know, but always inspired by a deep humanity, and not altogether unfruitful in themselves.

Though he would have enjoyed success in political life more than anything else, yet it was in the world of letters that he was most thoroughly at home, and his real intimacy was rather with writers and thinkers than with statesmen who might be neither. Certainly the most remarkable of these friendships was that with Carlyle. It was an attraction of opposites, for on the surface two men more utterly unlike could hardly have been found. It was Charles Buller who brought them together, in 1836, when the *French Revolution* was being written. A little later Carlyle paid several visits to Fryston, and a frequent though irregular correspondence passed between the two. They often argued, but, in the well-known phrase which Carlyle used in another connection, '*except* in opinion not disagreeing'; and in the words of Venables written after my father's death: 'His cheerful paradoxes often dissipated the moral indignation of Carlyle'. Both must have met frequently at The Grange, and, as the Milnes Notebooks show, he appreciated the charm and wit of Lady Ashburton as highly as did the philosopher himself, though, with his wider experience of *salons*, they may not have seemed to him so absolutely unique as they did to his friend. Altogether his relation with the Carlyles stood on a footing of its own.

Besides those on the Cambridge list who rose to distinction in the world of letters, Alfred Tennyson in particular, he was intimate with Thackeray and Dickens, while the tale of his friendly acquaintance among men of letters up to 1870 would be little more than an exhaustive catalogue of the workers in that field. Though he never had a specially full purse, even after his father's death, he helped many writers to the utmost of his means. And any of us who know something of the working of the Literary Fund, are aware how dire is sometimes the need of writers whose books are on every stall, and whose names are on every tongue. But he did much more than give. He took endless personal pains to get one man out of a scrape, or to find congenial work for another. In 1860 the young Scottish poet, David Gray—not a Keats or even a Chatterton, but a humbler counterpart of either —romantic and consumptive, with a real gift of song, came to London, and was saved from misery, though not from the inevitable death which claimed him within a year, by successive acts of thoughtful kindness. My father earned at last an alarming reputation for benevolence to aspiring writers, and his writing table was littered with appeals from all points of the compass. Such a correspondence produces but few David Grays, but the recipient of the letters showed a patience and humanity in examining the cases and giving a helping hand whenever possible, to which there cannot be many parallels. To quote once more the words of his friend Venables, ' If Wordsworth was right in defining the best operations of a good man's life as consisting of

> His little, nameless, unremembered acts
> Of kindness and of love,

Lord Houghton need not have feared comparison with the most pretentious philanthropist'.

I make no attempt to do more than enumerate my

father's writings up to the last quarter of the century, because this is no more a critical than it is a biographical essay.

Between 1834 and 1844 he published five volumes of poetry, that entitled *Palm Leaves* appearing in the last of these years. I especially note it, because though single pieces in some of the other volumes may appeal more strongly to a critic of to-day, if there is one, who does not regard all Victorian poetry as trash, yet to my mind, the fruit of his travels in Egypt and Syria fairly stands the test of time, and shows an insight into the Eastern mind which few later writers have attained. After this he produced but little verse, though one or two single pieces included in the collected edition issued in 1876 ought not to be forgotten. During the succeeding years he wrote a series of articles in the more important *Reviews*. He plunged into the Tractarian controversy with *One Tract More*, favourably mentioned in Newman's *Apologia*, followed in 1842 by a rather paradoxical brochure styled *Purity of Election*, and later by the *Letter on the Events of 1848*, of which I have already spoken. But he returned to the region of his earlier affections by the *Life of Keats*, published in 1848, the work which has been his best remembered book. It has, indeed, never been superseded, though it has been supplemented by later discoveries and comments illustrating the good taste of some and the bad taste of others.

I have mentioned a series of figures well known in politics and letters, but, naturally, some of my father's most intimate friends were not of this sort. A lifelong correspondent was Charles MacCarthy, first known as a young theological student at Rome, who abandoned Roman Orders for the British Civil Service, and ended as Governor of Ceylon. Another was William Watkiss Lloyd, a scholar of remarkable attainments in Greek archaeology, and also in Shakespearean lore; and a third was Sir James Colvile, distinguished as an Indian judge. A somewhat younger friend was Henry Bright, a Liverpool shipowner, one of the torchbearers of a tradition perhaps peculiar to this country, of combining, like Praed and Bagehot, business capacity with the love of letters. He was a close friend of Hawthorne, a regular contributor to the *Athenaeum*, and the author of that delightful little book *A Year in a Lancashire Garden*. The mass of letters that passed to and from these correspondents tells more of my father's life and personality than anything else. His later letters to his family were usually briefer, because his absences were not prolonged, and gout began to make writing inconvenient to him.

But it will not do to pass over the friendships with women, which filled an important place in his life—Florence Nightingale, whom in his younger days he had hoped to marry, but who was reserved for a greater destiny, and who maintained a close friendship with him and his wife; the successive hostesses of Holland House; the two Lady Ashburtons; Mrs Norton and her sisters; Lady Westmorland; Lady Palmerston; and, not least, the Miss Berrys, in honour of whom he wrote one of the best of his occasional poems. It is safe to say that the society in which these different luminaries shone was that in which he found perhaps his keenest enjoyment.

Such was the course of my father's life up to the age of sixty, though I have necessarily been guilty of some anticipation of dates. He continued to spend most of the winter at his country home at Fryston, where there was a perpetual flow of guests for long or short visits. It was in some ways a misfortune to him that he had no real taste for the country, or for country pursuits. He rode most days, whether in Yorkshire or in London, but, though his nerve was good, he was in no way an accomplished horseman; and a pronounced astigmatism made him abandon shooting in quite early days. He had no interest in gardening, and, though he farmed on a considerable scale until the disasters of the late 'seventies made a farm a ruinous possession, he never took the trouble to study agriculture or livestock. In the country, as in London, his interest was centred round human beings, and the books written by them, and about them. I hope some people still read *Piccadilly*—that engaging satire on life in the 'seventies, of which the earlier scenes are set at Fryston, where Laurence Oliphant, I remember, really did meet a distinguished Colonial Bishop, and an eminent Oriental of the highest reputation, of both of whom he presents a most comic travesty. Another visitor of those days was Swinburne, who had been a guest some time before *Atalanta* began to make him famous—his worship of Landor, whose friendship my father had long enjoyed, having brought the two together. I remember how my sisters and I, as children, were sometimes puzzled and sometimes attracted by the young poet, with his half-shy, half-boisterous manners, and his moments of inexplicable excitement. I remember, too, the figures of Anthony Trollope; Herbert Spencer (whom I had once heard Carlyle describe as 'that never-ending ass' when I went with my father to Cheyne Row); Sir William Stirling Maxwell and Julian Fane, two friends to whom my father was deeply attached; Dean Stanley and Lady Augusta, also close friends of my father and mother; Sir Francis Doyle, regarded almost in the light of a relation; Fawcett and Forster, the latter a frequent guest; and John Morley, just coming into notice as a journalist and writer.

The Franco-Prussian War, with which the decade opened, could not but absorb my father's interest. He had countless friends in France, but, though he had been intimate with the Emperor Napoleon III when he was an exile in England, his sense of public right, which, with all his tendency to make allowance for the follies and shortcomings of mankind, could assert itself firmly when a line had to be drawn, was outraged by the *coup d'état*, and he had barely seen its author except on official occasions in Paris. Beyond this, by a vein of sentimentality which ran through his complex character, he was attracted to the German nature, and to one type of German literature, rather than to the cleaner cut mentality of France. His sympathies, therefore, were drawn to the German side, at any rate in the earlier stages of the war, until he was moved by the privations of Paris, and the sufferings of some of his personal friends.

He maintained a fairly regular attendance at the House of Lords during this period, but had no excitement to match that which befell him just before it opened, when his intervention in favour of *Essays and Reviews* brought about the famous duel of words between Lord Westbury and Bishop Wilberforce. All this time he was one of the principal champions of the measure for permitting marriage with a deceased wife's sister, and when, years after his death, the law was changed, his devotion to the cause was not forgotten.

As the years passed, he found composition less easy, apart from the physical difficulty of holding a pen, and dictation never came naturally to him. More than thirty years before, Carlyle, enthusiastically praising my father's article on Emerson in the *Westminster Review*, had added, 'You will write a book one day which we shall all like, in prose it shall be, if I may vote. A novel, an emblematic picture of English society as it is? Done in prose with the spirit of a poet, what a book were that!' His family and many of his friends had long expressed a similar wish, feeling that in some respects he possessed a better

balanced aptitude for depicting social life in England than
Disraeli or Bulwer Lytton, than Thackeray or Trollope,
however far he might fall behind any one of them in
particular gifts as a writer. But this book was never to
be written. In 1873 he brought out a volume of biographical sketches under the rather cumbrous title of
Personal Monographs. It was always hoped that he
would write a volume of autobiographical reminiscences,
but he was content to reshape, mainly from articles
appearing in the quarterly *Reviews* many years before,
the portraits of some men and women he had known
intimately, and whose careers he admired. Those who
would still like to hear at first hand something of Sydney
Smith, Landor, and Harriet Lady Ashburton, to mention
but two or three, might do worse than spend an
hour over this volume. The bones of a book which he
might have built up into a fabric which would have been
sufficiently solid without being ponderous, exist in the
fifteen volumes of MS. commonplace books which he left.
They extend over a series of years, and are largely composed of extracts from books which attracted him at the
time of reading, interspersed with anecdotes, with some
short records of conversations, and with a limited number
of personal reflections. Some extracts from these books
are to be found as an appendix to Sir T. Wemyss Reid's
Life of their author.

In 1874 his home was broken up by the death of my
mother, after twenty-three years of the happiest companionship. Until her marriage, which was not in her
first youth, her parents having been dead for many
years, she lived with an aunt, partly in London, and
partly at Madeley, the Crewe family place in Stafford-
shire. It was an old-fashioned bringing up, chiefly in
what was left of the Whig world—of which Crewe Hall
had been one of the minor pivots early in the century—

together with the lettered society attached to that coterie. She was well read, being in particular a devoted student of Shakespeare, and the few living people who can remember her would testify to her personal charm. Leigh Hunt said of her that her smile was like a piece of good news, and after the marriage Disraeli wrote to her father-in-law an enthusiastic account of his first meeting with her. For a number of her last years she was the victim of a nervous illness, with which modern science might have been able to deal more effectively. Her most devoted husband, while trying every possible cure at foreign watering-places, was unable to conceive that any remedy could be equal to the agreeable society which she adorned when she was in good health, and could not always understand how much happier she would have been, left with her children, her garden, and her pony carriage, instead of receiving even the most delightful of house parties. When the end came, he felt that he had lost not only a loving wife, but the most appreciative and comprehending friend a man could have.

Less than two years later he made an expedition to Canada and the United States. He had many friends in the latter, and his sympathy with the Northern cause ensured a warm welcome from many outside the lettered circle to which most of them belonged. The journey afforded just the tonic which he needed after his trouble at home, and his health, in which recurring attacks of gout had made almost the only breach, stood the long journey well. A year later a fire at Fryston, by which a considerable part of the house was destroyed, and his beloved library received rough usage, though little was actually lost, broke another link in the chain of his existence. He was able to say that he had 'always liked keeping open house in one sense, and was now doing it in another'. But the shock was severe. Thinking more

of the future of others than of his own present, he set to
work at once on rebuilding and improvement. Thus the
'seventies closed for him. Like other landowners, he had
suffered severely from the agricultural depression which
marked their end. When the new decade opened, his
children soon married, and he spent a great deal of time
with his devoted sister, herself widowed, whose affection
had meant much to him throughout his life. Two of his
aunts, who had been more like elder sisters to him, and
had always spent some months of the year at Fryston,
still survived. So that, though much had been taken
from his home, something was still left. Nor did a younger
generation neglect him. The Prince of Wales greatly enjoyed his company, and he received much hospitality and
kindness from Lord and Lady Rosebery. Lord Rosebery's
gifts and tastes were specially congenial to him, and
having been closely intimate with several branches of the
Rothschilds, he was happy to continue the friendship
with a daughter of the house.

But the end was not very long delayed. In 1882, when
at Athens after a visit to his eldest daughter in Egypt,
he was prostrated by an attack of angina pectoris, which
passed off quickly, but was a warning which could not be
ignored. He spent most of his time in London, where
Lady Galway and he kept house together, and he was
able to carry on many of his usual activities, notably
speaking with much charm at celebrations in honour of
Coleridge, of Gray, and, last of all, of Wordsworth. His
cardiac trouble, as sometimes happens, afflicted him with
a certain physical restlessness, which made it difficult for
him to remain quietly in any one place, and led him to
undertake social and other engagements which made
almost painful calls on his strength and vitality. But there
was no restlessness or uneasiness in his mind. One day,
when still he had a year of life before him, he said, with

his usual smile, to Sir Wemyss Reid, who was visiting him at Fryston, 'I am going over to the majority, and, you know, I have always preferred the minority'. In Monsieur Henri de Régnier's little book of reminiscences and reflections he tells of a man-servant who, speaking of his employer's last illness, said: 'Monsieur le Duc a attendu la mort, comme sa voiture quand il l'avait commandée'. My father, showing the same placid spirit, had not to wait long before the carriage was announced. He went to Vichy with his sister in August, 1885, and having gone late to his room, after a day of pleasant conversations with French friends, he sank into a chair, and never recovered consciousness.

It is not at all easy for those who never knew him, and have not even read some of his familiar letters, to realise the sort of charm which he exercised on a vast number of people of the most varying degrees of culture and knowledge. To quote Venables once more, 'he was a fanfaron—not of vices, but of paradoxical fallacies which seldom deceived himself. Like other genuine humorists he had some mannerisms which irritated and misled strangers and dull observers. Dull humours took his off-hand utterances for his real opinions, and resented the intellectual vivacity which found it impossible to rest in commonplaces and truisms'. His friend Stirling Maxwell called him 'a bird of paradox', and it is impossible to delineate him in a few sentences without appearing to be paradoxical. To say that he was superficial, with the great mass of his knowledge of many subjects, would be ridiculous, yet, on the other hand, there was no subject of which his knowledge could be precisely called profound. He was fond of pleasure in various forms, and had no contempt for luxury, but he was quite happy to live very simply for long together, if there were compensation to be got in the way of interesting travel or intellectual converse. He had few personal extravagances, but he never could see why anybody should stint himself in the purchase of books—short of collecting Caxtons and Groliers—and he would always have thought it foolish not to travel to any part of the world that a man might wish to see. As I have observed, he had no taste whatever for country sports of any kind, but he could enjoy a modest gamble, and if he had had a larger command of ready money, and had not been haunted by the memory of his spendthrift uncle, he might have liked to have an interest in a racing-stable. But on one side of his character there were no contradictions. His tolerance, and his wish to see people happier, and his hatred for cruelty and harshness, never varied except to grow stronger as the years went on. If he had been more methodical and systematic he might have cut a finer figure in the world, and have occupied a larger niche in English history. He could hardly have enjoyed so many friendships, or have left behind him such a gracious memory.

Novelists of the 'Seventies

By Hugh Walpole

I cannot hope in the very short time at my disposal to give more than some fragmentary notes on this intricate and confused subject. That it *is* intricate and confused no one can possibly doubt, because these were the very years, from 1870 to 1880, when the English novel, having run a rather direct course for a considerable period, began suddenly to feel ashamed of its simplicities and show a rather touching desire to grow up and become a Man.

These ten years cover the most markedly transitional period of the English novel, and they show so curious a meeting of opposite waters, so violent a contrast of men, methods, ideas and morals that there has been no other confusion quite so great in all the history of English Letters. Consider for a moment some names and dates.

Between the years 1870 and 1872 Dickens died, a young architect called Thomas Hardy published his first novel *Desperate Remedies* and received neither cash nor credit for his pains, a young rebel in Edinburgh called Stevenson was sending essays to the English magazines and a novel called *The Adventures of Harry Richmond* appeared and created no stir at all.

At the other end of the ladder, in 1871, Thackeray and Dickens were dead but George Eliot was sixty-two years of age and published in 1870–71, as I think, her masterpiece *Middlemarch*, Disraeli was sixty-six and was to publish *Endymion* nine years later, Charles Kingsley was fifty-two, Henry Kingsley only forty-one, Sheridan Le

Fanu fifty-seven, Charles Lever was sixty-five, George Macdonald was forty-seven, Payn was forty-one, Charles Reade was fifty-seven, 'Mark Rutherford' was forty-two, Shorthouse was thirty-seven and Anthony Trollope was fifty-six.

Between the years 1872 and 1882 these works of fiction were published among many others: *The Coming Race* in 1871, *Erewhon* in 1872, *Far from the Madding Crowd* in 1874, *The Prime Minister* in 1876, *Travels with a Donkey* in 1879, *Endymion* in 1880, and *John Inglesant* in 1881.

Here then is the confusion, both of men and works out of which, if possible, some common principle, direction or inspiration has to be found.

Now in the first place it is my firm conviction that in studying the art of any country at any period it is quite absurd to look for any clear and uninterrupted line of progress. Art does not progress and its history must be always in the main the history of certain artists who have by the inspiration of their genius given an impetus, a twist, a fire to the artistic movements of their day. It is the critic's business to discover why the work of an artist has the colour, the shape, the influence that it has and he makes his discoveries by his study of the work of art itself, the personality and circumstances of the artist and the conditions of his time. These may indeed be platitudes, but it is curious and interesting to observe with what obstinate pertinacity the critic is forgetful of them.

In the history of no art is there any progress and most certainly not in the history of the English novel. Nor, let me add, is there retrogression either. When *Ulysses* looks in the face of *Tristram Shandy* does a blush rise on the cheek of either? Most certainly not. We cannot doubt but that Parson Sterne would be deeply intrigued by the discoveries, and most especially by the vocabulary of Mr James Joyce. What would Thackeray have to say to the author of *Orlando*? May we not be sure that the author of *Pendennis* would rejoice at the moral freedom of this year of 1928? he would not in these days be compelled to tell lies about Pendennis' little laundress even though Sir William Joynson Hicks were his Home Secretary.

On the other hand we may conceive that Walter Scott, studying the new books in Mr Wilson's handsome bookshop in Oxford Street would, in spite of his generous mind and noble ability to discover the best in everybody, wonder where his own genius of narrative and action had gone to. He would find, I fear, at this moment, not one single worthy example of that enthralling aspect of the novelist's art.

We are in fact allowed neither pessimism nor optimism. If, with Mr Guedalla and Mr Desmond McCarthy, we believe that the art of the novel is dying, it is only because our studies of the modern novel in England have been limited to a few altogether indifferent hours, our real interests being elsewhere. On the other hand the torrent of fiction that to-day deafens our ears and frightens our stability does, I must confess, make it difficult for us to believe in the survival of the fittest; at times even the most ardent novel reader among us must wish that the form had never been invented; it is only the novel writers who are never weary.

With our eyes on the 'seventies, however, looking as we must both back and forth, certain facts must be noticed. One is that, up to 1870, the English novel was the most English thing in England, another that it had been consistently regarded as a happy accident rather than an Art, and a third that it had in general grown so virtuous that it kept touch with real life only with great difficulty.

This *Englishness* of the English novel has not I think

been sufficiently emphasised by the historians of our
literature. It is an Englishness of background, of form
(or rather the lack of form) and above all of a kind of
creative zest, innocent, gay and physically rather boisterous. In the novels of Fielding, Scott, Thackeray, Dickens,
we are constantly aware of the physical condition of the
characters, and this physical condition is, even though
they are like Quilp or Barnes Newcome morally diseased
with sickly bodies, robust and healthy and humorous.
So unmorbid is the world of Fielding, Scott and Dickens
that sunlight seems to pierce into every nook and cranny.
The very weather plays a healthy part; in the novels of
Jane Austen for instance so soon as the day is unfair
everyone takes to the fireside; every page of those delightful works glows either with sunlight or firelight.

But the English atmosphere spreads farther. It isolates
these novels from the rest of the world. In Fielding's
stories Squire Western's scorn for the Hanoverian dynasty
seems to cover all the scene. English country, English
street scenes, English interiors are the only surroundings
for these intensely English characters.

The robustness of the atmosphere is also felt in the
many physical mishaps that occur to the characters.
Mr Pickwick's misadventures on the ice form a kind of
symbol of the moral jollity of this robust world. Food
and drink reach a sort of high ecstasy that no other
literature in the world can quite show. Even in the
'Horror School' Mrs Radcliffe and 'Monk' Lewis make
their horrors physical rather than moral or mental. Lewis
tries indeed to involve his readers in a simple sort of
morbidity but his black characters are so black and his
white so white that no one is taken in for a moment.

That the novel in England was not considered an Art
is another of its characteristics before 1870. Richardson
was the father-confessor of his readers, Fielding the jolly

companion, Scott the fireside story-teller, Thackeray the moral teacher, Dickens the exuberant improviser. Of them all only Jane Austen can seem to our time the deliberate artist and she was, it is clear from her words about the novel in *Northanger Abbey*, quite unselfconsciously so. No one, even Hazlitt, wrote about the novel as an Art. It was considered a pleasant minor occupation for self-indulgent persons who had not quite as much work as they ought to have.

The implications of this simple and natural innocency were many. In the first place there was no necessity for any kind of Form or Shape. Form for many of the mid-Victorian novelists indeed was forbidden by their manner of publication. What hope of technical Shape could you have when your novel appeared in shilling numbers month by month to be continued indefinitely until readers were weary? What Shape could you have when, like Dickens, you were concerned with perhaps the creation of four or five masterpieces at the same time? This manner of publication led also to a co-operation of reader and writer which is to-day alas unknown. It is true that a novelist of to-day may find his post loaded with letters informing him that the moon has risen at the wrong time or that his heroine's baby is eating bacon six months too early, but this is a co-operation *post hoc*. In one of Lady Ritchie's delightful prefaces to her father's works she describes how a young lady in the country, weary of Amelia and Dobbin, wrote to Thackeray requesting him to omit them for a number or two, and he was only too glad to do so, for was not the young lady in a manner writing his novel with him? I can only emphasise the sad change from then to now by asking you to allow your imagination to picture the indignation of a modern novelist requested by a reader to abandon his leading idea or alter his favourite grotesqueries! We are not, I fear, so humble as once we were. This absence of plan and excited mingling with eager readers produced beyond question a fine free ecstasy of creation. When the book might go as it pleased with nothing to check it, characters sprang up on every side and carried the writer along with them. No wonder we are told that Thackeray and Dickens laughed and cried with their creations, were grieved for days after they had killed one of them and attended, festooned with flowers, all the inevitable marriages. It is indeed one of the most serious questions that we have to ask as we watch the change in the character of the English novel, whether our increased sophistication has not largely killed our old creative force. It is a question that the 'seventies is, as a period, a little too early to answer, but the portents can be found there casting their shadows before them.

Secondly, there is the simplicity of moral psychology. In all the Victorian novels until at least George Eliot we have no kind of difficulty in distinguishing the sheep from the goats. If we are at all in doubt the illustrations, whether from Thackeray's own pencil or Cruikshank or 'Phiz,' will tell us, and, if after those, there be any question the *fate* of the characters is enough for us, the Victorian goat, however he may prosper, falling always into total ruin, the Victorian sheep, however he may suffer (and, shades of Paul Dombey and Little Nell, how he *does* suffer!) always, if death does not intervene, reaching the secure and eternally happy haven of matrimony.

This moral convention of the Victorian novel had, often enough, serious effects on the would-be artist. For Thackeray especially it was often disastrous. He knew so much more than he was allowed to say and, in a kind of violence of self-disgust, hurled cheap moralities at his audience and, in his heart, scorned them for accepting them.

But it may be that this moral simplicity led also to the strengthening of creative zest. Unworried by psychological subtleties the novelist could fix his eye on the swift current of events and could allow his characters, like the Czar's subjects before the war, every sort of freedom save the political one. We may suppose also that Victorian readers were not quite so innocent as they seemed and knew a thing or two that their novelists were allowed only to whisper in their ears.

Through all this there was practically no sign of foreign influence. The French novel might be read furtively but its significance was never literary. When we read the lives and letters of Thackeray, Dickens, George Eliot, Charlotte Brontë, and Anthony Trollope, we find that all of them enjoyed fun and freedom on the continent but never allowed the novel to be contaminated. French backgrounds are often painted but French morals always reprehended: Charlotte Brontë can give us the life of Brussels with wonderful vigour, but hers is always an English figure pointing an almost defiant contrast.

I said before that this insular morality was leading the English novel away from reality, and the principal drama of its adventures in the 'seventies lies precisely in this—its struggles towards honesty of statement, its fight for a new kind of realism.

The men concerned in this battle divide themselves quite clearly into three groups—the elders who are too old to learn new tricks, the writers who are still young enough to be plastic, the youngsters whose work is as yet almost unnoticed by their contemporaries although specially important for ourselves. Of the older novelists Charles Dickens, Disraeli, Wilkie Collins and Anthony Trollope stand out in a group of their own. It should not be the purpose of this paper to emphasise the characters of men concerning whom already almost too much has been written; it is waste of time merely to re-establish familiar standards, but the influence both of Dickens and Wilkie Collins on the novel of the 'seventies was particular and peculiar.

Everyone knows how the influence of Collins forced the later Dickens into a sort of plot strait-jacket with which he was never really familiar or happy. The novel that showed most favourably his attempt to squeeze his horde of characters into the bottle-neck of a plot was very possibly *Bleak House*, the worst quite certainly *Little Dorrit*. Yet it is *Little Dorrit* that I would choose as the true forerunner of the new world that the novel of the 'seventies was timidly setting out to explore.

Little Dorrit however is not my subject here. I would only remark of it that its queer dusky melodrama involved in the cobwebs of dark rooms, the ominous rumbling of trembling walls combined with the socialistic propaganda of the Marshalsea, the humours of Mr F.'s Aunt, the sentimentalities of Little Dorrit herself and Arthur Clenham, and the remarkable attempt to come to grips at last with life that is real and not sugarly fictitious, contains almost all the opposing forces that make the English novel of the 'seventies so strikingly the opening struggle between unfettered creative zest and sophisticated self-conscious Art, a struggle not yet finally decided.

And I would remark in passing that these three later novels of Dickens—*Little Dorrit, Our Mutual Friend* and *Great Expectations*—have not been sufficiently studied in their strange and almost uncanny relationship to certain aspects of the modern novel. There is interesting work here for a zealous investigator.

If we take the elements of *Little Dorrit* and divide them into Melodrama, Naturalism, Pathos and Humour, we discover at once the classes into which the 'seventies novel naturally divides. These are the old influences surviving from the earlier simpler creative age of which I have already spoken. Against them, meeting them with all the bright scornful cocksureness of the triumphant young we find the poetry, realism and intellectuality of the modern novel. It is the opening charges of this battle that gives the novel of the 'seventies its character and drama.

About Wilkie Collins a word must be said. By 1870 he had reached that sad decline into contemporary neglect that clouded all his later years. It is a sad story not to be told here: he, the intimate friend of Dickens and a citizen of the inner circle of letters, was now already deserted and almost forgotten. It is true that two of his very best novels appeared during the early 'seventies, *Poor Miss Finch* in 1872 and *The New Magdalen* in 1873, but the decline after this was very swift, and five years later novels like *The Two Destinies* and *A Shocking Story* proved how ruinous to any talent over-production and scamped work must be.

He is, however, the best melodramatist of the 'seventies if we allow that Charles Reade was something more than that. Whether there has ever been a better detective novel in English than *The Moonstone* I cannot say. For my part I believe not. We are at this very moment suffering from a flood of detective romances produced I believe mainly for Cabinet Ministers and the more superior literary critics. God forbid that I should throw scorn on them, but I do feel that for the most part their authors might study the better work of Wilkie Collins with advantage; most of them are algebraical problems, clever and adroit on occasion and on occasion not clever and adroit at all. Collins has Count Fosco, Miss Finch and many another memorable lady and gentleman to his credit. 'The Woman in White' is a real woman and not a mere numerical clothes peg.

His influence on the 'seventies was quite clear and definite. He brought no new thing into the English novel; he rather perfected a very good old thing. He made the Plot of so devastating an importance that all the novelists of the 'seventies felt compelled to have some sort of dealings with it—and a number of them dealt with nothing else.

On the other hand he hampered himself with one of the curses of the 'seventies' novel, and that was the quite intolerable demon of Propaganda, the demon that almost throttled poor Charles Reade, the demon who was drowned once and for all in a butt of the selfish amoral indifference of the early 'nineties. Collins, whether it was the abuse of private asylums in *The Woman in White*, the marriage laws of *Man and Wife*, the injustice to the prostitute in *The New Magdalen*, anti-vivisection in *Heart and Science*, or drunken nurses in *Basil*, could not check his most inartistic moral indignation. This moral indignation is the curse of the English novel of the 'seventies; it is the element that makes it hardest for us to be patient with many of the liveliest writers of that period.

It is interesting to notice, however, that the propaganda and the melodrama almost invariably go hand in hand. The pill is disguised with jam, the contrasts are painted in most violent colours, the sheep and the goats are separated more fiercely than either Thackeray or Dickens ever dreamed of dividing them. In any case there could not be clearer examples than some of these novels of Wilkie Collins if we wish to see the devastating effect on art that an honest determination to do good to your fellow-mortals can have.

Two other melodramatists should be mentioned in passing, Whyte-Melville and James Payn.

Of Whyte-Melville I shall say very little and for two

very good reasons. One is that he contributed nothing at all to the development of the novel. His stories were, I suppose, sentimental, melodramatic, false in dialogue, sugary in conclusion and wooden in character. I say 'I suppose' because I have been told all these things about them but have not, myself, read them since my childhood. And that is my second reason for saying very little about them here. Shades of cathedral closes, of reading in bed by the uncertain light of a tallow candle, of sitting elbows on knees in the midst of all the discordant babel of the Lower School Room while paper darts thickened the air and small boys toasted chestnuts over a reluctant fire—into the dust and discordance of scenes like these came Sarchedon with his majestic dignity, the Queen's Maries with their fatal beauty, Royal Charles a prisoner in Holmby House, the cruel Roman mob turning thumbs down as the gallant gladiator waits their judgment—and last and best of all the breezes and English backgrounds of *Katerfelto*; brazenness was I suspect his finest virtue, gusto his grandest card. At least he has given me too many gallant and romantic hours for me to dare ever to disturb those pages again.

James Payn too! Did I not read *Lost Sir Massingberd* in the high branches of an apple tree and *By Proxy* on a glorious summer holiday on Talland Sands? I have my copy of *By Proxy* yet, and there seems to me to linger about its pages a mingled aroma of hot sea sand, blackberry jam and shrimps. These pages also I will not disturb. Nevertheless I have not the same romantic delicacy for Payn that I have for Melville. He did not mean so much to me then nor I fear does he mean anything at all to anybody now. He was one of the stock novelists of his day, a gallant, good-humoured, generous figure with no illusions about his talent. He is interesting to me in my present connection only because re-reading him to-day he shows how little the minor melodramatist of the 'seventies had changed in eighty years. Might not this passage from *The Clyffards of Clyffe*, one of his better novels, have issued straight from the romantic heart of Mrs Radcliffe? I would add that the period of the story is late eighteenth century. Would you have guessed it had I not told you?

Raymond's eyes followed his brother with genuine sympathy until the door had closed behind him.

'Poor Rue! Poor Rue!' he murmured. 'God grant that thou mayst not bring the curse down on thine own head! It is no wonder that such prophecies work out their own fulfilment, when they have minds like thine to deal with. I wish with thee that thou and I could but change places. Rubbish of that sort might be shot *here*, I fancy,' striking his broad chest a sounding blow, 'without much damage. I am none of your dreamy ones, thank God! It is eleven o'clock. There are one, two, three good hours of fishing before me; and then, ah then! for my sweet Mildred!'

The dark face lightened as he spoke, and the eyes, somewhat too stern for boyhood, softened like the black waters of a mountain tarn touched by the moon, as he strode gaily from the sunken chamber, and through the vaulted passages to the hall, whistling his merry tune. So blithe he shone amid the general gloom, it seemed as though the haunting shadows of the place fled at his sprightly step, and gathered together after him more darkly than before, like clouds behind the sun.

Is not this exactly Thackeray's parody of Bulwer?

But it is at this point that we encounter two personalities who show to what remarkable heights of melodrama those novelists of the 'seventies could rise—two figures who both in their faults and their virtues are products only of that period; writers of their kind, of their *naïveté*, their force, their absurdities and their gusto will, we may safely say, never appear in the world again. They stand, big symbolic figures of that odd half-real half-imagined Victorian world—the close of it—figures at the gates about to be shut for ever.

When one considers the present industry in the

reinvestigation of minor and forgotten Victorians it is rather astonishing I think that these two men have found neither critics nor biographers of merit.

This paper will be justified should it lead an investigator—such a one as Mr Michael Sadleir for example —to a detailed thorough study of the work and personality of either.

The men of whom I speak are Charles Reade and Henry Kingsley.

Charles Reade is crying out for his biography, for his novels are both curious and perplexing in their combination of quite opposite qualities, and his personality in its odd violences, generosities, impetuosities both provoking and endearing.

He was a melodramatist of the theatre and in that he followed both Dickens and Wilkie Collins. There was in him a great deal of that odd mixture of sawdust, variegated waistcoats and amateur theatricals that belongs to Mr Crummles at one end and *The Frozen Deep* at the other.

But it was not merely *amateur* theatricals that held him; he had a very real traffic with the *real* theatre and it was unquestionably this *real* theatre—felt at a time when the English drama was at its lowest ebb—that was responsible for the gravest faults in his tempestuous novels. His fame also has been hampered by the excessive popularity of his most famous novel. Had he never written *The Cloister and the Hearth* there is no doubt but that *Griffith Gaunt, Put Yourself in His Place* and *Foul Play* would be awarded a higher critical position than they are. In many ways indeed *Griffith Gaunt* is the best novel that he ever wrote; it has less of his melodrama—although there is plenty—and more real tragedy having its source in character rather than in event, than any of the others. And it is strangely typical of its period.

It is full of the old false tricks, false violence, false pathos, false situation. It has that odd air of a city and smoking footlights that came in with 'Monk' Lewis, persisted with Lever, Hook, Ainsworth, Lytton, Dickens, Collins; it is one of the finest achievements of Meredith, Hardy and Stevenson that they took this very false paste and glitter and changed it into something quite different. It is perhaps that transformation that is the most interesting feature in the English novel between 1870 and 1885.

But *Griffith Gaunt* has signs of the new world as well as the old. Gaunt himself attains, as Reade's figures do, a gigantic height, and so having created him twice man's size Reade is able to apply to him words and phrases that would be absurd in other contexts but are normal here in this abnormal world.

Some of the dialogue in this novel has an almost Elizabethan ring: we are caught back into the world of Webster and Cyril Turneur. This fragment of dialogue, for instance:

> Mrs Gaunt threw her arms round Father Francis's neck, and wept upon his shoulder.
> 'Ah!' she sobbed, 'you are the only one left that loves me.' She could not understand justice praising her: it must be love.
> 'Az,' said Griffith, in a broken voice, 'she writes like an angel; she looks like an angel. My heart says she is an angel. But my eyes have shown me she is naught. I left her, unable to walk, by her way of it; I came back, and found her on that priest's arm, springing along like a greyhound.' He buried his head in his hands and groaned aloud.
> Francis turned to Mrs Gaunt and said, a little severely: 'How do you account for that?'
> 'I'll tell you, father,' said Kate, 'because you love me. I do not speak to you sir, for you never loved me.'
> 'I could give thee the lie,' said Griffith, in a trembling voice, 'but 'tis not worth while. Know, sir, that within twenty-four hours after I caught her with that villain, I lay a-dying for her sake, and lost my wits; and when I came to, they were a making my shroud in the very room where I lay. No matter; no matter. I never loved her.'

'Alas! poor soul,' sighed Kate, 'would I had died ere I brought thee to that!' And with that they both began to cry at the same moment.

This is not, although it ought to be, fustian. I think it is saved by a certain almost noble sincerity which Reade has worked into the fabric of it. There is also in the psychology of Griffith Gaunt much that is most interesting and moving and he is one of the best examples of what the later Victorian melodramatists can do when they are stirred by some self-experienced human emotion. This is a wild, deeply coloured, securely formed book and thoroughly deserves revival.

Henry Kingsley is, in my opinion, a yet more important figure than Reade. It is quite certain that he is most undeservedly neglected. The space allotted to him in the *Dictionary of National Biography* as compared with that given to his brother Charles is scandalous; it is more and more generally recognised to-day that he is in every way a novelist of greater importance than his brother.

His life was romantic enough with its swift transitions from Worcester College, Oxford, to the Australian goldfields, thence to England, then to the Franco-German War where he was present at the battle of Sedan, then back to England and novel-writing again. He was the author of at least six remarkable and memorable novels—*Geoffrey Hamlyn, Ravenshoe, The Hillyars and the Burtons, Silcote of Silcotes, Mademoiselle Mathilde* and *Stretton.*

He is an especially good example of the novelists of the fading Victorian tradition who was almost untouched by the theories and aims of the coming modern novel. He is, in a way, the most old-fashioned novelist in English literature. One might say that he would have been old-fashioned in whatever age he wrote, and that very fact, so long held against him, is now beginning to be his principal charm. He is a remarkable example of what zest can do for a novelist. Practically every fault that a novelist can commit Henry Kingsley commits. He is inconsequent, verbose and casual; he is desperately sentimental and a frantic moralist; he is for ever thrusting his own opinions and personality before the reader; he uses every possible device of melodrama and every impossible one; his characters are so black and so white that they blind the reader with their simplicity. He adores noble heroes with brawny chests, athletic parsons, weeping heroines and, worst of all, earls soaked in the traditions of Oxford and Cambridge. He is so proud of being an Englishman that one blushes for one's patriotism, and his affection for cold baths deserves all Laurence Oliphant's sarcasm. He has no technique, no powers of construction and only a theatrical sense of effect. Nevertheless with all this, his best books survive and survive amazingly.

He has neither the priggishness nor the intolerance of his brother and he is far, far stronger in the creation of character. It is indeed his creation of character that carries him through. How or why his characters survive his emotional exposition of them it is difficult to say, but survive they do.

His two best novels, *Geoffrey Hamlyn* and *Ravenshoe*, exhibit all his faults and all his virtues, but I would advise any reader of them not to stop with those two books but to experiment farther. *The Hillyars and the Burtons* and *Silcote of Silcotes* are becoming, I think, of increasing value as they provide pictures, in their tumultuous casual way, of a London and an England that seem already historically remote.

But it is his own interest in his own subject that gives Henry Kingsley his power; in this he is an object lesson to a number of very clever novelists to-day; again and again he makes us ask the question which is the supreme question forced upon us by the typical 'seventies novel—

how is the novelist to reconcile his creative zest and his self-conscious sense of art?

It is the age-old question to be asked about the novel: how to use your brains without stifling your heart, how to give your emotions full liberty and yet not make a fool of yourself! Only the greatest masters in this difficult art have answered the question for us and they have answered it without thinking of the rules of the game. It is instructive to realise that none of the great novelists of the world have written treatises on the novel—they have other things to do.

Henry Kingsley makes us ask almost in accents of despair about our own modern novel—must we always be compelled to choose between the novelist who is all heart and no brains and the novelist who is all brains and no heart? Happily there are one or two with a mixture of both and, for my part, it is they who win the prizes.

It would be untrue to say that Henry Kingsley had no brains; he was often brilliant, always eager, always courageous, but he remains the type novelist of the 'seventies—kindly, melodramatic, no artist but the tumultuous creator.

The type novelist of the 'seventies on the other, quiet, domestic side—and these two quite opposite types practically share the 'seventies' normal novel between them—must be divided between the persons of William Black, Besant and Rice, George Macdonald and Blackmore. There are of course many ladies of the same school and a number of other men—Grant Allen, Justin Huntley McCarthy, Rider Haggard in his domestic manner, and even Sheridan de Fanu, an excellent novelist who was both melodramatist and domestic. *Uncle Silas*, glorious book of my childhood, seemed to me when I re-read it the other day to be more domestic than melodrama, which was not at all what I had expected to find it.

Of these domestic novelists I do not propose to say very much. Frankly, I am disappointed. I had hoped, by delving among these old novels to discover a number of masterpieces unjustly neglected by our generation and to make these the subject of my paper. But they do not exist, these neglected masterpieces. It may be that they will appear in the paper concerned with the women novelists of the 'seventies. The men cannot provide them. In fact if one thing rather than another is clear from a study of the novels of this period it is that the average novel of to-day is immensely superior to the average 'seventies' novel. There are no more giants to-day than there were then—although I think there are as many—but there is a far larger body of fiction that can be read without irritation by the sophisticated reader now than then.

It is the fate of the domestic novel of the 'seventies that it is composed of milk and water. Besant when he combined with Rice had fun and gaiety. Le Fanu was eerie, Macdonald was piously Scotch (his fairy stories are quite another affair). Black was open-air and breezy. But oh! the thinness of the tale, the conventionality of the characters, the stale moral background of the parable!

Here is a short extract from *McLeod of Dare*:

McLeod looked tall as he came through the small drawing-room. When he came out on to the balcony, the languid air of the place seemed to acquire a fresh and brisk vitality: he had a bright smile and a resonant voice.

'I have taken the liberty of bringing you a little present, Miss White—no, it is a large present—that reached me this morning,' said he. 'I want you to see one of our Highland salmon. He is a splendid fellow, twenty-six pounds four ounces my landlady says. My Cousin Janet sent him to me.'

'Oh but, Sir Keith, we cannot rob you,' Miss White said, as she still demurely plied her fork. 'If there is any special virtue in a Highland salmon it will be better appreciated by yourself than by those who don't know.'

'The fact is,' said he, 'people are so kind to me that I scarcely ever am allowed to dine at my lodgings; and you know the salmon should be cooked at once.'

That gigantic salmon that has passed through the hands of the landlady and Cousin Janet and 'should be cooked at once' is the hero of most of William Black's novels.

There remains Anthony Trollope. I will say little of him here partly because so much has recently been written about him and partly because I do not think that he is a typical 'seventies novelist. He published in these years some of his very best novels—*The Vicar of Bullhampton* and *The Prime Minister* among others. He showed also in *The Way We Live Now* and *An Eye for an Eye* and *Ayala's Angel* a consciousness of the new colour and psychology that was coming, but the real kingdom that he conquered was an earlier one, and, in the 'Barchester' stories at any rate he was much more than a 'period' novelist.

I have tried briefly and I fear very inadequately to form some picture of the novel in the 'seventies as it typically was. Now I should like to turn for a moment to the forces on the opposite side, the forces that were, in one fashion or another, to effect the magic transmutation from the homely exuberant lusty 'innocent' to the polished, shining, sophisticated citizen of all the world that we now know.

First the satires. There was Laurence Oliphant and his *Piccadilly*, Butler's *Erewhon* and a delightful work now quite forgotten but most worthy of re-issue, the gay and ferocious *Ginx's Baby*.

Whether Laurence Oliphant was truly a novelist or not I do not know; I am sure that I have no ability to define *Piccadilly*. It is a book *sui generis*, and as it has just been very handsomely republished it can be in everybody's hands. Oliphant himself was an extraordinary figure and can be ranged with Reade and Henry Kingsley, also extraordinary figures, in his adventurous audacity, eccentricity and half-baked mysticism. He travelled the world over, had a brief sensational career in London society, was, like Henry Kingsley, a war correspondent in the Franco-Prussian War and was utterly subject to a crazy charlatan of an American prophet.

His attack on the fashionable 'sixties (it could be argued that he killed the mid-Victorian society novel) is brilliant, inconsequent, crazy and always alive. You seem as you read *Piccadilly* to sniff the air of a passing phase of social life. There is corruption, decadence, all the elements of transition. Its gaiety is bitter, its satire savage, the spirit behind it closely allied to madness.

Erewhon also is or should be in everybody's hands. Samuel Butler is not a typical 'seventies figure nor is *Erewhon* greatly concerned with the satirising of the fiction of that period. But we feel in *Erewhon*, as in another way we feel in *Piccadilly*, the emphasis of a dying fashion. It is always certain that if a period is changing socially, politically, morally, these changes will be found in all the interesting art of that period, and so *Piccadilly* and *Erewhon* are portents that concern us. *Ginx's Baby*, however, is a more direct portent still. Of its author, Mr Jenkins, I fear I know nothing. He is not in the *Dictionary of National Biography* although he ought to be. His book is the story of the son of Mr and Mrs Ginx. He was their thirteenth child, one of triplets, and Mr Ginx, feeling himself overburdened with family, desired to drown him. The baby is rescued by a nun who takes him to a Sister's Home. The matter is then made a public quarrel between different religious sects, spreads to the Law, to Parliament and so on. Finally, the baby grows up and, badgered on every side by Society, drowns himself in the river where his father once wished to extinguish him.

The satire is vigorous and at times savage; it is remarkably alive to-day, not at all out of date and one's feeling, as one reads, is that civilisation has progressed not at all—a pessimism unjustified but natural.

Here are one or two agreeable little pen-pictures:

The Constable's dilemma.

Unhappily the baby was on his beat, and he was delivered from the temptation of transferring it to the other by the appearance of X 101's bull's-eye not far off. What was he to do? The station was a mile away—the inspector would not arrive for an hour—and it would be awkward, if not undignified, to carry on his rounds a shouting baby wrapped in the largest daily paper. If he left it where it was, and it perished, he might be charged with murder. He was at his wit's end—but having got there, he resolved on the simplest process, namely to carry it to the station. No provision was made by the regulations of the force to protect a beat casually deserted even for a proper purpose. Hence, while X 99 was absent on his errand of mercy, the valuable shop of Messrs Trinkett and Blouse, ecclesiastical tailors, was broken into and several stoles, chasubles, altar-clothes and other decorative tapestries were appropriated to profane uses.

At the station the baby was disposed of according to Rule. Due entry was first made in the night-book by the superintendent of all the particulars of his discovery. Some cold milk was then procured and poured down the child's throat. Afterwards, wrapped in a constable's cape, he was placed in a cell where, when the door was locked, he could not disturb the guardians of the force.

The same night, in the next cell, an innocent gentleman, seized with an apoplexy in the street but entered on the charge-sheet as drunk and incapable, died like a dog.

Is not this rather pertinent to-day?

Sir Charles Sterling resumed his interest in the boy. He had been gallantly aiding his party in other questions. There was the Timbuctoo question. A miserable desert Chief had shut up a wandering Englishman, not possessed of wit enough to keep his head out of danger. There was a general impression that English honour was at stake, and the previous Fogey Government had ordered an expedition to cross the desert and punish the sheikh. You would never believe what it cost if you had not seen the bill. Ten millions sterling was as good as buried in the desert, when one tenth of it would have saved a hundred thousand people from starvation at home, and one hundredth part of it would have taken the fetters off the hapless prisoner's feet.

And does not this concluding paragraph strike home to-day?

Our hero was nearly fifteen years old when he left the Club to plunge into the world. He was not long in converting his spoils into money, and a very short time in spending it. Then he had to pit his wits against starvation, and some of his throws were desperate. Wherever he went the world seemed terribly full. If he answered an advertisement for an errand boy, there was a score kicking their heels at the rendezvous before him. Did he try to learn a useful trade, thousands of adepts were not only ready to underbid him, but to knock him on the head for an interloper. Even the thieves, to whom he gravitated, were jealous of his accession, because there were too many competitors already in their department. Through his career of penury, of honest and dishonest callings, of 'scapes and captures, imprisonments and other punishments, a year's reading of Metropolitan Police Reports would furnish the exact counterpart.

I recommend *Ginx's Baby* to some enterprising publisher. Meanwhile in its pages one hears sounded the doom of Victorian uplift and moral behaviour. On every side the new forces come sweeping in. *Harry Richmond, Beauchamp's Career, Travels with a Donkey, Far from the Madding Crowd.* These, however little it was recognised at the time, were the books of the modern world. The old novel was killed by three destructive forces—the sense of Form that came with the aid of Mr Vizetelly, Mr George Moore and others from France, the sense of Reality given to us by Thomas Hardy and George Gissing, the New Morality introduced to us by the New Woman.

The sense of Form taught us that it mattered whether our books were well-constructed, whether our sentences were well-balanced, whether our sequences were inevitable without being arranged. That our sense of Form has not yielded to the senses of Philosophy and Poetry is a subject beyond this present article.

Our sense of Reality has led possibly too easily to a sense of grime. Our noses are too close to the ground to-day just as in the 'seventies our chins were too high in the air.

But it is the sense of Morality that has yielded the greatest changes. In the 'seventies the novelists took it for granted that once you were married you were happy for ever after. In the 'nineties the novelists took it for granted that once you were married you were done for. In the modern novel as none of the characters are married at all the old question scarcely arises.

But there *are* other questions. We have lost something. What? Shades of Charles Reade and Henry Kingsley answer us! I see them standing in their Olympian shrouds gazing down upon us. On their genial countenances there are shadows of admiration, but also implications of pity.

Can it be that they pity us because we are so clever?

§ 3

Some Women Novelists of the 'Seventies

By Walter de la Mare

As any particular period of time steadily recedes into
the past, its content in human memory suffers a series of
rapid and inevitable transmutations. It fades in patches,
it continues but changes colour, lightens in one place,
darkens in another. It becomes contorted, distorted and
shrunken; here, flattered in retrospect; there, belittled or
defamed. Though the whole of that content, we vaguely
suppose, is still 'there', as precisely fitting its original
receptacle as a nut its shell, even of the personally experienced only fragments are recoverable, and they not
as they actually were, but as they now look to be. For
the rest we must depend upon memorials in print or
writing, in stone or wood or canvas, and attempt to
translate them into something resembling the original.
But many even of these memorials have been the outcome
of a close or heedless sifting, selection or condensation,
and they cannot but be modified or falsified in some
degree by the perspective of the present, in quality,
meaning and impressiveness.

So with that brief section of time known as the
'seventies. From our crow's nest of the passing hour we
gaze out in its direction over the sundering flood in
search of landfall and sea-mark. It is a period for many
of us (a many rapidly dwindling to a few), just remote
and just retrievable enough to be singularly beguiling.

What was its general appearance? Who and what was 'going on'?

During the last few days of 1869 a thaw had set in after a hard frost, and readers of the 'agony column' in *The Times* were greeted on New Year's Day with this message: 'R—D to B—S. Thanks dearest. Delighted. All right. 6. 8. 10. 11 will suit—not 7, prefer 6. Your own R':—a cryptic utterance that might at any moment be addressed by humanity itself to the fatal Sisters. For larger affairs, Europe was on the verge of the Franco-Prussian War—a fiery Phoenix that of late returned to the sole Arabian tree. On the 8th of June Charles Dickens, that supreme magician, then fifty-nine, after working all day on *The Mystery of Edwin Drood* died suddenly of a stroke. The School Boards were established in the same year, and Thomas Huxley was one of the original members for London. The Bank Holiday Act, Darwin's *Descent of Man*, Ruskin's *Fors Clavigera* and Guild of St George and *The Adventures of Harry Richmond* were of 1871, *The Ordeal of Richard Feverel* having appeared twelve years before. In '71 Henry Irving opened at the Lyceum with *The Bells*; in '71 T. W. Robertson died, in '73 Lord Lytton, in '75 Charles Kingsley, in '76 Harriet Martineau. In '74 Whistler exhibited his portrait of Thomas Carlyle. And precisely midway in our period 'A Young Lady' implored the Editor of *The Times*, the great Delane, to lend his aid in the releasing of ladies from segregation when travelling by rail. The doors and windows, she said, were obstinate. She had hurt her hands and ruined her gloves in the attempt to open them. 'Men and women', ran her challenging postscript, 'are meant to go through life together, to separate them is a poor way of getting over any difficulties there may be.'

Though Girton College had been founded in '69 and Bedford College followed ten years afterwards, the

'Girton Girl' (who 'views with horror a slim ankle and a pointed toe') was still an object of derision to Mr Punch even in '86, the year of the establishment of the 'National Society for Women's Suffrage'. Four years afterwards he began to ogle the 'Undomestic Daughter'. In '78 England secured 'peace with honour' at the Congress of Berlin, Parnell became the uncrowned king of Ireland, and *Pinafore* was produced. In '79 John Henry Newman received the cardinal's hat. In 1880, a year before his death, Benjamin Disraeli's last novel, *Endymion*, was published.

In the 'seventies the rich and various work of the great English illustrators—how rich and various Mr Forrest Reid has lately revealed—began to decline. And it would be difficult to say how much in form and design they owed to the happy accident that the feminine attire of the time was a rather full skirt and a rather tight bodice with natural sleeves, and a tendency to shawls. Shallow, brimmed hats, or ovals of fur or velvet, crowned heads with the hair bunched out behind in a chignon. Between these and the ferocious English sun a little fringed parasol afforded a pleasing and becoming shade. In the following years monstrous flounces began to multiply, the train to expand, the 'waist' to contract. Indoors was awaiting a cap (or 'lappets') to ensure respect for the matron of thirty and upwards, who, says Mrs Alexander, might still be called charming even at that advanced age; and who might then solace herself at the pianoforte with such sentimental ballads, I fancy, as *Love's Old Sweet Song* or *In the Gloaming, O my Darling!*

About 1880 whiskers, curly or weeping-willow-wise, and, if need be, dyed, were vanishing from the scene, together with that 'fantastic velvet vestment', the smoking jacket. The crinolette was 'in'. I recall, too, a sort of tongs which were worn dangling from the hips to keep

the train from out of the dust. Little 'buses, with a con-
ductor hanging from a strap behind, or with a hole in
the roof for the collection of fares, and with straw in the
interior, roamed the streets, which rang merrily with the
strains of the butcher boy whistling *Tiddy-fol-loll* or
Tommy, make room for your Uncle! A few years later he
began shrilling *We don't want to fight.* ...

The bell of the horse tram had first tinkled in London in
'71; Charles Peace—who preferred the solitude of a gig—
met his end in '79. The lamp-lighter with his little ladder
still went his dusk and daybreak round—even in Holywell St. and Seven Dials; and Valentines, exquisite and
otherwise, burdened the peak-capped postman's back on
the 14th of February. Jack-in-the-Green jigged through
the streets on May Day, and occasional roving Frenchmen
scared every horse within scent of them with their dancing
bear. Third-class railway passengers after dark took their
ease on narrow wooden seats under a single oil lamp, its
ooze softly swinging to and fro in a glass container over
their heads. Smoke as of the infernal regions asphyxiated
the hardy subterranean adventurer whose route lay from
Bishop's Road to Farringdon St.; the merry-go-round of
the Inner Circle being not as yet completed.

The typewriter, friend of the printer, was of '73; the
telephone, foe of the unready, of '76; and the phono-
graph, a rich blessing though one then in disguise, was
patented by Mr Edison in '77. Life was in process of
being mechanised, 'speeded up', made noisy and mal-
odorous—though in other respects deodorised. Yet, in
spite of a fivepenny income tax, of the School Boards
and of the blessings of science, a steady increase in the
mortality from suicide began to show itself even in '76.
But, as all things must, the 'seventies came to an end.
The penny-farthing bicycle and electric light its chief
novelties and the fall of the Tay Bridge its final disaster,

1879 went out with the storm 'cones' up in most districts, and in worsening weather.

Last, but not least, all persons now between fifty and sixty years of age, who in our period helped to raise the population of England from twenty-three to twenty-six millions, were then engaged in being born. Providentially for many of them the average number of children in the families of the professional classes in the United Kingdom had not then sunk to what, I believe, the statistician now shows it to be—a figure in the neighbourhood of 0·9.

It is fortunate for a hazy and fragmentary historian that this paper is concerned not with life in the world of the real and actual during this decade, but with its reflex in the looking-glass of fiction. None the less, any attempt, and even one so superficial as this, to recall what those years 'looked like'—and to this end the trivial is as evocative as the important—may be of service in the company of that fiction. It vaguely presents the scene; it gives the reader his bearings. It may help to preclude prejudice.

'Some Women Novelists of the 'Seventies'—the phrase has the cadence of a lullaby, and conjures up in the fancy a trim walled garden in June, bee and flaunting butterfly, pinks in bloom and tea roses, candytuft and mignonette. A closer view proves this to be a delusive picture. The walled garden leads out to where the vegetables grow; cherry trees and gooseberry bushes give place to the prickling briar and the grieving thorn, cypress and yew. And at length a waste appears, no rill of living water musical on the ear, bindweed and viper's bugloss its few clear flowers, bleached slender bones their only company in its sands. And of all things in this world, what is less easily retrievable than that which once breathed the breath of life and has now not only passed away but vanished out of remembrance?

In space our theme is confined to the British Isles, and that is fairly simple. It is in respect to the arbitrary division in time and still more to the division in kind imposed by it that difficulties abound. Even in history a decade is no more than a convenience, a fold whose hurdles prove extremely defective, and even when facts are the only sheep. But authors and books—it is impossible to segregate objects once so lively as easily as that. Its date of publication is hardly even a book's birthday. That was when in one of the closest privacies known to man its first words appeared on paper. The seed of it may have been quickening in timeless dreams for half a lifetime.

Ten years of childhood, too, not only in mere appearance of duration, surpass a hundred of maturity, but have more influence on the mind and imagination than any that follow. Next in virtue of influence are the years of a man's youth. These are the well-spring of his after-life. 'By their fruits ye shall know them', but it was the season of blossoming that set those fruits to ripen. It is, too, what goes on in ourselves rather than what goes on in the outer world that makes our days significant. Its near and dear, its detested and its little usually affect us much more than its far, its multitudinous and its large. We buy newspapers, first to scan, and then to light our fires with.

The work of every writer therefore varies in quality and meaning and value at different times of his life; its last state may be worse than its first. But the greater he is as an artist, so much the more signally, within certain limits, is that work the revelation of his own mind and spirit. The creative impulse, the visiting spirit, is essential. His external surroundings, to whatever degree they may affect him, are by comparison of lesser account. What curiously diverse and individual reflections of the 'seventies, for example, are *Literature and Dogma, The*

Unknown Eros, and *Thrift, Character* and *Duty* by the author of *Self-Help*.

The civilised world may be pursuing the even tenor of its way across the flats of tradition while one man whose privy thoughts are fated to have the effects of an earthquake on that tradition may be living in complete obscurity. On the other hand, since great novelists occupy the world of their own day, that world must to some extent occupy them. But they transmute it into their own terms. And so it comes about that the London of Dickens's day is for most of us chiefly Dickens's London; just as Chaucer is largely our fourteenth century, and Malory, who flourished seventy years after Chaucer died, seems to have been his senior by centuries. Even though, too, a fine novel be markedly the product of its own period, it is apt to continue to live because it little seems so. Or conversely, a novel that continues to live and shed its influence, to interest, engross and amuse must in its own kind have something of greatness in it. It is no mere parasite of its period.

While then any particular decade can be said to illumine the annals of literature only with its best and brightest, it should modestly refrain from taking on that score too much unction to its soul. Apart from Thomas Hardy himself, to whom and to what do we owe *The Dynasts*? To Wellington, Nelson, Napoleon and their satellites, and to the first ten years of their century, or to the first ten years of this? Or to the chance that introduced a child of eight to a cupboard containing a lavishly illustrated copy of *The History of the Wars*? Is *Arabia Deserta*—the author of which, when he was invited to contribute to a grace-offering to the poet of *The Dynasts* on his eightieth birthday, quite innocently enquired, 'And who is Thomas Hardy?'—is *Arabia Deserta* the patchoulied nosegay of artifice we associate however unfairly with the 'naughty 'nineties'?

Novelists, too, tend probably to write of what they were familiar with when they were younger. However hospitable they may be to new ways, new ideas, new views, these are not their spiritual home. But to sort their achievements on this basis would be a feat for the kindly ants in a fairy tale.

If, then, any great novel had been written by a woman during the 'seventies it would not much concern us now. So far as I can discover none was. George Eliot's finest work had been done in the 'sixties, and only *Daniel Deronda* appeared during the next ten years. Of other than great —of sound, gifted, amusing and edifying fiction there was an abundant supply. How much of it is read nowadays, I cannot say; probably, little. For each generation in turn gracelessly discards the fiction of its immediate predecessor. We begin to read grown-up novels in our later 'teens, and then read those written for the most part by novelists many years our seniors, but hot from the press. A novel-reader upwards of forty, then, may be vividly familiar with the fiction current when he came of age, and yet have the vaguest acquaintance with that of his childhood. For this reason any little private excursion such a reader may nowadays make into the minor fiction of the 'seventies will largely be into almost virgin country. A variegated scene will spread itself around him, a curious adventure may prove his ample reward. If he is tempted to be condescending let him remind himself that current criticism cannot but be affected to some extent by current taste; that that veers with the wind; and that a personal judgment, also, is seldom innocent of prejudice, and may be as temporary as it is assured.

In 1897, for example, a large flat volume appeared entitled *Women Novelists of Queen Victoria's Reign*. It was written by a number of ladies 'who had been concerned

for some years in the publication of works of fiction'; and
it was intended as a loyal tribute to Queen Victoria on the
celebration of her second Jubilee. It declined to 'assess
the merit' of living 'lady fictionists' (apparently pre-
ferring that toast-and-water phrase to so simple if
sibilant a neologism as *novelistesses*). Its hospitality was
otherwise restricted to those women writers who did all
their work after the Queen's accession.

While, then, such 'famous novelists' as Mrs Gore,
Mrs Bray, Mrs Hall and Mrs Marsh were given no niche
in it, the works of Mrs Archer Clive, of Anne Manning,
and of Mrs Stretton were duly appraised, and among its
actual contributors were Mrs MacQuoid and Mrs Parr,
whose pen-name was 'Holme Lee'. In spite of the fact
that Queen Victoria's second Jubilee is so recent an
event that all novelists now aged thirty-three were born
amid the rumour of its drums and tramplings, in how
many minds, I wonder, will these names awake positively
rousing echoes.

'Views' on fiction, we might assume, however, would
not at that time differ very much from our own. Nevertheless we find so shrewd and vigorous a critic as Mrs
Oliphant asserting, first, that in 1897 homage to the
Brontës exceeded that accorded to Dickens, Thackeray
and George Eliot; next, that Charles Reade and Trollope
were almost forgotten; and last, that the 'nobler arts' of
fiction are all of them missing from the Brontë novels.
When, however, in the course of her paper she refers to
Charlotte as a demure little person, silent and shy, 'plain,
even ugly—a small woman with a big nose, and no other
noticeable feature—not even the bright eyes of genius',
and when finally she expresses the hope that Miss Brontë's
'memory will be allowed to rest'; we become conscious
of a certain bias. Whether or not, straws like these show
not only the way the critical breeze is apt to blow, but

how the wild west wind of popular opinion and caprice may sweep a fiction once alive and beloved into the seemingly lost, if not into the irrecoverable.

The distance that in fiction lends re-enchantment to the view, has indeed to be considerable. The once expensive furniture, glass and china of the 'seventies has as yet won only half-way to the goal of what the American Customs Officers recognise as the 'antique'. First editions of its women novelists are in even worse case. As rank on rank, dwindling in perspective, they repose on their metallic shelves in the London Library and meet the faltering eye of the enquirer, they may shed a tranquillising calm—but they are unlikely to be collected. This is no proof however that they are unworthy of being *re*-collected.

'The demon of Chronology' being in our midst, only the dryest statistics can suggest the actual situation. In the year 1875, then, when *Comin' thro' the Rye* appeared and Thomas Hardy had recently published *A Pair of Blue Eyes* and *Far from the Madding Crowd*, when Meredith was forty-seven and Henry James thirty-two, when Mr Wells, Mr Galsworthy and Mr Bennett were not yet in their 'teens, the following novelists were more or less engrossed in the production of fiction: George Eliot, Mrs Henry Wood, Anne Manning, Mrs Alexander, Mrs Oliphant, Rhoda Broughton, Charlotte Yonge, Charlotte Tucker, Mrs Lynn Linton, Jean Ingelow, Julia Kavanagh, Amelia Edwards, Mrs Annie Edwardes, Miss Betham-Edwards, Mrs Craik, Mrs Marshall, Mrs Hungerford, Mrs Riddell, Elizabeth Charles, Harriet Parr, Hesba Stretton, Mrs Archer Clive, 'Ouida', Mary Elizabeth Braddon, Rosa Carey, Charlotte Dempster, Rosa Kettle, Mrs Linnaeus Banks, Florence Montgomery, Lady Augusta Noel, Mary Linskill, Eleanor Poynter, Florence Marryat, Mary Roberts, Mrs Hibbert Ware, Mrs Robert Stuart de

Courcey Laffan, Anne Thackeray, Jessie Fothergill and 'Rita'. Adeline Sergeant was as yet busily engaged only in sharpening her quill. Of these novelists nine were alone responsible for about 554 publications in all, chiefly in three volumes. An average of sixty-one each, that is, with a remainder that would suffice in mere paper for the complete works of Flaubert.

Such a catalogue (and one no doubt far from complete), however reviving or otherwise its incidental effects, has very little connection with fiction as an art or even with books as literature, and it is no more of a map than is a collection of place names. It is also a confession of failure. For confronted with this vast reservoir I must confess that I have merely dipped and dipped again. Its deeps and its shallows seem inexhaustible. During the 'seventies alone 'that wicked Ouida' was responsible for nine novels, including *Puck*; Mrs Henry Wood for ten, including the *Johnny Ludlow* series, and Miss Braddon for sixteen, including *Vixen* and *Joshua Haggard's Daughter*.

A hardly less arid and harrowing means of hinting at the situation is to mention a few titles—a title being at least as indicative of the character of a novel as of a man. A large number of the novels of the nineteenth century written by women were called after their heroines—or their heroes. It matters little which, since both usually imply a pursuer and the pursued—only a slight jar of the kaleidoscope, whatever the consequent form and 'pattern'. For the rest, *Miriam's Marriage, No Saint, Only a Woman, Two Little Wooden Shoes, A Rise in the World, Goodbye, Sweetheart! Can This be Love? The Doctor's Dilemma, Half a Million of Money, Wee Wifie, Her Dearest Foe, Pearl Powder, Above Suspicion, Ought We to Visit Her? The Beautiful Miss Barrington*, may surrender a glimpse of their general trend.

Compare them with *The Dove's Nest, The Light House*,

Dangerous Ages, Told by an Idiot, Skin Deep, The Tramping Methodist, Poor Man, Studies in Wives, Seducers in Ecuador, The Maternity of Harriett Wicken, Why They Married, Tents of Israel, A Pitiful Wife, Secret Bread, Precious Bane, and, say, *The Sheikh,* and a difference in theme and aim, if not in quality, clearly discloses itself.

Seriousness whether it be a condition of the spirit or an attitude of the mind is closely akin to sincerity, and in some kind or degree, though it may parch bad fiction like the sirocco, it is essential to fine fiction, though a novelist may smile and smile, and yet not be frivolous in virtue or in villainy. George Eliot was so serious as to be by conscious intention didactic, and to declare that her mission in life was that of 'an aesthetic teacher and an interpreter of philosophical ideas'. Yet her fiction survived the strain. Seriousness indeed (however airily variegated), prevailed in the minor novels of the 'seventies. It may be in part explained by the fact that women had been compelled to fight for the liberty of becoming novelists at all.

'Novel writing', said Mrs Parr, writing in 1897, and she can scarcely have realised that a quarter of a century afterwards well over 300 women would be following her own dreadful trade,—'Novel writing has now become an employment, a profession, distraction, I might almost say a curse.' 'The mania to see their names in print' had seized upon her sex. But when in 1833, Anne Manning burst into her father's study with the announcement that she had finished a tale entitled, *Village Belles*, 'Papa', said she, 'I don't know what you will say, but I have written a story!' 'Ho, ho, ho!' was what Mr Manning said. He nevertheless read the tale, and afterwards remarked, 'My dear, I like your story very much'. But as he seems never to have referred to it again, the problem of what actually passed in Mr Manning's mind is left unsolved.

It was still something of an event in literary annals so late as 1846 when, at the age of twenty, Mrs Craik fled to London from Stoke, 'conscious of a literary vocation'. 'Women in her day', says Mrs Parr, 'were in intellectual imprisonment.' Even in the later 'fifties, and in spite of the enthusiastic encouragement of John Keble, when Charlotte Yonge announced to her parents that she was about to publish a novel, a family council immediately followed, and its sanction to so daring a 'departure from the ladylike' was granted only on condition that Charlotte should not herself profit by any financial reward that might come of it. She agreed; and a large part of her ill-gotten gains enriched missionary work in Melanesia.

Not that such little hindrances were confined to one sex, for even in the 'seventies we find Amelia Edwards ironically enquiring, 'Can a painter by any possibility be a gentleman? Might a gentleman without loss of dignity, write poetry, unless in Greek or Latin?' By that time, however, women's great challenge had been definitely issued, though quality in the ranks was still more conspicuous than numbers, and the battle was not yet to the strong.

Long before December 1869, for example, the tint of the bluestocking, it might be supposed, had to be very dark to justify the ascription of the term. None the less in 1877 a novel of this title was published by Mrs Annie Edwardes. Clementina Hardcastle, the bluestocking herself, had been brought up by her parents with no startling originality. They hoped to see her well married, and were convinced that 'under-educated men desire over-educated wives'. In consequence she writes to her long-absent lover a letter (beginning 'Dear Sir John'), which is restricted to enquiries relating to the geology of the

Channel Islands. Bluestockings in those days, we are told also, wore a fringe and spelt humanity with a big H. Clementina's lively appearance does not suggest anything very formidable. She has reddish brown eyes, reddish brown hair with a golden tint 'probably due to Auricomus Fluid at twenty-one shillings and sixpence a bottle', very black lashes and eyebrows, aided it may be by 'antimony and a pencil', and she is wearing for a walk along the sea-shore 'a skirt, O, so narrow that it would take a year's study to learn to walk in it at all; a fan-shaped train carried over one arm', and a Mother Hubbard hat.

The New Woman, though, maybe, as yet unlabelled, was not unknown. She, too, in the guise of a 'writing woman' named Mattie Rivers, appears in the same novel as 'the customary accessory' of a smart yachting cruise. She is described as 'an emancipated sister of twenty-nine, with a cavalier hat worn distinctly...over one ear, a rakish-looking double eye-glass, a cane...a palpable odour of Havana smoke clinging to her gentlemanly yachting-jacket, and short-clipped, gentlemanly hair'.

But even if the Havana smoke was of her own making, the heralds of the Keynote Series were in Mattie's day still in their nurseries, only playing with pen and ink, and it was not until the end of the century that the 'sex-problem'—dismallest, surely, of all drab phrases—had become, according to Mrs Oliphant, 'the chief occupation of fiction', and that Mrs Linton could refer to 'unveiled presentations of the sexual instincts which seem to make the world one large lupanar'—a term which I was relieved to find no trace of in *The (Concise) Oxford Dictionary*. However that may be, the novels written by women in the 'seventies were still for the most part either love stories, not very subtle, perhaps, but simple, and not usually sensuous, or passionate; or they were tales like

Bridget, by Miss Betham-Edwards, or *Debenham's Vow*,
or *The Mistress of Langdale Hall* by Rosa Kettle dealing
with the domestic affections, and welcomed by the family
circle, phrases nowadays perhaps needlessly tepid in
effect. If 'I don't *think* Papa would mind your being
poor,' is one extreme of the situation; 'I am quite sure
Mamma wouldn't mind your being a marquis,' might
well have been the other.

In *The Wooing O't* Mrs Alexander tells us that Maggie,
her chief character, a young woman (the daughter of a
chemist), whose 'brave little heart' is not less endearing
and delightful company than her sound little head, was
guided in a certain crisis by 'the fixed underlying feminine
instinct which has probably kept more women straight
than religion, morality and calculation put together, the
true instinct that woman "should not unsought be won"'.
A brilliant and charming man of the world having rescued
his titled cousin from marrying her, has himself won her
heart—and she, though she knows it not, his. 'She cried
shame upon herself for thus casting her full heart before
a man who didn't want it....' 'That', Mrs Oliphant
agreed, 'is somehow against the instinct of primitive
humanity.' So too would most of the heroines of our
period. Nor did the women novelists who created them
cast *all* that was in *their* full hearts before the public. The
public had to wait awhile.

That public—an otherwise extremely hospitable one—
had lately been presented, though only temporarily, with
Poems and Ballads, and Rhoda Broughton had not only
skimmed its pages, but had observed its reflex in life
itself. For Nell's sister Dolly L'Estrange, in *Cometh up
as a Flower* (Miss Broughton's first novel, of '68), with her
'passionate great velvet orbs', was, we are told, 'the sort
of woman upon whom Mr Algernon Swinburne would
write pages of magnificent uncleanness'. She has a

nefarious finger in the plot of the story—she forges a
love-letter; but otherwise occupies little space in it; and
I cannot recover what Mr Swinburne thought of her.
Even Nell, her Tennysonian sister, was probably in the
nature of a bomb-shell for mothers with daughters. It is
her own story, and she tells it in the first person, not
always as the purist (in grammar) would approve—
'every English gentleman or lady likes to have a room to
themselves'. And its more dramatic episodes are narrated in the historic present, a device at times discon-
certing: 'Great tears are standing in his honest tender
agonised eyes—tears that do not disgrace his manhood
much, I think...and as he so kisses and clasps me, a
great blackness comes over my eyes, and I swoon away
in his arms'.

Nell's pretty face varies in beauty according to her
fickle moods. At one moment her 'curly red' hair falls in
'splendid ruddy billows' over the clasper's shoulder, and
at the next, in her looking-glass, she scrutinises a 'wide
mouth' in 'a potato face'. But even when that 'huge
loose knot of hair' is 'crowned by a sevenpenny half-
penny hat' she always 'looks a lady'; and when she
enters a drawing-room, she is bound to confess, 'several
people (men especially) looked at me'. What would be
the precise equivalent of the quoted phrases in an 'advanced' novel of 1929?

Nell's seriousness, amply encouraged by her creator,
takes the form of impassioned little discourses on such
expansive themes as Death, Fate or Eternity. But simply
because as a novelist Miss Broughton is so witty, high-
spirited, generous and headlong, however serious she may
be, she is never so sober, never so solid as most of her
contemporaries.

If, indeed, kisses be the food of love, then Cupid is on
famine commons in Jessie Fothergill's *Probation*. It is a

tale remarkably well told for a girl in her twenties, of life
in Lancashire. The Civil War in America has converted
the plenty of 1860 into the dearth of 1862. 'King Cotton'
has for the moment abdicated his throne. As in many of
the novels of our period, and in few of our own, wedding-
bells—a double peal—ring out its last chapter. None the
less, only two kisses, so far as I can recall, are recorded in
the complete three volumes, and one of them is the forlorn farewell of a rejected but still gallant admirer. In
Cometh up as a Flower, which, like many other novels of
its day has a sad ending steadily foreseen, they are as
multitudinous as dewdrops at daybreak on a briar rose.
But both novels are 'love-stories', and both are representative of their time.

In general, perhaps, our novelists' heroines are left safe
and sound on the outskirts of an 'untroubled future such
as women ought to enjoy'—wedded bliss, that is, with
a loved one who usually has income enough for comfort;
though Leah in Mrs Annie Edwardes' caustic, sharp-cut
novel of that title, dies of heart disease half an hour after
a wedding by which she renounces not only a nefarious
peer but a substantial fortune. But Miss Fothergill, like
Amelia Edwards, the author of *Robert Orde's Atonement*,
would have agreed, I fancy, with Mrs Humphry Ward's
summary in *David Grieve* that, 'The most disappointing
and hopeless marriage nobly borne is better worth having
than what people call an ideal passion'.

Nor was beauty in the heroine of the 'seventies indispensable. 'She was one of those women, who are not anything, neither ugly nor beautiful, until one knows them,
and then they are lovely for ever.' That is a memorable
thing to say of anybody, and remarkably well said.

All this is by no means to suggest that the fiction whose
chief concern is with questions of sex, and whose first
green leaf, it seems, was raised from a seed that may have

escaped from Aphra Behn's pocket, but was assiduously watered by Charlotte Brontë, was not already in vogue. The intention was different. Love, as Miss Storm Jameson has recently declared, is an emotion that concerns not only the body, but the mind, spirit and imagination of man or woman. This seems to have been the view shared by most women novelists in the 'seventies, and it gives their treatment of the theme, balance, proportion and depth. Women of the world they may have been, and women (as Rhoda Broughton puts it) 'too thorough... not to enjoy household work', but in their explorations of the House of Life they did not lavish an unconscionably protracted scrutiny on the drains. Some of them were a little prudish; a few paddled in the shocking; but that as yet was not a difficult feat. Nowadays novelists bent on the same adventure and in search of low tide cannot but 'weep like anything to see Such quantities of sand'. A day may come when the ultimate shore will loom into view and the artist be left to work in peace.

As for the 'free' woman in another sense, she was rather frowned upon than otherwise. 'I thought', says Sebastian, one of the two heroes of *Probation*,

'I thought that if Miss Mereweather disapproves so strongly of men in general, it would annoy her to be mistaken for one of that odious and inferior sex; and, moreover, would only be a sign of how very different she must be from most women.'
'She is very superior to most women' [replies Helena, her devotee]. 'If that is what you mean, I concede the point willingly.'
'Well, if such a superior woman is often mistaken for a man, is not that a piece of negative evidence of the inferiority of women in general?' Sebastian asked politely.

Then, as now, I suppose, the majority of assiduous novel-readers were women. None the less, note neither exclamatory nor interrogatory bedecked my library copy of *Probation* at this remark, and annotators appear to have been grossly free with the pencil in those days.

Miss Mereweather finally marries a clergyman, the headmaster of 'a sort of college', and in face of this betrayal of her ideals, Helena refuses to regard her any longer as a friend. But by this time, bravely facing the grief and distress that have come into her life, she has realised what from the beginning has been clear to the reader—that she is in love with Sebastian, while his own love for her has convinced him that 'no man and no woman pitted each against the other could do any good, but that "the twain together well might change the world"'.

Not all strife between the sexes in the fiction of the 'seventies ended as peacefully as this. Though the craving for a latchkey and similar emblems of emancipation was not yet vocal, though 'the shriek of the Sapphos for love' seldom echoes in its courts, and even 'the longing', in Mrs Oliphant's words, apropos of Mr Joseph Taylor and Charlotte Brontë, 'for life and action, and the larger paths and the little Joes', is seldom vehemently expressed, there were other prevalent problems.

The monk from the monastery was still a romantic danger; the deceased wife's sister among the forbidden fruits (there are two such sisters in *Hannah*); and ritualism might wreck a home. *Under Which Lord*, by Mrs Lynn Linton, is a lengthy and rather acid discourse on this theme. It tells of the conflict for parochial ascendancy between the Hon. and Rev. Launcelot Lascelles and Richard Fullerton, for the fealty of Richard's wife, Hermione. Richard has for many years of his married life devoted his leisure to the study of mythology and protoplasm. Too much, or too little, science has converted him to 'free thought'. Mr Lascelles (having himself chosen the guests) boldly denounces him at Hermione's dinner-party as an atheist and an infidel. And Richard Fullerton, courageous and urbane opponent though he may be, is in a position which he realises too late is hideously weak. For owing to his father-in-law's sagacity in tying up Hermione's money, her worldly goods were only on sufferance his. For this reason, perhaps, he addresses her as 'My wife', or 'My Lady-hood'. When he wished to amuse her in the evenings, 'he told her some facts of natural history'. Robbed at length of his daughter, of his influence, of his agnostic working-men, and even his bank account, he bows his head and retires.

His enemy, Mr Lascelles, is a sort of hieratic volcano, gaunt, frigid, capped with snow, yet menacingly eloquent of the suppressed and awful fires within. One of his flock, after an hysterical outburst at a harvest festival, dies of his dark influence. He secures most of Hermione's money, though she herself returns and is reconciled at last to poor Richard on his death-bed.

The effect of the story is oddly and garishly unreal; a bright hard theatrical daylight dwells on the scene; and both men are little more than waxworks. Yet its author's violent prejudices, though apparent, are ingeniously screened. Quite apart from Mr Lascelles, she is no friend of man, as such; nor, being one herself, of strong-minded women neither. The cleverest woman in her story is easily a match, in both senses, for the vicar, but even she has 'the curiosity of her sex'—in relation to octo-genetic evolution. 'Men', we are told, 'never know any-thing of what goes on about them. It is only women who find the truth.' 'As if', again, 'the cleverest man in the world is not as helpless as a babe, when the right kind of woman, who knows how he ought to be managed, takes him in hand.'

A faint hope of refuge from this sad extremity springs up with Mr Lascelles' tragic suggestion: '"So few women understand the deeper thoughts of men. Some supplement us, but it is given to very few to really understand us." "I know that", murmurs Hermione, "being one of the few."' But, alas, this is merely the old fable of the fox and the goose.

That Mrs Linton was not only serious but intensely in earnest *The True History of Joshua Davidson, Christian Communist*, is overwhelming proof. What is more astonishing nowadays, perhaps, this book had an immense popular success. In spite of its intention, it is not a winning tale, nor is *Under Which Lord*. Mrs Linton's most impressive female characters combine the chill of the crocodile with the austerity of the priestess and the cunning of the fox. They suggest a sort of neuter sex, being at the same time queens of the hive and parish workers. Her intention is ardent, but her ink is cold, and at times corrosive, and her attitude towards man is shared by a lady in Mrs Oliphant's *The Three Brothers*. She 'was endowed with that contempt for the masculine understanding that most women entertain'.

Such, so it seems, was the general reflex of life in the feminine fiction of the 'seventies. And this reflex concerns of course its kind, not its quality. When woman rules, her rod, there as everywhere, is adamantine. When she shares the throne, and takes her Queen for her model, or meekly submits to an autocrat, a little feminine tact or manageableness, or the love that finds out a way, or downright guile, or Lilith-like seducements, come to her aid. A few tears are still a resource, and not to one sex only; a good cry is still an anodyne and a tonic, though the swoon and the vapours are going out. The women novelists themselves, if judged by their work, do not seem to have been made desperately unhappy because in Eden Adam needed a help meet for him. To read their fiction is to be refreshed by the courage, the fidelity, the wits, the loving insight, and above all the sovran good

B

sense of the women depicted in it. Silliness, gush, sentimentality; the minx, the cat, the scold, the harpy, the
gosling; the complete Grundy family may add their tang,
but it takes all kinds of femininity to make the world
as it is, and even a faintly realistic fiction.

Yet, for the most part these novels seem soon to have
faded out of remembrance. In 1904 Mr W. L. Courtney
published his *Feminine Note in Fiction*, a critical survey
of eight women novelists of his day, John Oliver Hobbes,
Mrs Humphry Ward, Lucas Malet, Gertrude Atherton,
Mrs Woods, Mrs Voynich, Miss Robins, and Miss Mary
Wilkins. The abhorred shears had been busy, and the
wind had changed since 1879. Of the twenty-three
writers who wrote or were written about in *Women
Novelists of Queen Victoria's Reign* his index mentions
only four.

In his introduction he maintains that feminine fiction
in general suffers from a passion for detail. It is 'close
analytic, miniature work', usually limited to a narrow
personal experience, with a tendency to the self-conscious
and a limitation of ideals. 'Would it be wrong to say that
a woman's heroine is always a glorified version of herself?' Her fiction is too strenuous, worn out with zeal,
the labour of the half-educated. A woman is that kind
of human being, he quotes, 'who thinks with her back-
bone and feels with her nose'. Her historical evolution
may be summarised in a quintet of terms, three of
which are derogatory, 'slave, hausfrau, madonna, witch,
rival'.

This is a withering summary, though it is honey of
Hymettus compared with the views of Mrs Oliphant on
the Brontës. Mr Courtney's tests of the fiction of the
'nineties were severe; the great, and for the most part,
the man-made novel was his standard. We may if we
please submit the fiction of the 'seventies to similar tests.

Does it, in Mrs Oliphant's own words, concerning its
'nobler arts', exhibit a masterly combination, construction, a humorous survey of life and a deep apprehension
of its problems? Is it of imagination all compact, that
imagination which, as Jean Ingelow said, is 'the crown of
all thoughts and powers', though 'you cannot wear a
crown becomingly if you have no head (worth mentioning) to put it on'? Is it the creative outcome of a central
and comprehensive experience of life, and rich and vivid
and truthful in characterisation? What ardour of mind
went to its making, and what passion of heart? What
kind and quality of philosophy underlies it? Are these
novels puppet work, but exquisite, a variegated patch-
work of cleverness, a relief to 'fine' and exclusive feelings,
a rousing challenge or a deadly malediction? And last—
the question that covers most ground—are they works of
art?

A little quiet reading makes many of these questions
look rather too solemn and superior. Few novels written
by anybody will survive so exacting a catechism. High
standards are essential; but what wilts beneath their test
may still have a virtue and value of its own. And we can
be grateful even for small mercies. In general the novels
that enjoy a brief but vigorous heyday—the idolatry of
the few, or the intoxication of the many—so succeed
simply because they deal with current themes and theses,
or are a lively and entertaining peepshow of their passing
day's fads, fashions, fantasies and fatuities. Having
served their purpose ill or well, they perish, or, rather,
escape from view. And man has had as active a hand in
this manufacture as woman. May to-morrow's brilliant
masterpiece then be as modest as it can!

The rôle of the rival however, in literature as in life, is
a restless and invidious one, and the mere steady approxi-
mation of the work of either sex to that of the other would

be cumulatively distressing. As that astonishing and precocious young man, Otto Weininger, maintained, the sexes may be not simple but compounded, not two but many. If any particular human being, that is, may be said to consist of ten-tenths, some of the tenths may be masculine and some feminine, though it may be difficult in any particular case to fix the precise proportion. The man of genius is said to be compounded of himself, a woman and a child. It is the colourless medium that would be most deplorable. What was Emily Brontë or Christina Rossetti or Queen Elizabeth compounded of? Chromosomes apart, we all have as many granddams as grandsires in our heredity. An Orlando may not be unknown to life, though he is at present unique in fiction.

None the less, 'man and woman created He them'. And a burning and secret hope may be forgiven that woman will discover in herself some inward faculty or power unpossessed by man, and one of which we as yet know little. Reality covers a large area. There may be complete provinces of it awaiting her exploration—truth, beauty, 'meaning'; as yet but faintly dreamed of.

There is little in the fiction of the 'seventies, one must hasten to add, to suggest this. Still, it nourishes the fond belief that woman as woman, and apart from other sovran graces, is gifted with her own fine faculty of divination; that she can flit like a fire-fly from A to F-F-F-*Fool*—as Whistler once reiterated—without bothering about B, C, D and E; that her common-sense, in the old meaning of the word, is peculiarly her own. It suggests, too, that she tends to be a practical idealist. For of all the divinities made in man's or woman's image, none that I am aware of has been solely of feminine workmanship. An assertion a little less sweeping might be made in respect of domestic inventions, those labour-saving devices which are sometimes the joy but usually the secret scorn of the modern housewife. In this fiction, at any rate, ardour for science, pure or applied, is as little manifest as the transcendental. If *The Time Machine* had been written in the 'seventies its author would still, I think, have been a man. So also with *The Return of the Native*. On the other hand, neither Thomas Hardy nor Mr Wells was the author of Jane Austen's novels or of *Villette*.

Voteless, 'unskilled', man-dependent though the women of the 'seventies were, there is surprisingly little of *Lamentations* and of *Ecclesiastes* in their fiction. Its liveliest interest is in human beings as social creatures rather than as pilgrims of eternity. Revolt was in the air—if a very partial and unmethodical survey be a safe guide—but extraneous 'purpose' seems to have been rare, and still more rare, challenge and battle-cry. For the most part these novelists were eager, absorbed, diligent recorders. They were assured of what they believed in. They were happy in the company of their characters and delighted in merely telling a story, though even that simple and seductive achievement cannot but involve a good deal of 'life' in solution.

The ghost drifts or shambles in; the psychic intrudes. But the effect of the spectral in Rhoda Broughton's *Twilight Stories* is a little deadened by the terse postscript, 'This is a fact'. Mrs Oliphant's solemn and memorable *A Beleaguered City* was of 1880. But nowhere apparent in this fiction is man's peculiar inclination to regard an infinite (or finite) universe as though it were a concatenation of miracles, or an over-populated mousetrap, or an 'unweeting' machine, or an excruciating jest. One becomes conscious of a vague difference in intention, in the views given of life, and in what one most wants in it. There is more wit and irony than humour. Fantasy finds small place in it, and there is nothing—unless unintentionally—grotesque. The smart, the self-conscious, the too clever is uncommon, and where it is found it is, like old rubber, desperately perished in appearance and effect. Even the sentimental seems to outlast the meretricious; and the rather commonplace love story, quietly and serenely narrated, or even the mildest record of the domesticated may keep enough of its interestingness to make it still readable by the not too fastidious.

In matter many of these novels are singularly substantial; in style, sound, workmanlike, practised, and a little formal. If anything, their authors appear to be a little over rather than under-educated; or, rather, too well-informed. For the fine novelist is in most (that he needs most) self-schooled, self-taught. As a child with his hornbook, Nature stood him, not always very kindly, at her knee; for the rest he went, mind and heart, to the world at large. Its gallery is enormous and open to all. *Knowledge*, however valuable it may be, may prove imaginatively indigestible.

Of the men characters in the 'seventies the *paterfamilias* and his generation are usually natural and vigorous enough. The romantic hero, the Lothario, the daredevil, the man of fashion or about town, the Bohemian, is apt to be less so. These novelists are seldom completely at home in their younger men. They are making them up; the creative breath is faint that should free them into life. Even a hero, who is 'good, rich, handsome, clever, and kind'—and nowadays these epithets would appear in a different order—may remain inadequately vitalised. We watch him, but remain uneasy and incompletely transformed. It must be remembered, however, that fiction consists solely of words, more or less evocatory, and that it rests in great part with the reader to decide on the more and the less.

There may be artificial hindrances. Richard Harold

M'Gregor, for example—with his dark grey eyes and great yellow or 'heavy tawny' moustache, his head of curly yellow hair, a sabre cut on his cheek, a meerschaum pipe between his lips, his severe Greek beauty gilded by vespertinal carriage lamps, or starlit as he sits with his sweetheart, 'each on their several tombstone'— is it credible that if this ravishing young man were yet alive he would still be only in his early 'eighties? Others of his contemporaries too, with their arch or sprightly or solemn conversation, their elegance, or their boisterousness or their boorishness or their artisticalness, or the exquisite aroma (or stifling reek) of the tobacco that clings about them— all this suggests tapers at a shrine, or a sensitive shrinking from the embraces of a bear. Because our novelist is unusually a little self-conscious in their company, so are we. We must strip off this mask of the period and evade this trepidation before we can use what else we are given, and out of these fragments and what they imply make of such characters explorable wholes.

But though even the finest fiction consists only of words, every such word may have been the outcome of an impassioned choice. Its maker himself, therefore, cannot but be immanent in it, though usually he is not at hand. He influences the scene as may the intangible presence of a divinity, whose all it is, and whose presence is everywhere, even though it remain unheeded. In fiction which falls short of this standard, but not too far, that presence is more obvious and externalised. The reader is on private property, and evidences of its owner are everywhere conspicuous. At an extreme, such a story becomes a mere essay with illustrative puppets. And what if the lord of the Manor be a lady?

Whatever the converse may be, I am inclined to think that when a man is reading a novel written by a woman, he is more or less pervasively aware that he is in feminine

company. This awareness cannot depend on any lack of
artistry since, surely, it is never absent when Jane Austen
is delighting us with her company. It has a subtle and
pervasive effect extremely difficult to define. Rhoda
Broughton—vivid, impulsive, romantic, satirical; Mrs
Oliphant—cultured, fervent yet amused, courageous and
austere; Mrs Lynn Linton—mordant, daunting, cold;
Mrs Alexander—sympathetic, equable, just, tender-
hearted; Jessie Fothergill—earnest, reserved, aspiring, a
little stilted; Mrs Annie Edwardes—bold, acute, worldly;
Ouida—witty, cynical, flighty, odd; Rosa Carey—observant, sentimental, scrupulous, lover of scene and season;
Jean Ingelow—oddly unreal, meandering, but with occasional glints of penetrating imagination—mere glimpses
all of them, and of but a few of many, and on how slender
a foundation. But how in a few words convey the phantom of personality, which in every one of us has so many
strands, as it disengages itself from a piece of pure invention concerned with imaginary scenes and characters,
and whose influence when it is entirely unpremeditated
is only the more effective.

But apart from this various and often delightful companionship and apart from all pleasures and interests of
a literary kind that await the reader of this bygone
fiction, it affords another diversion—and one which was
certainly not aimed at by its writers. At the mere
thought of it, indeed, the busy pen might at once have
fallen idle from the nerveless fingers. None the less, alas,
it may possibly prove the most entertaining—the charm,
that is, and the illumination afforded by the old-fashioned.
Here it is the realist, the copyist, who suffers most, or at
any rate suffers most for the time being. Centuries hence
the antiquarian may fall upon his work as if it were the
funeral memorials of a Tutankhamen. After an interval
of fifty years its appearance is merely odd and queer and

pacifying and, if one was then a child in these matters, a little pathetic. Manners, habits, hobbies, dress, furniture, food, frivolities—how swiftly the dreadful charge of quaintness can be brought against them.

Here, for example, is an interior, admirably informed, but closely resembling the pell-mell of an auction-room, yet still as inhabitable as a dream. We have mounted the steps into a prosperous city man's London mansion, in the days when dozens of young stockbrokers, 'more or less jewelled, white-hatted and blue-cravatted, were to be seen flitting to and fro about Mark Lane...any sunshiny morning between March and October'.

There was the suite of reception rooms, three in number—the yellow damask room, the blue satin room, and the crimson velvet room—all panelled with enormous looking-glasses, lit by chandeliers like pendent fountains, and crowded with gilded furniture, pictures in heavy Italian frames, tables of Florentine mosaic, cabinets in buhl and marqueterie, ormolu clocks, and expensive trifles from all quarters of the globe. Here was nothing antique—nothing rare, save for its costliness. Here were no old masters, no priceless pieces of majolica, no Cellini caskets, no enamels, no intagli, no Etruscan tazza, no Pompeian relics; but in their place great vases of the finest modern Sèvres; paintings by Frith, Maclise, Stanfield, Meissonier, and David Roberts; bronzes by Barbedienne; Chinese ivory carvings, and wonderful clockwork toys from Geneva. The malachite table in the boudoir from the International Exhibition of 1851; the marble group in the alcove at the end of the third drawing-room was by Marochetti; the Gobelin tapestries were among the latest products of the Imperial looms. Money, in short, was there omnipresent—money in abundance; and even taste. But not taste of the highest order. Not that highly trained taste which seems to 'run' in certain classes of society, like handsome hands or fine complexions.

It is a museum piece, after Gibbon, but, alas, the intervening years seem to have put it under glass.

A dining-room, on the other hand, from *The Wooing O't* exhibits taste of an order high enough at least to satisfy the first-cousin of an earl, and a fastidious cousin at that:

...A most dainty apartment it was: the walls a pale grey,

richly but lightly decorated in the Pompeian style; the hangings
of soft amber, fringed and relieved with borders of red-brown
velvet.

The dinner was perfection. The poetically-arranged dessert, with
its delicate service of engraved glass and silver, the profusion of
flowers, the noiseless attendance which seemed to anticipate every
want, the easy elegance, the quiet simplicity, made one forget, by
the absence of effort, the immense cost at which this completeness
was attained.

But Maggie, one of the guests at this feast, is not quite
at her ease, for her rival shares its perfection, and this is
her *demi-toilette*:

...rich, dull, thick silk, of the most delicate spring-like green,
with quantities of priceless white lace, and emeralds sparkling at
ears and throat—a sort of half-subdued sparkle in her great eyes,
and a rich colour in her clear brunette cheek.

'Can the force of civilisation further go?' thought Trafford, as
he unfolded his napkin and prepared to enjoy his *potage à la
printanier....*

And here is Mr Lascelles' drawing-room, the Mecca of
his 'spiritual harem':

The table was deal, with heavy, plainly-squared legs and a plain,
unornamented 'autumn-leaf' table cover; the old oak chairs were
stiff, hard, and straight-backed, and there was not an arm-chair, nor
a lounge, nor a sofa anywhere. The cold grey walls were hung with
a few pictures—all sacred subjects; some in oils, copies from the
Old Masters, and some of the Arundel Society set in plain white
frames, without even a gilded edge. A few flowers in *grès de
Flandres* vases gave the sole signs of living life there were; but
these were only on two brackets which flanked the feet of a large
carved ivory crucifix—an antique—that hung against the wall....
It was a room that suggested more than it expressed....

And last, here is Lady Lanchester's country-house
dining-room bedecked for an improvised 'hop'.

I don't wish to see a more cheery scene than the Wentworth
dining-room—transmogrified with pink calico and Union Jacks and
wreaths of evergreens and flowers, it hardly knew itself, the band
consisting of a big fiddle, a little fiddle, harp and bones.

As for dress, an old lady in *Poor Pretty Bobbie* by
Rhoda Broughton tells how in her day young people
damped their clothes to make them stick more closely to
them, 'to make them define more distinctly the outline
of form and limbs'. 'One's waist was under one's arms,
the sole object of which seemed to be to outrage nature
by pushing one's bust up into one's chin, and one's legs
were revealed through one's scanty drapery with startling
candour as one walked or sat.' Not quite so in the
'seventies:

> How lovely she was! None but a very lovely woman could have
> stood the dull ivory satin dress she wore, fitting tight, without a
> fold or a crease in the waist...trailing straight and long behind
> her. She wore a black lace fichu, and elbow-sleeves with black lace
> ruffles falling from them. The fichu was fastened with a golden
> brooch; beyond that was not a ribbon, not a frill, not a jewel
> or a flower about her. And her beauty came triumphant through
> the ordeal.

And Hermione, at the dinner party when her husband,
the atheist, is unmasked:

> She had never looked so well and had never been dressed with
> such a prodigality of wealth and luxury. Her dress was 'moon-
> light'-coloured satin...with a good deal of fine white lace and
> silver embroidery about it. She wore diamonds in her hair and
> round her neck.... She didn't look more than twenty five years of
> age with her fair innocent face, crowned with the curly golden hair.
> ...Her beautiful arms with one diamond band on each; her softly
> moulded figure which had bloomed into generosity without losing
> its grace.

If the 'seventies be any guide, then, the novelist who
falls short of the best and brightest must beware of a too-
precise descriptiveness. 'Art is coy and loves a secret.'
And Time caricatures the lately past in precisely the same
fashion as Mr Punch scoffs at the just-arrived.

No longer does a young married woman flush with
timidity at meeting a strange young man in a field of
barley, or steal out for a 'dawdle and scramble' into her

kindly, detested, land-owner husband's park in the dowdiest cloak and hat she can find—having first removed her wedding-ring. And as for the Dolly who reminded Miss Broughton of *Poems and Ballads*, she has recently appeared (though in a different walk of life) as the heroine of *Gentlemen Prefer Blondes*, and there has been explored. Yet even she would have been a little scandalised perhaps at the thought of reading *Humphrey Clinker* to her father in her 'teens, as did the old lady of 1820 told of in *Twilight Stories*.

How oddly reviving, too, are passing references in this old fiction to what was then 'the latest thing out' or to the taken-for-granted in that smaller, bygone, darker, gayer, unevener, homelier London: to the pre-Raphaelites, to Wagner, to Mr Tennyson, to the craze for Bach, Botticelli and blue china, to gas that mortified the atmosphere and blackened the ceiling, to tea at ten o'clock, to card games (Commerce and Chow-chow), to antiquated criminals. Rush ('Pig to-day, and plenty of plum sauce'), Palmer and Townley, to bonnet and shawl (a combination which poor man has never forgotten having succumbed to), to the learned lingo of the latest science, to the gentleman's sunshade, to the hansom cabman 'in his Sunday black', to the new-fangled mowing machine, to Solitaire, to waltz and galop and mazurka, to opiates and cosmetics, to 'pipesticks' and silk slipper tobacco-pouches, to Martinis (the rifle), to personal letters from Worth to his choicest clients, to neuralgia—the 'malady in vogue', to children who 'fear' their parents, and servants who refuse to stay in service more than the 'conventional year'.

We gaze wistfully on these fading memoranda of a vanished scene. We are amused. But now and then we may surprise ourselves smiling a little wrily at the discovery that many of the novelties of which we are most

conscious in our own disillusioned era are not quite so
dewy and verdant as we suppose. One novelist assures
us, 'No young gentleman who is a gentleman ever *is*
eager about anything now-a-days'; another, 'It was not
that he felt at all happier or satisfied or contented—not
that life appeared much brighter to him, only *it had to
be lived*'. That is hardly a sentiment alien to our time.
The objection of the dowager of the 'seventies 'to the
newest kind of dancing', may be no surprise, but it is
little short of a shock to chance in *Probation* on such a
passage as, 'I fancy the children are as good as their
parents would like them to be....The new education
theory is that when children are allowed their own way
they always do right, or if they do wrong someone else
is to blame for it'. And we are by no means in strange
surroundings when we read:

Hugo and his companion left the mill-yard, and paced down the
street in the bitter cold of the March twilight, now rapidly becoming darkness. The lamps were being lighted; some shops were open;
the passengers along the streets were not many; the great factories
were silent, there was no cloud of smoke to obscure the frostily
twinkling stars.

These and many similar curiosities will be the unforeseen
harvest of an adventure into the novels of the women
of the 'seventies. If the reader disdain them, he will be
less well rewarded. All fiction, however little its author
may have intended it, becomes at last a picturesque
annotation of history. The very prejudices displayed
in it are revealing. But as with many other things in
life, what may be an advance is not necessarily progress.
Time puts things into proportion, or at any rate into a
clearer relation one with another. The novelists attempt
a similar feat, but Time has his way with them too.

For which reason, and apart from the work of the
masters and mistresses of the art, there must be of fiction,
as of most things civilised, a constant supply laid on, like

gas, like water, like beauties and celebrities, like leading articles, like politics. Yet though the fashion changes, in essence fiction changes not very much. And even though it flourish as briefly as a poppy in the wheat, it may have consumed the very soul of its maker. The press rings and rings again with carillons of congratulation and flattery, or damns with faint praise. The critic gently or severely displaces the reviewer. A hurricane may sweep across the insular scene from France, from Russia, or from Germany maybe. A Henry James may widen the range, refine the technique, and multiply the difficulties; and the censor may add to the price and increase the sale of some forbidden and even possibly purging dainty which he intended to destroy.

But when all is said, the actual experience of sharing the company of these once living and eager and now half-forgotten 'lady fictionists'—and even of the less endearing of them—is a rather tragic one.

> Blow, blow, thou winter wind,
> Thou are not so unkind
> As man's ingratitude....

A dead book is a more pathetic, a more forlorn object than a tombstone. It strikes nearer home. In the reading of many such books, even though in the process life stirs in them again, one's mind, if it is capable of sentiment, becomes haunted at last. These are ghosts. A clumsy interloper has pushed open a door only just ajar, and his heavy tread resounds in the still, abandoned rooms. The phantom tenants, once eager and warm-blooded, would, I believe, gladly keep him out. They are less alien to him than he to them. But the wan dismantled house, the wind in its willows, the owl in its cold chimney, night-skies of the nowhere overhead, remains defenceless. It cowers in silence, but cannot eject the trespasser.

And the distant rumour that thrills the air is not only

the sound of Time's dark waters, but is mingled with the roar of our own busy printing presses. 'As we are, so you shall be!' The very years we now so actively occupy will soon be packed up in an old satchel and labelled, the 'twenties; and our little, hot, cold, violent, affected, brand new, exquisite, fresh little habits of mind, manners, hobbies, fashions, ideals will have thinned and vanished away, will steadily have evaporated, leaving only a frigid deposit of history; a few decaying buildings, a few pictures, some music, some machine-made voices, an immense quantity of print—most of it never to be disturbed again.

In the midst of the battle maybe it is indiscreet to muse on the tranquil moonlit indifference of the night that will follow. Yet one cannot but be reminded of it as one grubs and burrows in these old novels—re-animating old heroines, not merely dead and buried (for no novelist has power to keep them so) but forgotten. It may be that many devotees still visit the derelict scene. If it is not so, may I be forgiven for disturbing its peace. Walter Savage Landor was confident that his work would be remembered. 'I shall dine late; but the dining-room will be well-lighted, the guests few and select.' That too may be the postponed joy of some of our novelists. But Landor knew also that such a destiny is unusual:

—Laodameia died; Helen died; Leda, the beloved of Jupiter, went before. It is better to repose in the earth betimes than to sit up late; better, than to cling pertinaciously to what we feel crumbling under us, and to protract an inevitable fall. We may enjoy the present while we are insensible of infirmity and decay: but the present, like a note in music, is nothing but as it appertains to what is past and what is to come. There are no fields of amaranth on this side of the grave; there are no voices, O Rhodope, that are not soon mute, however tuneful; there is no name, with whatever emphasis of passionate love repeated, of which the echo is not faint at last.

§4

Andrew Lang in the 'Seventies —and After

By George Saintsbury

It will pretty certainly be known to any R.S.L. audience that even before 1870 the Press had quite got rid of most if not all the disadvantages which in earlier years had hung about it, and which had deterred men of some social and undoubted intellectual rank from doing it service. No more had not merely the neophyte but the journalist of some experience outside as well as inside journalism to think himself lucky if he could clear ten shillings by a full morning's work: only in the remotest country villages did old ladies deplore the fate of their nieces who married contributors to penny papers. The lift which had been given, in respect of more or less known contributorship, by the *Edinburgh* and the *Quarterly*, by *Blackwood* and *Fraser*, had, with less or more of the element of 'known-ness' extended its influence to daily and weekly prints; and men leaving Oxford and Cambridge had for a full generation, though perhaps as a rule under some pretence of by-work on their way to Bench of this or that kind, taken the Press's sovereigns.

Anybody of tolerable intelligence could of course see that this new Island which had risen from the waves, though providing comfortable colony-places and whole-some food for respectable people in a very satisfactory manner, was in a way a sort of Island of the Sirens—of the Sirens in their proper vocation, which it must be remembered, though it often is not, was not so much to gobble sailors up or drown them as to keep them from their business and prevent their reaching nobler goals than it could itself provide. I believe there are some people who regard or affect to regard my friend of nearly forty years, the late Mr Andrew Lang, as having been to some extent a Victim of this Sirenity of the Press, and it may be worth while to consider this, with some other points about him.

I did not know Lang in his very earliest literary days, for though he was a fellow of my own College, Merton, his Fellowship only began some months after my Postmastership ended; and though it actually followed from this that we had been for some years undergraduates together, it happened that I was very little in his college, Balliol. He had come up rather late, having passed through two Scotch Universities, St Andrews and Glasgow, but I doubt whether anybody ever spent, either in northern or southern Academes, days more preparative for a literary life than he had when he first listened to the Siren's voice. Indeed my doubt would be audacious enough to extend itself further, and question whether anybody, undergraduate or don, Oxonian or Cantab, about the year 1869 possessed knowledge of ancient and modern literature as literature, coupled with power to make use of that knowledge in a literary way, to a greater extent than Lang.

At the same time nobody was ever less of the typical imaginary pedant or merely bookish person than he was. Some physical defects—at the very time when he had just published his first book in 1872 considerable doubt was entertained by the faculty whether he was not hopelessly consumptive—prevented him from being a great practical sportsman. But he used to inform his friends, with just pride but perfect consciousness of the double

edgedness of the classification, that authorities in cricket
had ranked him as 'a change bowler' and he never lost
interest in the game or (though to a somewhat less extent)
in several others, during the whole of his life. In what
used to be, and perhaps always should be the greatest of
all Press subjects whether on the more abstract or still
more on the party side, he could with difficulty be got to
show any interest. I used to say of him that he couldn't
be a Liberal and wouldn't be a Tory. He did not with
any willingness treat religious subjects, while Science in
the more limited sense but with the largest capital, was
not his business, yet the *Encyclopaedia* held few other
subjects on which he could not write something worth
reading.

I do not know in what paper Lang made the first of
his many thousand appearances in periodicals. He had,
I think, family connections with the *Saturday Review*,
which had already for some years exemplified and har-
boured the great though rather indefinable change in
English journalism. New papers, which did not always
live to be old, were constantly starting in the late 'sixties
and early 'seventies: and to one of them at least—most
virtuous and hospitable but ill by any profit rewarded,
though it kept itself alive and contributed to the alive-
keeping of its contributors for a considerable period—to
the *Academy*, he was, I think, a supporter from the beginning. But the fact was that no editor who had the very
slightest fitness for his business could hesitate about
annexing anything of Lang's that was offered to him and
promptly demanding more. I have had myself no short
or small experience of editing or assisting to edit; a very
large experience in contributing; and, until quite recently, what it is not, I think, extravagant to call an
immense experience in reading this division of literature.
I do not hesitate to say that, allowing for his not taking

service in the political, the religious and some technical departments, Lang was quite the king of all the contributors to 'the papers' that I have known. His vessel did not carry—thanks to the limitations just mentioned it did not require—such heavy metal as H. D. Traill's; I fancy that it may itself have been of slightly too heavy a draught in respect of knowledge on the part of the reader to be able to skim the waves of universal popularity as did, especially latterly, the craft of our common friend Sir Edmund Gosse. But for a compound of scholarship and lighthandedness, of multilegence and complete freedom from pedantry, of what may be called literary good manners, infinite wit and a peculiar humour he had, I think, in his own generation no equal—certainly no superior.

And wherever it was first shown there I am sure appeared, though it could hardly be separately recognised till it was followed by something else, a peculiarity which has not yet been mentioned but which depended without doubt on things that have been. And this was Lang's extraordinary individuality. You could not, after you had seen a little of his writing, mistake it for any one else's or any one else's for his. Nor did this individuality depend upon any tricks of style in the lower sense like the snipsnap of Macaulay; the chaotic riches of Carlyle; the repetitions and word-groupings of Arnold; the infused blank verse (in their so different kinds) of Ruskin and Dickens; the elaborate rhythm and colouring of Pater. It was most commonly said to be like Thackeray's, and no doubt there was a strong resemblance of spirit; but I really doubt whether the greatest similarity between their manners was not the fact that neither had *any* manner easy to analyse or capable of being pinned out and down. Only great incompetence or great prejudice—for choice perhaps a skilful combination of the

two—could fail to recognise this idiosyncrasy. I remember talking about him, not long after his death, with
a person by no means incompetent but the contrary, a
scholar, a man familiar with society, an expert in various
kinds of press-work, but one, I think, who did not like
Lang either personally or critically as much as I did. He
had been indulging in some little drawbacks and *dis-
tinguos* to some of my commendatory remarks; but when
I came to this point of absolute individuality he boggled
no more. He fully admitted that what Lang could give
you nobody else could; that he copied nobody and that
nobody had ever succeeded in copying him. I have
indeed been told that some wicked men in clubs have
ticketed others as 'Sham Langs', but the resemblance was
merely caricatural in personal ways and simply non-
existent in literary form.

Curiously, but rather conveniently and almost immediately after writing the preceding paragraph, I saw
in print a description of Lang's style as 'a waggish drawl'.
The context, unless it was ironical, seemed to show no
hostile intention in this; but hostile or friendly, serious
or ironical, it was extremely, though no doubt not quite
unintentionally, illuminative. As adequate, or even as
partially correct, one could not accept it for a moment.
Lang's speech might from anybody who did not intend
to be specially complimentary be called a drawl; I have
been told that his consciousness of it was one of the
reasons for his refusing professorships, though he did
sometimes lecture. But how his printed matter could
produce on any one the effect of drawling is a mystery to
me—the drawl must have lain in the mind's ear that read,
not in the mind's mouth or pen that wrote. And this
explanation, so frequently applicable in changed applica-
tions to misestimates and misunderstandings, is even
more valuable as regards the 'waggish'. Of course if

anybody takes this word to be a synonym for 'humorous'
we begin to see a great light—for humorous 'in a quiet
way' (as a good-for-nothing satirist-contemporary of
those days observed of something else) Lang always was,
except perhaps sometimes, though rarely, when humour
was doubtfully in place. But 'waggish' he was never or
very seldom, on a few occasions when I think he did it on
purpose by way of throwing more contempt on his
subject. Yet the description is, as was said, valuable. It
explains his immense popularity, especially in the number
of miscellaneous and non-political matters that he wrote
about for so many years in the *Daily News*, because it is
quite possible that a certain proportion of the *vulgus* did
take this quiet humour for a variety of the drawn-out
joking they admire on the stage. And it is possible that
others may have disliked and may now dislike it because
they took it at the same 'angle of the moral oxygen' and
did not like that angle, not being able to see round it.

It was not till just this side of the middle of the
'seventies that I actually met Lang; for during their
earlier years I had been living first in Guernsey and then
in the north of Scotland. But I had, of course, seen a good
deal of his work in different places, and it so happened
that his first book, *Ballads and Lyrics of Old France*, dealt
with a subject which (partly I suppose owing to my residence in the Channel Islands with Hugo for neighbour
though not acquaintance) I had myself taken up some
years earlier. The title, however, which has just been
given was not the whole one; for 'and other poems' was
added, and these other poems supply a considerable part
of the matter. To begin with a book of verse has always
been more or less the proper thing—in fact I believe it is
not improper even now. But it was not the proper thing
as yet, though it came to be so before very long, to begin
with a book of prose compacted of short newspaper

articles. I have sometimes been sorry that the double entry did not then prevail: for the contrast-combination in Lang's case would have been very remarkable, and might have 'set' the idiosyncrasy of the writer with a useful decision at an early period, before the reading world. As it was the world read the articles with eagerness as they appeared and then forgot all about them individually, while rather neglecting the verse which is certainly not negligible.

Probably few people have had a better right to claim, as though in different words he did claim, the benefit of Anne Evans's great definition of humour, 'thinking in jest but feeling in earnest', than Lang: but the 'feeling' never got proper recognition. Its verse expression was somewhat unlucky in point of time. There is not very much in this particular book, though some of the translations necessarily employ it, of the formal French versification which a little later became so common from his and other hands: but the whole is more or less of that pre-Raphaelite colour which was having its day if it had not fully had it, and much more than less of that great school of nineteenth-century poetry which after starting under Keats and Shelley, and restarting after a short interval under Tennyson and Browning had, with no interval at all, taken the pre-Raphaelite turn.

Now fashion (which if not exactly a synonym for 'day' is closely connected with it), though not necessarily either a bad or a good thing, is well known to have perhaps more bad than good effects and consequences. However good it is in itself it can be exaggerated or caricatured, and by unskilful imitation turned to bad. If it is bad in itself, why it *is* bad, and there's no more to be said. Whatever its intrinsic quality, people are apt to get tired of it to its own unfair disadvantage; or to make mistakes about other things which are not the fashion or, worst of

all, to take more fancy to these *because* they are not the
fashion. Comparatively few are those—and profoundly
grateful to Providence or the Muses, or Fate or Chance
or whatever object of gratitude takes the place of these
in their Scheme of Things, should those few be—who can
appreciate all poetry which is poetry whether it be Job's
or the present Poet Laureate's, Donne's or Dryden's,
Sappho's or Christina Rossetti's, Cowper's or Mr Swinburne's. To these fortunate ones—perhaps there is no one
who possesses this best of good fortunes entirely and
absolutely, but there certainly have been some who had
it in large shares—date and subject, form and language,
are of comparative unimportance: many instances have
been given, some certainly not merely jocular, of recognition of the poetry without understanding of the
language.

Their critical appreciation has something in it of
water—divining or reaction to atmosphere—the rather
hackneyed but beautiful word *aura* would be better still.
I do not think many people who possess this sense—for
one can give it place in the rather numerously occupied
room of the sixth senses—have refused its satisfactory
exercise to Lang's verse work—though some of them may
not think that he had the faculty in its highest degree.
Much is translation, and translation of famous things in
pure lyric, where, it has sometimes been said, you must,
to succeed, be as good a poet as your original was, and
even then you will give another good thing, not the same.

Therefore when you find the poetical atmosphere or
aura in a translation the translator must be entitled to
the credit of some of it: and I think it is to be found in
the book I am speaking of as well as in the more definitely
and temporarily fashionable *Ballades* of some years later.
And a very uncommon talent, not easily distinguishable
from genius, was displayed in the prose translation of the

Odyssey which he did in collaboration with another friend, and for some of the latter years of his life a colleague of mine, S. H. Butcher. I think I have heard this book described by a person professionally connected with bookselling as one of the most popular translations from the classics he has himself known. That it was at the same time one of the most scholarly might be put down, not merely by Lang's enemies but by a not ill-natured reader, to the fact of Butcher's participation, but that his attribution would be insufficient ought to be seen by any one scholar enough himself to appreciate not merely the singly turned out Theocritus, but almost every part of Lang's work. That he was not, in certain restricted senses of 'scholarship', a great master of it, may be true enough. But he was penetrated, in a way which was getting rarer in his own time and has been increasing its rarity ever since, with a sense of Greek and Roman literature which, when it was more common, was frequently disjoined from any extensive knowledge of English, and was very seldom conjoined with any knowledge of other modernity except perhaps French which itself did not ascend beyond the *grand siècle* with Montaigne or Rabelais or both. There was, of course, in a few cases and at one time a certain acquaintance with Italian, the coming in and the going out of which have always both been rather mysteries to me. Every girl from Scott's heroines to my own sisters seems to have been taught Dante and Petrarch and Tasso and even Ariosto as a matter of course. Have these been changed for civism and genetics?

Now how many modern languages Lang knew, in a fashion capable of satisfying the examiners, I do *not* know. But I do know that all his work was, as I have said, saturated with knowledge of literature ancient and modern.

Of course some one may say: 'As far as the printed

Lang of the 'seventies is concerned, we can form our own
opinions: we only need you for your accidental and
illegitimate advantage of having known him personally'.
There may be something in this, but not much. In the
first place, by far the larger part of the printed 'Lang of
the 'seventies' never got reprinted at all, and though the
extraordinary 'kenspeckleness' of his manner might
enable a tolerably keen-sighted person to follow him all
through the files of the *Daily News* and the volumes of
the *Saturday* as well as in the signed matter of the
Academy and elsewhere—that is not exactly everybody's
job. There is, however, something more to be said of the
work before one turns to the man, I have seen this very
'dispersedness' (as Shakespeare or Shakespeare's stage-
direction-maker might call it) brought as a sort of charge
from quite early dates to almost or quite this day against
him. There is no doubt that the public does like to have
something definite by which—if we are amiable we say
'to remember', if not quite so 'to call' a man. It is not
mere nastiness to say that Gray owes more than half his
fame to the less intrinsic advantage of being 'the author
of the *Elegy*'. There is particular luck in this because a
whole department of poetry and of literature is thus
conveniently pinned to a man's coat or *vice versa*: 'Gray?
Oh yes! he wrote the *Elegy*'. '*Elegy*? Oh yes, that's the
thing that Gray wrote'. And so with many others. Now
in all the small and closely spaced type of the columns
that stand under Lang's name in the catalogue of the
London Library you cannot, I fear, pick out a single
entry with which Lang can be thus differentially and
monopolisingly ticketed. There are or were people who
would tell you that he intended *Helen of Troy* to be such
a ticket, and that it is only a failure of one. I venture to
differ with the first half of this: but there is a certain
amount of truth about the second, though I think the

book deserved more success than it obtained. What was said above as to ill luck of times and seasons comes in here with quiet force. But if anybody desires to test Lang's poetic value in the first instance, at less expense of effort, let him read the 'Ballade of his Choice of a Sepulchre' and the Burnaby sonnet. At the worst he will not have wasted his time: for a result of dissatisfaction will show that he does not himself know poetry when he sees it and had better let it alone. Some people not so hopeless prefer, I believe, one or other of the Gordon epicedes to the Burnaby one: but that is only an instance of the common error of judging by subject, not treatment.

The mention of the Sepulchre piece—one of the most charming things of the kind that, in a tolerably wide familiarity with verse, I know—will lead with peculiar propriety to what may be called the specially epitaphic part of this paper. Dismissing for a moment Lang the architect, and artist, what was Lang the man? There has been some talk about this lately: and as only a comparatively small minority of the hearers, that is to say, readers, of this talk can be supposed to be in a position to check it by extensive personal experience it is perhaps just as well that those who *are* in such a position should put in their evidence. I may have said it before in print— but what I say twice is not necessarily untrue—that I do not think anybody outside his own family knew Lang by frequent companionship and conversation much better than I did. For not a few years we walked together— people walked then and consequently talked—for about three parts of the length of more specially habitable London, two or three times a week. And if any one should say: 'Ah! he couldn't get rid of you!' this is futile: for he could easily have done so. Being a faster though not a much more legible writer than myself he had always done his leader ten minutes or a quarter of an hour before

me: and needed no other excuse, if any at all had been
wanted, to go.

This frequentation continued on the scale mentioned
from nearly the middle of the 'seventies to not far from
that of the 'eighties and on a somewhat reduced scale (I
had given up contributing to one of the papers concerned)
for another ten years, with all sorts of miscellaneous com-
panionships. When I moved to Scotland in 1895 our meetings were necessarily fewer and farther between: but I
don't think he often missed coming to see me in Edinburgh
on his annual way to St Andrews. Now I cannot say as
Rupert, Lord Derby, said on being sarcastically asked as
to the qualities of a member of his cabinet that he 'had
heard no complaints'. At no time in his life I should
think, and at none of the greater part of that life which
I knew, was he universally popular. I have always
thought more or less, and since the complaints have
multiplied and become acrimonious I have thought still
more, of two incidents, one in literature, and one in life,
which bear upon the matter. The first is the case of the
immortal Scrub, who was sure that people in the company
were talking of him because they laughed consumedly.
It was not Lang's habit to laugh consumedly: but he
sometimes had an air of not being violently interested in
things and persons, which people who were not oversure
of themselves might mistake. It is curious that in such a
case it should not occur to anybody that perfect immunity
from discomfort is provided by simply not troubling
yourself whether the other person is interested in you or
not: but unfortunately it seldom does occur. The other
story, which in fact had nothing to do personally with
Lang, is still perhaps illuminative. A thousand years
ago, or perhaps a little less, there happened in a country
drawing-room, about afternoon calling-time, to be present
a sufficiently ordinary company—say, one married couple,

one at least temporarily single man and four or five ladies, married and unmarried. The coupled male having some appointment or other left his wife and went forth, bestowing a quite amiable, but not theatrically enthusiastic nod-bow on the other man, whom he did not know very intimately. When he met his wife at home later she said (I fear, laughing), 'Ah! *you* don't know what a state of mind you put Mr Dash in this afternoon. As soon as you had shut the door he got up and began to walk furiously up and down, saying, "Why won't that fellow shake hands with me?"' Now it happened that 'that fellow' had very recently left Oxford where, a thousand years ago or a little less, hand-shaking was, whatever may be the case now, quite out of fashion. With men of your own College you hardly did it at all. With outcollege men, as a civility, you probably did it if you met them at the end of term just before they were going down, and perhaps at the beginning of it when you met them for the first time. At casual meetings, unless there were formal introductions, never.

Now this not quite unamusing story came to my knowledge before I ever knew Lang: and as I have already said he had nothing personally to do with it. But not very long after I did know him I began to think of him in connection with it, and recent things have brought the remembrance and resemblance freshly home. Several people seem to have interpreted Lang's manner as that of one not thinking them worth shaking hands with, when, as a matter of fact, he was probably not thinking about them at all except as coincidences of existence. I suppose he could not be called invariably affable; but your invariably affable person requires a certain extra touch from Providence to prevent him from being frequently intolerable. Now in all those years—many of them thickly frequented years, of which I have spoken—

I never found his company other than agreeable. In the
earliest days he did tell somebody—at least the somebody
told *me* so—that I laughed like a character in *Les Cloches
de Corneville*. But as I didn't know how the person in the
Cloches de Corneville laughed and he didn't say it to me,
I fear that I was not much moved.

As a rule you could not have better company, of your
own sex; I have known no better story-teller. To this
day, speaking as a critical literary Epicurean, I do not
know for which of two heard story-tellings I ought most
to thank my stars—Mr Anstey Guthrie's *Vice versa* told
on the eve of publication by Lang who knew it in process
of manufacture, or one of Mr Kipling's, recounted by its
author before he had actually put it to press. But the
first experience was, of course, an exception: and Lang
was quite as good at ordinary conversation on a great
number of subjects: politics and religion, as above, being
almost the only ones excluded. Providence had further
been kind in prearranging that though I was utterly
unfitted for either of his two favourite sports, cricket and
angling, I have never been tired of reading reports of
cricket and possessed a brother-in-law who was sometimes allowed (except by the others) to be the best fisher-
man in Hampshire—so that I was not a philistine or an
ignoramus on either subject. And as for books, one more
thing at least is specially worth saying on that head. I
do not think I ever met a man so utterly free—I am sure
I never met one more so—from one of the commonest
and most contemptible of the plagues that beset the
'littery gent' be he poet or proseman or both—jealousy
of others who write about the subjects which he himself,
more or less, specially prefers. 'That's *my* thunder', is
the motto of the Dennises all over literary history. I have
known lifelong hatreds spring from no apparent cause but
this. But I never saw a touch of it in Lang after I knew

him: and I am entitled to speak on the matter because, as I have mentioned already, he and I both began with the same subject—Old French—and I was before very long luckier in getting hold of creditable and profitable employment on this subject than he was. And he actually introduced me, if not directly to these, to others which were likely to lead to them. But it was quite impossible for him to do anything ungenerous, even as it was impossible for him to do anything unliterary. And this last word may give us a keynote to a brief conclusion or summing up of the whole matter of Andrew Lang both in the 'seventies and as long as I knew him. I have said and now repeat that with him literary did not mean pedantic. I don't think I ever knew any one whom it would be more absurd to call a pedant: it was not much more adequately synonymed by 'bookish', for that word generally implies limitation to books. The Muses have, with the vulgar, a bad reputation for neglecting the garments, the manners, the age, and other trimmings (as one may call them) of their lovers; they did not do so with Lang. And the quality of his literariness itself was, if not as unique as his delivery of it, very unusual. It was pervasive but not obtrusive; varied but not superficial; facile to a wonderful degree, but never trivial or trumpery. It may be that in one way it did not concentrate itself enough—did not leave two or three big books instead of thirty or forty little ones; and in another concentrated itself too much by writing not very small books on subjects which might have been adequately treated in not very long essays. So also in his behaviour there may sometimes have been a little too much abstraction, and too much indifference to the existence of those agreeable folk who always put the worst construction on everything. I once heard him abused for affectation because he had lunched off two oysters and a pancake. What use to suggest to this kind of abuser or accuser that he probably confined himself to the two because he did not want a third, and to the one because he did not want a second. Yet I venture to imagine that explanations of this kind, lodged with the Recording Angel, would not be rejected; though that weary official might perhaps suggest that they were quite unnecessary. Meanwhile if Lang is (more's the pity!) gone, and some of his work gone with him or recoverable only with infinite labour and pains, there is a great body of it accessible, and the old 'Take it and Read it' may be said with unusual confidence to anybody hesitating about the matter. 'Selections', of course, suggest themselves and have been suggested. It is possible to conceive not merely one but more than one which would supply reading of the most refreshing kind. But it would be an extraordinarily difficult job; and while selections often fail to satisfy their readers, this selection would be so unlikely to satisfy the selector that he would probably never get it finished. So the *Tolle, lege,* had better be completed with the most elegant Latin available for whatever of Lang's you come across. It is ten to one you will not go wrong.

The Poetry of the 'Seventies

By JOHN DRINKWATER

THE conventions of criticism have imposed on our minds a habit which on the whole is helpful in organising our thought, but which needs an occasional challenge to keep it from taking more upon itself than habits should. In their application to English poetry the conventions have had a clearly definable effect. We all of us habitually think of that poetry as falling concisely into a series of epochs, each of which is readily separable from the rest in character. Thus the story presents itself with very plausible organisation; we have the Chaucerian Age, the pre-Shakespearean, the Elizabethan, Caroline and Restoration, the Augustan Age and the Romantic Revival, the Victorian Age, and so down to our own neo-Georgians. There is something in it; there is, indeed, a great deal in it, and criticism has not been really wide of the mark in devising these categorical labels. Each of the designated Ages has, in fact, some governing attribute or attributes that distinguish it in a general way from all others. Sometimes the contrast is rather an obscure one, as for example that between the lyric verse of such representative poets as Marvell and Landor; or again, it may be immediately striking, as that between the narrative poems of Shakespeare and Pope. But the distinctions may be maintained. Criticism on the whole is justified of its epochs.

Nevertheless, we have sometimes to remind ourselves that here, after all, is nothing but a critical convention,

and that this organisation is not so much a necessity
forced upon criticism by the art of poetry, as a convenience elaborated by criticism for its own purposes.
Seen in long perspective, poetry may be said with some
reason to assume this carefully regulated appearance, but
when we return to the actual study of the poetry itself,
poet by poet, we find that the sharp lines, to which we
have accustomed our critical thoughts, tend to readjust
themselves, to become blurred, and often to disappear
altogether. A very striking instance of this is to be found
in Wordsworth's poetic contact with the eighteenth-
century school of poetry against which his critical attack
was so memorably directed. Nothing, our critical habit
tells us, could be more decisively established than the
revolt shown by the poetic practice of *Lyrical Ballads*
against the manner of the preceding age. And then a re-
examination of that book, quite properly termed epoch-
making, reveals a strange intimacy between the new
gospeller and such marks of his confessed disapproval as
Matthew Green and John Armstrong and James Thomson
and William Shenstone. Why, even so stiff and dry a
formalist as William Somerville has to be allowed his
grain of influence upon the dawning ardours of 'the return
to nature'.

It is, therefore, no bad thing once in a while to fix upon
some quite arbitrarily chosen date, and see precisely what
was then happening in the art to which our classifications
may sometimes be too hastily applied. Those of us who
care for, and have taken some trouble to familiarise ourselves with English poetry, if asked to define its condition
in the eighteen-seventies, would probably answer off-
hand that it was then in the full tide of Victorian
ascendancy. Browning, Tennyson, Arnold, Swinburne,
Morris—these are the figures that would come instantly
before us, dominating the scene. The Victorian Age, we

B   7

should readily remember, survived in its vigour until the
exquisite but more tenuous manifestations of the 'nineties
and the Yellow Book. In the 'seventies the poets of Vigo
Street were at school, and the Victorian supremacy had
not yet begun to dwindle. Or so we should be likely to
assert without reference to the book. But we should be
inexact in doing so. Let us take our bearings.

In 1870, the Romantic Age, dimly surviving in the
aged Wordsworth, who died in 1850, had passed into
memory. Keats and Byron and Shelley were as far away
from the poetic realities of the time as are Morris and
Swinburne from those of our own. But a great deal more
had happened than that. We find, surely with some surprise, that by 1870 the great Victorians had themselves
come to the full assertion of their powers, and were
already in the enjoyment of reputations that their later
work would not enlarge. Forty years had passed since
the publication of Tennyson's first book, and in 1850 *In
Memoriam*, following the *Poems* of 1842 and *The Princess*,
established a fame that by 1870 was acknowledged by a
public such as in numbers and authority has seldom been
claimed by any poet. Nothing that Tennyson published
after that date, while much of it is of high excellence,
widened his appeal or enlarged the merit of his work.
Similarly, Robert Browning, with a less popular following, had brought nearly forty years of poetic production
to a splendid crowning achievement in 1869 with the
publication of *The Ring and the Book*. Henceforward
Balaustion and Hohenstiel-Schwangau and Fifine and
Ferishtah and the rest of them were to carry that un-
resting psychological ardour into a rich old age, but they
were hardly to prove Browning a greater poet than he
was known to be by 1870. At that date, too, Matthew
Arnold's *Strayed Reveller*, his *Empedocles*, and his three
volumes of *Poems* had for some years been before a public

that was slow to recognise what, indeed, has not been fully recognised even yet, that here was a poet whose work had in it less waste tissue than that of any of his contemporaries. William Morris's *Defence of Guenevere*, published in 1858, had been followed by his *Jason* in 1867, and in 1870 the last of the *Earthly Paradise* stories made their appearance. Here, it is true, was one of the great figures who was to add definitely to his achievement in the 'seventies, with *Sigurd the Volsung* which was published in 1876, and, in a lesser degree, with the *Love is Enough* of 1872. Swinburne was prolific in our period, but nothing that he then wrote can be said to increase his stature as measured by *Atalanta in Calydon* (1865) and *Poems and Ballads* (1866). Dante Gabriel Rossetti did not publish his first volume of poems until 1870, but the circumstances are well known in which he suppressed the work of the late 'forties and early 'fifties until that date. He, like Morris, made a substantial addition to his work in the 'seventies, with *Ballads and Sonnets* published in 1881, but he again had made his essential contribution to Victorian poetry before our decade opened.

Coventry Patmore had completed *The Angel in the House* by 1863, and its publication was followed by that of the *Odes* in 1868, though a considerable elaboration of these last was to appear in *The Unknown Eros* of 1877. Christina Rossetti with *Goblin Market* in 1861 and *The Prince's Progress* in 1866 had given ample proof of a genius that did not announce itself publicly in verse again until 1881, when *A Pageant and Other Poems* contained sufficient justification of Professor Saintsbury's statement that the 'astonishingly true and new note of poetry' found in her earliest work was 'sustained, and indeed deepened, varied, and sweetened' into the later years of her life. But her gift of poetry was notably a secluded one, and though her not very frequent utterance in the

'seventies and after was usually of an exquisite tenderness, it cannot be said to have materially enlarged the
Victorian achievement as a whole.

While, therefore, it may be conceded that several of
these poets did a certain amount of work that was worthy
of themselves after 1870, it can hardly be said of any one
of them that his death at that date would seriously have
impaired his reputation. And we may go beyond that and
assert that if from 1870 the major voices of Victorian
poetry had been silent, the achievement and significance
of that poetry would have remained very much what
it is.

Before leaving this tabulation, it may be worth while
to consider briefly the case of those lesser poets who made
some striking contribution of their own to the poetic age
of which those larger figures were the leaders. That fantastic fellow and notable poet, Richard Hengist Horne,
had published his remarkable 'farthing epic' *Orion* in
1843. Newman's *Dream of Gerontius* appeared in 1866,
and William Cory's *Ionica* in 1858. William Barnes in
1863 had completed the series of poems in Dorset dialect
which he had begun to publish in the 'forties; and Robert
Stephen Hawker, the Cornish poet, had been born as far
back as 1803. The voluble but highly talented Alexander
Smith had published his last book of verse in 1861, and
two years later Jean Ingelow had scored a great and not
unmerited popular success with her *Poems*. Fitzgerald's
Omar, though little noted at first, had appeared in 1859.
F. W. H. Myers's *Saint Paul* (1867) was a characteristic
example of the current religious fervour expressing itself
in ardent but somewhat nebulous verse. These poets, in
a large variety of mood, completed the Victorian harmony, and they too, as we see, had put forth their representative work by 1870. It may be added that George
Meredith's *Modern Love* had been published in 1862, and

it was not until well on in the 'eighties that he appeared again as a poet; and that although in 1871 Thomas Hardy was to come before the public as a novelist with *Desperate Remedies,* he was not to announce himself as a poet until towards the turn of the century.

It is difficult to say at what distance of time criticism begins to liberate itself from the mist of error and prejudice that notoriously impedes contemporary judgment. Does any summary that has yet been made of the literary achievement of the past thirty years, or, say, the first quarter of the twentieth century, bear the stamp of authority on its critical conclusions? Many individual writers of that period have been carefully and wisely assessed, but we may be sure that nothing like a true balance of the general account has yet been struck. If we push our date back a decade or two, it remains doubtful at least whether we can declare the truth with any certainty of vision. A great deal has yet to be adjusted in the final perspectives of a period when such poets as Lionel Johnson, Mary Coleridge, Ernest Dowson, John Davidson, Francis Thompson, with others who worked on well into the new century—Alice Meynell, Robert Bridges, William Watson and W. B. Yeats—were in the full exercise of their powers. Some of these poets were already out of childhood in the 'seventies, and here and there we find one of their names on a title page bearing so early a date; but they belong representatively to the later time, and it is a time still too near to us for decisive records to be made in the critical high court. That court is curiously constituted. No single mind ever governs it, nor is it quite under popular control. The truth seems to be that, while individual critics may be greatly at variance in their moods and tastes, there comes a time when a given object of criticism is absolved of all the circumstances that provoke disagreement and stands out

in a positive clarity about which there can no longer be
any dispute even among the most conflicting witnesses.
It is, for example, safe to say that all critics of poetry
to-day, however violent they may be in their differences
on contemporary topics, are agreed on the simple proposition that Keats was a good poet—a view, it must be
remembered, that was once hotly questioned by honest
and reputable opinion. There is, as I say, no principle by
which we can decide as to the moment when this elucidat-
ing process takes place. We can only speak arbitrarily as
each instance arises; and for our present purposes we may
say that, while the issues of the 'nineties are still un-
decided, we ought, with the material before us, to be able
by now to reach some general agreement as to the poetry
of the 'seventies.

And it must be confessed that we shall reach it by way
of an examination that affords no great excitement. The
major Victorian impulse was waning, and the new poets
of its dying fall were for the most part expressly minor.
No one has, I think, ever given a satisfactory explanation
of what is meant by a 'minor poet', and we are each of
us apt to invest the term more or less vaguely with a
meaning of our own. For myself, I think of a minor poet
not as one who does some small thing of his own extremely well, but as one who produces, often with considerable fertility, not from the resources of his own
nature but from the overflow, or perhaps the backwash,
of a poetic movement with which he happens to be in
contact. The greatest poets may be, indeed must be, influenced both by tradition and by their contemporaries,
but the influence is a condition and not the foundation
of their art, while with the minor poet the influence is
rather the source of his work than a subsequent condition.
A minor poet may be charmingly gifted, but he has no
originality. On the other hand, an original poet, who need

by no means be a great poet, may work within a very tiny
compass. John Banister Tabb, for example, is an original
poet, though no one would claim that he is a great one.
Similarly, Richard Barnefield, and Christopher Smart,
and George Darley, and Robert Hawker and Mary
Coleridge are original poets. It would be easy to name
half-a-dozen poets now writing who, with a very un-
ambitious scope, have this originality. It is not for us to
decide whether we have or have not great poets among
us, but we certainly have original poets whose claims to
greatness are never likely to be advanced, and it is, in
my view, a confusion of terms to call them 'minor'. That
we have our minor poets too is abundantly evident.

In the 'seventies, then, the new poets who took up the
Victorian note were mostly destitute of this saving
original grace. Verse writers like John Addington
Symonds and Philip Bourke Marston had talent and
sensibility, they came to no little mastery of their craft,
and they wrote a few things that can still be read with
pleasure. But they were, first and last, minor poets of the
Victorian era. Their best has worthily secured for them
a modest place in the great record which is English
poetry, and this is no small thing to have attained. But
their best hardly ever fails to remind us of the men who
had done better. We look in vain, or nearly always in
vain, for the personal accent that, however slight, may
give even the most traditional little poem a place in the
memory for ever. It is not that these men are consciously imitating their masters as an exercise. Among
the hundreds of people who at that time, as at any other,
were writing verse, only a very few could write it as well
as Symonds or Marston, who remind us that after all
minor poets may be poets. Nevertheless, the subjection,
little though they may have been aware of it, was one
from which they managed hardly any moments of escape.

And it is just by such moments that even the poets of strictly limited powers may prove their originality.

So far as the larger volume of poetry in England was concerned we find, therefore, that the 'seventies was a time somewhat hushed. And it was the hush rather of exhaustion than of expectancy. Some of the Victorian masters, as we have seen, were adding an authentic leaf here and there to their laurels; and already there was an occasional note that might, to an uncommonly shrewd appraiser, have told of a later generation that was to take the world with a new vigour. It is interesting to observe, although poetry is little enough concerned in this connection, that in the fugitive literature of the 'seventies the name of Bernard Shaw first announced itself. But, in poetry, the period of our discussion marks, with a precision that is rare in the annals of these things, the subsidence of a spent wave. The decade saw the assured arrival of no poet who was greatly to take up the succession. If English poetry had stopped short at 1880, it would not have enlarged the boundaries of 1870. And, further, if the poetry of 1890 down to our own time had done nothing beyond the indications of 1870–80, it would have been an immeasurably less considerable thing than it is.

There is, however, more to be claimed for our decade than this, and it is to be claimed by virtue of a few poets who, without enlarging the great Victorian tradition, or clearly preluding the achievement of our later age, made a personal contribution to the stock of original English poetry by moments of inspiration that have little to mark them as belonging to this age more than another. They are mostly lyric moments, and come of a fortunate dispensation that has always waited on English poetry, producing some grace of song here or the graver numbers of an unexpected philosophic seclusion there—the lyrics of a Richard Watson Dixon or a James ('B. V.') Thomson's *City of Dreadful Night*.

So that the chief interest of English poetry in the 'seventies is to be found not in any striking development or preparation in the larger activity of the art, but in the good things that, it might almost seem, have drifted into the time by chance, and from nowhere in particular. Finding our 'seventies to be of very little profit by the methods of comparative criticism, we may yet part from them not too discontented with a little anthology in our minds of those things that carry their own virtue plainly marked upon them, and make no pretence beyond it. They do not extend the tradition, and they do not open up new avenues for future effort. They are merely good poems, touched by a breath of spontaneity that keeps them fresh and gainly after fifty years. We may choose them without ordering, as they come to our hand. Here is Dixon, with his exquisite *Song*:

> The feathers of the willow
> Are half of them grown yellow
>   Above the swelling stream;
> And ragged are the bushes,
> And rusty now the rushes,
>   And wild the clouded gleam.
>
> The thistle now is older,
> His stalk begins to moulder,
>   His head is white as snow;
> The branches all are barer,
> The linnet's song is rarer,
>   The robin pipeth now.

We may see in that something of Dixon's early Pre-Raphaelite associations; or we may agree with Gerard Hopkins that in such work there is a kinship with Wordsworth such as has not been shown by any other later poet; but there is really little more to say of it than has been said by Dr Bridges: 'I should say that the destiny of this poem is that it will always be found in any collection of

the best English lyrics'. It is true that this actual poem
was published six years before our decade began, but
Dixon went on writing verse of the same tender and
subtly personal quality through the 'seventies and, indeed, for many years towards his death in 1900. His
output was small; Dr Bridges in his edition of Dixon's
Poems gives only sixty pieces drawn from a working
period of over thirty years. But in the 'seventies his gift
was at its maturity, and in those years its occasional
exercise added much of the best to his fastidiously restrained body of work.

Lord de Tabley was another poet who, having published verse—to the extent of six volumes—before 1870,
continued after that date to add at intervals to his most
distinguished poems. He wrote more freely than Dixon,
but with a less constant excellence. Though he has to his
credit one longer piece, the verse drama *Philoctetes* published in 1866, which is not unworthy of comparison with
the major poems of his greater contemporaries, his lyrical
talent was of very variable merit, and his *Collected Poems*
need careful sifting before they are relieved of tedium.
But his lucky moments, if rare, had the remote and timeless quality of which we have spoken, and in the 'seventies
many of these were bearing fruit that was to be gathered
in the two volumes of 1893 and 1895. *Misrepresentation*
says for itself all that is necessary:

> Peace, there is nothing more for men to speak;
>   A larger wisdom than our lip's decrees.
> Of that dumb mouth no longer reason seek,
>   No censure reaches that eternal peace,
>   And that immortal ease.
>
> Believe them not that would disturb the end
>   With earth's invidious comment, idly meant.
> Speak and have done thy evil; for my friend
>   Is gone beyond all human discontent,
>   And wisely went.

Say what you will and have your sneer and go.
You see the specks, we only heed the fruit
Of a great life, whose truth—men hate truth so —
  No lukewarm age of compromise could suit.
    Laugh and be mute!

In the 'seventies Thomas Edward Brown, the Clifton schoolmaster, was writing his *Fo'c'sle Yarns*, and other verses in which a schoolmaster's mind was contemplating nature and rustic character without pedantry. Slight, light things many of them, but nearly always sparkling with their own lyric freshness. Here is a snatch of song, dated 1878—*Vespers*:

O blackbird, what a boy you are.
How you do go it!
Blowing your bugle to that one sweet star—
How you do blow it!
And does she hear you, blackbird boy, so far?
Or is it wasted breath?
"Good Lord! she is so bright
To-night!"
The blackbird saith.

Arthur Edward O'Shaughnessy, who died in 1881 at the age of thirty-seven, published his *Epic of Women* in 1870, *Lays of France* in 1872, and *Music and Moonlight* in 1874. In the first and last of these he displayed an original talent that expressed itself with great technical subtlety, but after a brief creative period he lapsed into the silences of the British Museum. How sensitive he was in ear and mood may be seen in the *Song*:

Has summer come without the rose,
  Or left the bird behind?
Is the blue changed above thee,
  O world! or am I blind?
Will you change every flower that grows,
  Or only change this spot,
Where she who said, I love thee,
  Now says, I love thee not?

The skies seem'd true above thee,
  The rose true on the tree;
The bird seem'd true the summer through,
  But all proved false to me.
World! is there one good thing in you,
  Life, love, or death—or what?
Since lips that sang, I love thee,
  Have said, I love thee not?

I think the sun's kiss will scarce fall
  Into one flower's gold cup;
I think the bird will miss me,
  And give the summer up.
O sweet place! desolate in tall
  Wild grass, have you forgot
How her lips loved to kiss me,
  Now that they kiss me not.

Be false or fair above me,
  Come back with any face,
Summer!—do I care what you do?
  You cannot change one place—
The grass, the leaves, the earth, the dew,
  The grave I make the spot—
Here, where she used to love me,
  Here, where she loves me not.

James Thomson's *City of Dreadful Night* was first published, in a journal, in 1874. Thomson was a poet of very uncertain attainment. His shorter lyrical pieces are seldom if ever better than second-rate. It is not that they are weak imitations of other men's work, but that they come from an insufficient impulse. Many admirable poets have suffered from misfortune, ill-health, and even defects of habit and character, and have yet managed to reserve for their poetry some energy uncontaminated by these influences. Thomson was less just to himself, and wrote much of his verse when his hold upon experience was infirm. The consequence is a certain triviality of spirit, which leaves his lyrics for the most part poverty-stricken and tame. And yet that there was in him, how-

ever loosely it was employed, a poetic power of deep
originality, *The City of Dreadful Night* puts beyond
question. There is, perhaps, no long poem in the period
under consideration that is more clearly marked by individual genius. The accomplishment is uneven, the design rather precarious, and the pervading gloom of the
poem often seems to lack the bracing air of tragic art.
Nevertheless, the work is made memorable by fitful
gleams of intense though, as Professor Saintsbury has
observed, somewhat sinister emotion. With all its defects, it could no more have been written by anyone but
its author than the *Song to David* could have been written
by anyone but Christopher Smart. It is in many respects
an unsatisfactory poem to read as a whole, and yet its
merits can be realised in no other way. It would be use-
less to support by brief quotation the opinion that *The
City of Dreadful Night* is a very decided asset in the poetry
of the 'seventies.

There remains only to mention a few poets whose
names, for one reason or another, cannot be quite disre-
garded in taking leave of our subject. William Allingham,
whose epical *Laurence Bloomfield in Ireland*, published
in 1864, is a meritable poem of which Dr Johnson might
have said, as he did of Congreve's early novel, that he
would rather praise than read it, wrote freely through
our period. His lyrics, including the celebrated fairy
piece, *Up the airy mountain*, have a grace and sometimes
a poignancy that hold the attention, but they hardly ever
achieve the originality of which we have spoken. 'Sentimental' is a dangerous word, and a snare to criticism, but
Allingham is a poet who almost compels the use of it.
But we may at least allow that he turned sentiment to
very pretty uses, and his gift may be epitomised in a
fragment that could be disliked only by a very grudging
temper:

Four ducks on a pond,
A grass-bank beyond,
A blue sky of spring,
White clouds on the wing;
What a little thing
To remember for years—
To remember with tears.

In 1879 Sir Edwin Arnold published *The Light of Asia*. It is an exposition in narrative verse of Buddhist philosophy, running to some 5000 lines, and probably finds as few readers to-day as Philip James Bailey's *Festus*, an even longer philosophical poem of an earlier generation. And yet, if there were time for everything, the perusal of Arnold's poem would not be among our wasted employments. I cannot speak of it with any critical certainty; I happened to read it young, and I still retain, especially from such interludes as 'We are the voices of the wandering wind', a pleasing impression of somewhat drowsy but well-sustained romance.

In conclusion, we may note that Robert Louis Stevenson, William Ernest Henley, Edmund Gosse, Robert Bridges and Alice Meynell were of grown years when our decade began, as were John Davidson, Francis Thompson and William Watson by the time it closed. The names of Gosse, Bridges and Alice Meynell all appeared on title pages in the 'seventies, but in their maturity these poets belong to a later period. The account we have had to give is not a very inspiring one; but it is not without interest as a passage in the larger story of English verse.

The Women Poets of the 'Seventies

By V. SACKVILLE-WEST

WHEN I was first asked to prepare a paper for this Society on the women poets of the 'seventies, I accepted the invitation with a cheerful rashness. Such feminism as is latent in me—and I suppose a certain degree of feminism must be latent in all women, however reasonable—was flattered by this assumption that several women, and not Christina Rossetti alone, had been engaged in writing poetry in the 'seventies. That period, so exciting for the free male, so suffocating, so matrimonial, for the still comparatively enslaved female, perhaps might prove the genesis of the literary woman's emancipation after all? Women with a taste for literature, I reflected, had already been given a good lead: Jane Austen, the Brontës, and Mrs Browning lay behind them; demure and deadly, tragic and vehement, delicate and sentimental, they had persevered with their work under conditions of varying difficulty. Jane Austen, as we know, had been obliged to write uncomfortably in a corner of the common sitting-room at Steventon, with chatter going on all round her, compelled to keep one eye open in vigilance lest anyone should approach to see what she was doing, in which case the cover of the blotting-book must hastily be shut down—scarcely an ideal system for writing a novel; the Brontës, up at Haworth, ill, cold, harassed by poverty, domestic duties, and a half-blind father with a violent temper, discouraged by publishers, deciding to conceal under ambiguous pseudonyms the horrid truth that they

were women—the Brontës likewise had insisted on over-
coming all opposition. Mrs Browning, indeed, who by
1870 had been laid for nine years in an honoured grave,
had travelled a smoother path in pursuit of literature.
She had been taught Greek; her father had been a man
of culture; and she had married a poet. But even she had
had her troubles. She had been an invalid, and in order to
marry her poet she had been obliged to run away. All
these reflections encouraged me to think that the first
half and the middle of the nineteenth century had seen
the true beginning of women's desire to express themselves in other ways than in the management of a home,
the bearing and upbringing of children, and the humble
devotion to one all-but godlike man. By 1870, I thought,
the movement must have been well on its way.

There was another encouraging consideration. The
literary women of the early and middle nineteenth
century were quite ordinary women in one way: they
were morally respectable. No one had ever breathed a
word against Mrs Hemans, or against Adelaide Anne
Proctor. Now in a previous outburst of literary activity
among women, a hundred and fifty years or so earlier, the
same could not be said. Neither Mrs Aphra Behn, nor
Mrs Mary de la Rivière Manley, nor Mrs Eliza Heywood,
cared a straw about their virtue, nor were their works
such as might be left lying about on a Victorian drawing-
room table. You may remember that Dorothy Osborne,
writing to Sir William Temple, has some very sharp
things to say of women who use their pens for other purposes than that of writing to their betrothed. If I am not
mistaken, she goes so far as to use the word 'monster'.
But by the nineteenth century that attitude appeared to
have changed. The point was not perhaps a very important one, except in so far as it seemed to prove that
ladies whose ideas as to moral conduct were perfectly

correct, now considered the pursuit of literature compatible with a virtuous life; they could take up a pen
without first making a gesture of defiance; literature, in
fact, was not to be thought unwomanly. It was possible
for a woman to be an author, and yet in no way to depart
from the high Victorian standard of bashfulness. Obviously, this enlarged the field. If literature in the feminine
world was no longer to be limited to a few poor rakes,
whose almost avowed object was to scandalise the men
as much as they possibly could, or to a few great ladies,
such as the Duchess of Newcastle, whose social position
allowed them to write letters, diaries, and even biographies with impunity, then clearly the daughters of the
great middle classes and of the gentry might swarm
forward as recruits to the world of letters. And swarm
they did. They wrote fiction, they wrote poetry: it was
perhaps not all of it very good fiction or very good
poetry; but the main thing was that they wrote. The
proverbial ear which is keen enough to hear the grass
grow, might in the nineteenth century have been keen
enough to hear also all over England the gentle scratching
of a myriad feminine pens in boudoir and arbour.

But it is time for me to stop generalising about the
nineteenth century, and to come down to the 'seventies.
What was happening to women? for, after all, one cannot
begin to consider the poets until one has looked round at
the general situation. In order to find out what was
happening, we will not go to any learned work; no, we
will simply open an old volume of *Punch*. Instantly a
rustling of petticoats fills the air. 'The Chignon at
Cambridge', we read; and then we remember: of course,
Girton came into being in 1869; Newnham came two
years later; and two colleges at Oxford for women—
Somerville and Lady Margaret Hall—in 1879. Mr Punch
tried his best to be reasonable: but it is evident that he

did not approve; and Mr Punch represents the average Englishman much more truly than does John Bull, for John Bull is a fixed type, whereas Mr Punch is a mirror that perpetually shifts the angle of reflection, constant though the surface of that mirror remains.

The woman of the future! she'll be deeply read, that's certain,
With all the education gained at Newnham or at Girton;
Or if she turns to classic tomes, a literary roamer,
She'll give you bits of Horace or sonorous lines from Homer.

Thus said *Punch*; and added,

Oh pedants of these later days, who go on undiscerning
To overload a woman's brains and cram our girls with learning,
You'll make a woman half a man, the souls of parents vexing,
To find that all the gentle sex this process is unsexing.

Thus *Punch* complained; and complained perhaps all the louder because the fashion and necessity of the day had cut out one of his ribs and fashioned a Mrs Punch—a Mrs Punch, who, in the person of a Miss Matilda Betham-Edwards, had begun to interfere in his paper as early as 1868, and who had already ventured so far as to call man a 'despot to whom woman is a ministering slave'. Women were really becoming intolerable. The Married Women's Property Act was a serious topic of conversation; the Feminist Movement, and, with it, the woman's vote, had called for Mr Punch's notice as far back as 1857; Huxley, the great Professor Huxley, was actually lecturing to women in South Kensington in 1870; certain fanatics maintained that women ought to be admitted to the Bar; women were taking to games: to croquet and archery— well, that was just admissible; archery was a pretty sport, that in its gesture displayed the figure to its best advantage, and croquet gave to the dear creatures a generous opportunity to cheat, and to Mr Punch the opportunity for a standing joke—so far so good, but now lawn-tennis was threatened with feminine competition, and even

bicycling, though Mr Punch was sure bicycling was a
pastime utterly unsuited to the gentler sex. And rinko-
mania too—the daughters of the middle classes gyrated
wildly, with wheels on their feet much as Mercury had
wings on his ankles, in the arms of the sons of the middle
classes with whom the barest introduction had brought
them together. And women wrote—but compared with
these athletics, and compared with this Higher Education, a copy of verses was surely a harmless thing? Let
them write by all means; let them write even novels—
though Mr Punch must have a dig at Miss Rhoda
Broughton—the wielding of a pen, at any rate, did not
develop the muscles of the forearm or necessarily flatten
the chest. The whole agitation was deplorable; but if
women must assert themselves at last, after centuries of
convenient though perhaps rather humiliating subjection,
then possibly fiction and poetry were less offensive forms
of self-expression than Higher Education and bicycling,
which could have nothing but a disastrous effect on
cookery and the comfort of man.

But now I would ask you to observe what curious
creatures poets are, how little advantage they take of
opportunities offered them, and how remote they live
from the busy world and its doings. Here we are in 1870,
at the very beginning of all this stirring about women's
rights, and woman's equality, with Professor Huxley
lecturing to women in South Kensington, and Miss Rhoda
Broughton coming up as a flower, and women putting on
the gown of a Bachelor of Arts, and a thousand arrows
being loosed at the bullseye—by women—and a thousand
croquet balls being tapped through the hoop—by women
—and a Mrs Punch intruding on Mr Punch's paper—
which is as outrageous as a woman walking into a man's
club—and Miss Florence Nightingale terrorising Sidney
Herbert, and married women sticking to their own

8-2

property, instead of yielding it up *ipso facto* to their husbands, and women beginning to think they can interfere with the vote and the British Constitution, and Miss Charlotte Brontë having years ago induced the seventh publisher to accept the manuscript of *The Professor*, and Miss Barrett having run away years ago with Mr Browning, and Mrs Emily Pfeiffer writing

> Peace to the odalisque, whose morning glory
> Is vanishing, to live alone in story;
> Firm in her place, a dull-robed figure stands
> With wistful eyes, and earnest, grappling hands,
> —Oh woman! sacrifice may still be thine,
> More fruitful than the souls ye did resign
> To sated masters; from your lives so real,
> Will shape itself a pure and high ideal
> That ye will seek with sad, wide-open eyes...

all this, and what are the women poets doing about it? The answer is: Nothing at all. Poets are usually supposed to be in advance of their time; and women, especially, are supposed to travel by short cuts; but if the evidence of the women poets of the eighteen-seventies is to be believed, neither of these two platitudes has a grain of truth in it. Truth compels me to confess that the women poets of the eighteen-seventies, though numerous and prolific, are exceedingly dull. This was the conclusion at which I arrived after reading a large number of volumes. I may say that I read very little criticism, contemporary or otherwise; I read the authors themselves; I wanted to drink of the stream at its source. I read, in the hopes of making a discovery. But the only discovery I made, frankly—which was Mary Coleridge—I couldn't fit into our date. So how am I to go on, having made this confession? and what am I to say to you? You will complain that you have been brought here under false pretences; and unless I allow myself to be pushed back on to Christina Rossetti, who is too great and too famous to come within the scope of this paper, your complaint will be justified. So before you set me and my paper down as a complete fraud, may I say something in a general way about women and poetry? basing it all, to make it more admissible, on women and poetry in the 'seventies?

First of all—and this is important—what men were writing poetry in the 'seventies? The answer comes quick and obvious: Tennyson, Browning, Swinburne, Rossetti, William Morris, James Thomson; no need to mention any minor names. It is clear from these names alone that poetry in England was alive. Pre-Raphaelitism, however much out of fashion it may be to-day, and however unpopular cliques and coteries may be with those who stand outside them, existed as an armed force in the stronghold of Chelsea, a gathering of personalities to which even in our irreverent age we must still take off our hats. A woman living in the 'seventies, then, stood a good chance: poetry in England was neither flagging nor stale; women since the beginning of the century had set an example of literary activity; and, above all, the general emancipation of women, though resentfully derided by Mr Punch, had already progressed so far that he could no longer afford to ignore it. Notoriously, the English always turn a danger into a joke. They have a theory that that system diminishes the danger. Therefore, if *Punch* made jokes about the emancipation of women, it meant that English manhood at large was alarmed. I have already admitted, however, that there was no cause for alarm on the part of the poets: their position was not in the least degree challenged by the poetesses. Perhaps this accounts for the extravagant praises lavished on the poetesses by some of the reviewers; Hartley Coleridge for instance, reviewing Mrs Clive's poems in the *Quarterly*—though a little earlier, to be exact, than our date—said of them that 'the stanzas printed by us in italics are, in our

judgment, worthy of any one of our greatest poets in his
happiest moments', and Darwin, who had not opened a
volume of verse for fifteen years, on the recommendation
of Professor Ray Lankester read with enthusiasm the
whole of *Keynotes* by Mrs Louisa Guggenberger. The men
were generous, and they could afford to be. But their
generosity makes the women's lack of response all the
more surprising; and to those who like to believe that
women can hold their own against men, all the more
distressing. Here were women, whose sisters were going
forward in other branches; here were women with the
profession of letters open to them in all respectability;
encouraged, indeed, not only by the reviewers but by the
very men they had married—did not Mrs Emily Pfeiffer
tell Mr Japp that she regarded it as 'a duty to the
memory of her husband to do all that in her lay to
cultivate still further the literary gift in which he had
so firmly believed'?—yet they could produce nothing
better than ponderous texts or verses worthy of a keep-
sake album.

I am bound to add that they produced them in enor-
mous quantities. The list of poetesses who were busy in
the 'seventies is really formidable, and justifies Professor
Saintsbury's remark that the latter part of the nineteenth
century was more prolific of applicants for the position of
Tenth Muse than the whole earlier range of English
literature. Cecil Frances Alexander, Caroline Clive, Eliza
Cook, Isa Craig, Anne Evans, Dora Greenwell, Harriet
Hamilton-King, Isabella Harwood, Jean Ingelow, Violet
Fane, Dinah Craik, Emily Pfeiffer, Menella Bute Smedley,
Louisa Shore, Augusta Webster—these are only a few of
the names that appear in the biographies and anthologies.
Professor Saintsbury, true to the masculine tradition of
generosity, remarks that a number of them are 'entitled
to challenge a place with the masculine minorities'. This

may be so; his estimate does not alter, but rather in-
creases, the fact that their value is of a pretty low order.
As well be frank about it. There is scarcely a voice among
the whole bevy of them distinguishable from another
voice. It is not until we come to Alice Meynell's *Preludes*
—and who now thinks of Alice Meynell as a poet of the
'seventies?—that we can feel any revival of literary pride
in the sex.

Indeed one is tempted to ask, as one wades through
Isabella and Menella, whether there was any inherent
reason why those women should not have written better
poetry. I came across a crushing phrase, written by a
distinguished man of letters *à propos* of no less a person
than Christina Rossetti. 'Everywhere else', he says, the
exception being *Goblin Market*, 'she is, like most poetesses,
purely subjective and in no respect creative'. That, I
thought, was a hard saying; but I wondered how much
truth there was in it, not as applied to Christina, but to
the women poets as a general principle. These women in
the 'seventies, for instance, with their elegant or de-
votional pieces; their wordy and portentous moralising;
their dreary narrative poems; their descriptive pieces
which reminded one of nothing so much as a washy and
indifferent water-colour—what was essentially wrong
with them? Was it lack of education? No, for education
never made a poet. Was it lack of leisure? No, it
certainly was not that. Was it discouragement? No, for
by the 'seventies literature was, as I have said, a respectable occupation for women. One must conclude,
quite simply, then, that it was lack of talent? Apparently
one must. It was of course possible to argue that women
had only just begun to emerge from the muffled and
subjected state in which nature and men had kept them;
but that theory, although consoling, broke down immediately as one remembered the earlier women whose

genius had never allowed itself to be thwarted by obstacles. It is the critic's pet temptation to make out a case in favour of almost any argument; a little selection here, a little omission there, and the trick is done. I prefer to say plainly that if the women of the 'seventies did not write better poetry it was because they had not got better poetry in them to write. Some of it was graceful; some of it was even quite pretty; some of it was skilled; much of it was desperately serious; but there it stopped short. It was a disappointing conclusion to come to, but it was true. Christina remained, admirable, but solitary.

But if my hopes of a 'discovery' were dashed, I did nevertheless settle on some points of interest about the poetry of women. It seemed to me that there were various special pits dug for them, into which they fell one after the other, with a swirl of petticoats and a clatter of polysyllabic bangles. Women, I fancy, were so much afraid of being thought frivolous that they became heavy-handed. There were certain temptations, which they seemed quite unable to resist. Moralising in verse, for instance, manifestly had a charm which at any moment was liable to lead them astray. Curiously enough, they were more inclined to moralise than to sentimentalise. Now that, after all, might be attributed to the age—for could not Tennyson, when he was in the wrong mood, his prosperous, Laureate, edifying mood, out-moralise the most serious of women?—but somehow I suspected that the age and the natural temperament of the poetess had happened to coincide here in an unfortunate accordance. Religion no doubt was partly responsible for this general impression, for it was frequently religion which moved women in the nineteenth century to take to poetry. Christina herself, and Mrs Meynell, owed a great deal to this form of inspiration. Probably many people would be surprised to hear how many of the most familiar hymns were written by women in the nineteenth century —'Just as I am, without one plea', 'Thy will be done', 'Watch and pray', by Charlotte Elliott; 'Jesus lives! no longer now, Can thy terrors, Death, appal us', by Frances Elizabeth Cox; 'Nearer, my God, to Thee', by Sarah Flower Adams; 'Our blest Redeemer', by Harriet Huber; and a number by Mrs Alexander, including 'There is a green hill far away', 'The roseate hues of early dawn', and 'When wounded sore the stricken soul, Lies bleeding and unbound'—though Mrs Alexander, indeed, seems to have shown some reluctance to be regarded as absorbed entirely in her spiritual pieces, for when a tea-table visitor asked her, 'Don't you yearn on starlit nights to be upon the Alps, high above the earth, on the line of the eternal snow?' she rather tartly replied, '*No*, I don't'. But religion was not enough to account for that Sunday-school spirit in women, for it made itself manifest even where religion was not the avowed motive. Possibly, and leaving the freak of genius out of account, since that is an independent law to itself, the women of mere talent had not had time to grow accustomed to their increasing emancipation; they could not as yet take their activities normally and in their stride. Possibly the art of letters was too new an experience for them to accept naturally; and they regarded it less as an art than as a means of authority, as a great responsibility newly given into the hands of women. It was one's duty, perhaps, to improve the reader's mind; to give him delight was not enough. He must lay down the book, a better man. So Mrs Hamilton-King wrote:

> And now, what more shall I say? Do I need here
> To draw the lesson of this life; or say
> More than these few words, following up the text....
> And whoso suffers most hath most to give.

And Louisa Guggenberger wrote:

> What's the text today for reading
> Nature and its being by?
> Effort, effort all the morning
> Through the sea and windy sky.
>
> Is there nothing but Occurrence?
> Though each detail seem an Act,
> Is that whole we deem so pregnant
> But unemphasized Fact?

It was an unfortunate theory to hold; it drove Madame Darmsteter (Mary Robinson) into giving 'her triste muse' the task of 'inventing a delicate misery which, happily, has never existed', and it completely turned the head of Louisa Guggenberger, who is described in consequence as 'emphatically the poetess of evolutionary science'—which apparently explains the interest that Darwin took in her poems, though one would more naturally have expected it to make him throw her book across the room. Then there was Augusta Webster, perhaps the most serious of the lot, and Mrs Clive with her reflections on mortality; but it is time to say something about these ladies in rather more detail if the title of my paper is to be at all justified.

Augusta Webster, who was born in 1837 and was publishing verse all through the 'seventies, must have spent rather a queer childhood. Her father was a vice-admiral, who, we are told, but briefly and without detail, had 'won a reputation for his success in saving shipwrecked seamen'. He then held various coastguard commands, so that his daughter Augusta was brought up trailing in the wake of a naval career, now stranded in the north in the castle of Banff, now whisked down south to Penzance, at the extreme opposite end of these islands, now actually on board a ship, the *Griper*, in Chichester harbour. These odds and ends of biographical information float up to one,

like so much orange-peel and spume, from the pages of
Introductory Notes, and critical Forewords, in the manner
of such facts, telling one really nothing at all—how should
they?—about the girl who lived on board the *Griper* in,
I suppose, 1850, or about the father who had won such a
reputation for saving shipwrecked seamen. One would
like to make up a preparation for the future poetess, out
of such beginnings; but instead of that, several more facts
come rapping out: that she studied the classical authors,
notably the Greek dramatists; made translations from
Aeschylus and Euripides: was a member of the London
School Board; married Mr Thomas Webster, a solicitor,
at the age of twenty-six; and collected her essays into a
volume of prose called *A Housewife's Opinions*, which
contained a great deal of useful advice. To these facts one
may add some observations of one's own: that she had
read and admired Mr Browning, and that she was not
afraid of expressing herself in plain language on even the
more delicate subjects; 'if a fault can be found,' said one
of her annotators, 'it is that the delineation of Woman's
heart in the most appalling condition of Woman's life is
too painful'. Her volume of poems, which appeared in
1870 under the title *Portraits*, does indeed contain some
downright speaking; I will read you a few lines from the
poem called *The Castaway*, in which you will not fail to
notice the influence that Browning had had on her. The
speaker is a girl in trouble:

> Well, well, I know the wise ones talk and talk:
> 'Here's cause, here's cure'; 'No, here it is, and here';
> And find society to blame, or law,
> the church, the men, the women, too few schools,
> too many schools, too much, too little taught;
> somewhere or somehow someone is to blame:
> but I say all the fault's with God himself
> who put too many women in the world.
> We ought to die off reasonably, and leave
> as many as the men want, none to waste.

> Here's cause: the woman's superfluity;
> and for the cure, why, if it were the law,
> say, every year, in due percentages,
> balancing them with men as the times need,
> to kill off female infants, 'twould make room;
> and some of us would not have lost too much,
> losing life ere we know what it *can* mean.

You may say that that is not poetry; you may say that it reminds you of the remark passed on a novel of a certain type, also by a woman, 'Good, but powerful'. But at least we must concede that it is the vigorous expression of a woman who was deeply concerned with the lot of women throughout her life. It is just worth noting, in passing, that Mrs Webster printed her blank verse without capitals at the beginning of the lines. We have grown accustomed to this to-day, but in 1870 Mrs Webster was criticised for her eccentricity, and was told that 'to do this with English poetry was a great mistake'.

Mrs Webster's talent was not confined to these blank-verse pieces, which she probably regarded as vehicles for expressing her sociological opinions rather than as poetry. She was also the author of several plays, and of several other books of poems, in one of which, called *A Book of rhyme*, she includes English *stornelli*, after an Italian verse form which had taken her fancy. I should like to read you a lyric, from her book called *Yu-pe-ya's Lute*, published in 1874, which I think is pretty enough to deserve a place in anthologies:

> Too soon so fair, fair lilies;
> To bloom is then to wane;
> The folded bud has still
> Tomorrow at its will;
> Blown flowers can never blow again.
>
> Too soon so bright, bright noontide;
> The sun that now is high
> Will henceforth only sink
> Towards the western brink;
> Day that's at prime begins to die.

> Too soon so rich, ripe summer,
> For autumn tracks thee fast;
> Lo, death-marks on the leaf!
> Sweet summer, and my grief!
> For summer come is summer past.
>
> Too soon, too soon, lost summer;
> Some hours and thou art o'er.
> Ah! death is part of birth:
> Summer leaves not the earth,
> But last year's summer lives no more.

Isa Craig, or Isa Knox as she afterwards became, began her literary career by winning a competition against 620 rivals with an ode on Burns, on the occasion of the Burns centenary. Evidently she based but very slight hopes on her poem, for she did not even take the trouble to be present when the result of the competition was declared, and so missed the pleasure of hearing her ode read to thousands 'with fine effect' in the Crystal Palace. The ode is competent enough, but no more inspiring than one could reasonably expect it to be. Some of her lyrics, however, have merit and are worth rescuing from obscurity; for instance, *The Woodruff*, of which I will read you three verses:

> Thou art the flower of grief to me,
> 'Tis in thy flavour!
> Thou keepest the scent of memory,
> A sickly savour,
> In the moonlight, under the orchard tree,
> Thou wert plucked and given to me,
> For a love favour.
>
> 'It keeps the scent for years,' said he
> (And thou hast kept it);
> 'And when you scent it, think of me.'
> (He could not mean thus bitterly.)
> Ah! I had swept it
> Into the dust where dead things rot,
> Had I then believed his love was not
> What I have wept it.

Thy circles of leaves, like pointed spears,
My heart pierce often;
They enter, it inly bleeds, no tears
The hid wounds soften;
Yet one will I ask to bury thee
In the soft white folds of my shroud with me,
Ere they close my coffin.

And then there is another little poem, simply called,
Song, which just deserves to be quoted:

A greenness o'er my vision passed,
A freshness o'er my brain,
Rose up as when I saw them last
The glad green hills again.

Amid the streets' bewildering roar,
I heard the rushing stirs
Of vagrant breezes running o'er
The dark tops of the firs.

Far round, the wide and swooning view,
The bound of chained heights;
Far off, the dales my footsteps knew,
With all their green delights;

Far down, the river winding through
The valley, silver white;
Far up, amid the cloudless blue,
The slow sail of the kite.

A greenness o'er my vision passed,
A freshness o'er my brain,
Rose up as when I saw them last
The glad green hills again.

It is not a very easy task to single out poets for special
mention. For one thing, it is not easy to decide about the
dates: is it, for instance, legitimate to include Mrs Clive,
who was still living after 1870, but most of whose poems
were published a number of years earlier? Is it legitimate
to include Margaret Veley, who was born in 1843 but
whose poems were not published until 1888? Or Madame
Darmsteter, whose first collection did not appear till
1878? Then the temptation to bring in Mrs Norton is

very strong; certainly her last volume of poems appeared in 1862, but she herself survived it by fifteen years, and I find it hard to refuse admittance to so brilliant and lovely a lady. Perhaps you remember Fanny Kemble's description of Caroline Norton at an evening party, amongst the members of her family, these Sheridans so famous for their beauty? there were gathered together 'Mrs Sheridan, the mother of the Graces, more beautiful than anybody but her daughters; Lady Graham, their beautiful aunt; Mrs Norton, Lady Dufferin, Georgiana Sheridan, duchess of Somerset and queen of beauty by universal consent; and Charles Sheridan, their younger brother, a sort of younger brother of the Apollo Belvidere. Certainly I never saw such a bunch of beautiful creatures all growing on one stem. I remarked it to Mrs Norton, who looked complacently round her tidy drawing-room and said, "Yes, we *are* rather good-looking people"'.

This was the lady whom Lockhart in the *Quarterly* called the Byron of poetesses, but who lives in the memory chiefly for her looks, her misfortunes, and her wit. You may remember the story of how, when she was paying a call, she caught sight of the clock, and exclaimed, 'Good gracious, it's seven o'clock; I shall be late; please call me a cab at once'. Her hostess confessed that the clock was a quarter of an hour slow: the time was really a quarter past seven. 'Oh, in that case,' said Mrs Norton, 'please call me two cabs.'

And if we admit Mrs Norton, it is ungracious to exclude Mrs Clive, the author of that once popular novel *Paul Ferroll*; for though Mrs Clive, beside the glitter of Mrs Norton, was but a provincial and pathetic figure, with her lameness and ill-health, she was certainly the more considerable poet of the two. Not that her verse was inspired by any originality. One suspects that she had read Gray's *Elegy* a little too often—I am thinking especially of her long poem, *The Grave*—but one must allow her a melancholy dignity of her own. Her life seems to have been overshadowed by its final tragedy, for, a confirmed invalid, she was burnt to death through her dress catching fire as she sat working in her boudoir, surrounded by her books and papers. What a funeral pyre for a poet! Although her poem *Conflict* appears in the *Oxford Book of Victorian Verse*, I should like to reproduce it here, as I fancy it is but little known:

> As one whose country is distraught with war,
> Where each must guard his own with watchful hand,
> Roams at the evening hour along the shore
> And fain would seek beyond a calmer land;
>
> So I, perplex'd on life's tumultuous way,
> Where evil pow'rs too oft my soul enslave,
> Along thy ocean, Death, all pensive stray,
> And think of shores thy pensive billows lave.
>
> And glad were I to hear the boatman's cry,
> Which to his shadowy bark my steps should call,
> To woe and weakness heave my latest sigh
> And cease to combat where so oft I fall:
>
> Or happier, where some victory cheer'd my breast,
> That hour to quit the anxious field would choose,
> And seek th'eternal seal on virtue's rest,
> Oft won, oft lost, and O! too dear to lose!

But I must pass on, and come down the century in time, for there are names to mention, even if there is no need to linger over them: Mary Howitt, the Quakeress, a writer of ballads; Eliza Cook, a tradesman's daughter, who frankly wrote for the people and enjoyed great popularity for her sturdy patriotic verse; Dora Greenwell, a friend of Christina's; Dinah Craik, the authoress of *John Halifax, Gentleman*, who also wrote in verse; Ellen O'Leary, an Irishwoman, the author of simple and patriotic songs and ballads: George Eliot herself, who adventured, but not very successfully, into poetry with her *Spanish Gypsy*, her *Brother and Sister*, and her *Legend of Jubal*; Isabella Harwood, who under the pseudonym of Ross Neil was responsible for fourteen dramas; Emily Pfeiffer, the translator of Heine; and Jean Ingelow, who although she is best known for her children's stories, is also the author of one really excellent poem, *Divided*, from which I may perhaps be allowed to quote an extract:

> An empty sky, a world of heather,
> Purple of foxglove, yellow of broom;
> We two among them wading together,
> Shaking out honey, treading perfume.
>
> Crowds of bees are giddy with clover,
> Crowds of grasshoppers skip at our feet,
> Crowds of larks at their matins hang over,
> Thanking the Lord for a life so sweet.
>
> Flusheth the rise with her purple favour,
> Gloweth the cleft with her golden ring,
> 'Twixt the two brown butterflies waver,
> Lightly settle, and sleepily swing.
>
> We two walk till the purple dieth
> And short dry grass under foot is brown;
> But one little streak at a distance lieth
> Green like a ribbon to prank the down.

Then lastly one must mention Mathilde Blind, by birth a German, by adoption an Englishwoman, traveller, biographer, and translator, evidently a woman of character, to whom poetry was but one facet of many activities. It is the commonplace of criticism to condemn her poems as machine-made, and wholly inadequate as an expression of her personality; nevertheless I think her gift has been slightly under-rated; her sonnets over-esteemed, and her vision of Nature esteemed not sufficiently. I must not dwell too long on Mathilde Blind, for the majority of her publications in verse lie outside the 'seventies, but perhaps I may include a few verses from her poem *The Sower*:

B   9

The winds had hushed at last as by command;
The quiet sky above,
With its grey clouds spread o'er the fallow land,
Sat brooding like a dove.

There was no motion in the air, no sound
Within the tree-tops stirred,
Save when some last leaf, fluttering to the ground,
Dropped like a wounded bird;

Or when the swart rooks in a gathering crowd
With clamorous noises wheeled,
Hovering awhile, then swooped with wranglings loud
Down on the stubbly field.

For now the big-thewed horses, toiling slow
In straining couples yoked,
Patiently dragged the ploughshare to and fro
Till their wet haunches smoked.

So, with an effort, the 'seventies have produced for us—
what? Some pretty lyrical verse; a great deal of senten-
tious verse; nothing of any remarkable value; and a
general sense of women scribbling, scribbling—which
perhaps in itself, apart from all question of merit, is the
most encouraging sign of all. For as a modern poet wrote,

It doesn't much matter *what* you do,
So long as you do it, and mean it, too.

But the trouble with life is, that it is exceedingly difficult
to know what you do mean; and the trouble with poetry,
and indeed with all forms of literature, is that it is exceedingly difficult to express it even when you know it;
and the trouble with women in the 'seventies was that
they, all bewildered, knew less than anybody where their
proper place really was in relation to life; so who can
blame them if they took refuge in prettinesses or in
sermons? Heaven knows, that we ourselves are only just
beginning to grow out of it.

But in the few minutes that remain to me, may I whirl
you away—to America? I have taken liberties with

chronology; may I now take a liberty with geography? For in America, an almost exact contemporary of Christina Rossetti, was living a poet, a woman, who had no respect whatever for the literary figures of her age, and who said what she meant in the roughest and fewest of possible words. She lived in complete seclusion; she would lower baskets full of fruit or sweets on a string from her window to the local children, but if the editor of *The Atlantic Monthly* wanted to see her he must come to her home, for she would not go to Boston. She believed profoundly in herself; and language was to be her instrument, not she the instrument of language. The result was odd sometimes; twisted; ungainly; she paid the price of those who, like Thomas Hardy, say what they want to say rather than that which poetry wants them to say. She was alive to both the advantage and the disadvantage of this determination, for if she could write,

> The thought beneath so slight a film
> Is more distinctly seen,
> —As laces just reveal the surge,
> Or mists the Apennine,

she could also write

> I felt a clearing in my mind
> As if my brain had split;
> I tried to match it, scene by scene,
> But could not make them fit;
>
> The thought behind I strove to join
> Unto the thought before,
> But sequence ravelled out of reach
> Like balls upon a floor.

I refer, of course, to Emily Dickinson, the one woman poet of that time, or so it seems to me, who had truly felt 'a clearing in her mind, as if her brain had split'. For though the others, the English women, wrote and wrote, always copiously and often competently, it was not in their brain that the split had occurred, but in the fashion of their day. And the fashion of their day was really in advance of them. Far from being prophets, they were almost anachronisms. Literature was permitted them as a respectable pursuit, but in the glue and treacle of literary convention they had remained embedded. Still, by their mere energy they were dragging their footsteps upward; for this we owe them our gratitude; and since symbolism may be twisted to serve almost any end we may conclude with these verses of the 'seventies, written by Alice Meynell:

> O mother, for the weight of years that break thee!
> O daughter, for slow time must yet awake thee,
> And from the changes of my heart must make thee.
>
> Know that the mournful plain where thou must wander
> Is but a grey and silent world, but ponder
> The misty mountains of the morning yonder.
>
> The one who now thy faded features guesses,
> With filial fingers thy grey hair caresses,
> With morning tears thy mournful twilight blesses.

The Theatre in the 'Seventies

By Sir Arthur Pinero

WHEN Macaulay was itching to make a start on his *History of England* he recorded in his diary that 'the great difficulty of a work of this kind is the beginning'. 'How is it', he asked himself—'how is it to be joined on to the preceding events! How am I to commence it! I cannot', he goes on to say, 'plunge, slap dash, into the middle of events and characters. I cannot, on the other hand, write a history of the whole reign of James the Second as a preface to the history of William the Third; and, if I did, a history of Charles the Second would still be equally necessary as a preface to that of James the Second.'

Now, I am conscious that this is a somewhat portentous beginning to a slight discourse on what many may regard as a trivial subject; but the difficulties of great men are intensified in the case of little ones, and in confronting my difficulties I may claim excusably some kinship with Macaulay. For the theme I am given to lecture upon is 'The Theatre in the 'Seventies', and at the outset I am brought face to face with the fact that the theatre of the 'seventies was influenced in no small degree by a man who wrote and did his best work in the 'sixties. I allude to Thomas William Robertson. I propose, therefore, with your permission, to speak at some length of Robertson before I get to the period with which I am asked particularly to deal.

Robertson was born at Newark-upon-Trent in the year

1829. He came of a hardworking, struggling theatrical family who followed their calling for the most part in the lesser provincial towns, and his education was of that sort which is vaguely, and often evasively, described as having been gained at 'private schools'. In Robertson's case there is indeed a specific account, in a brief Memoir written by his son, of his attending, in 1836, the 'Spalding Academy', and subsequently, in 1841, a school at Whittlesea; but when he was barely fifteen his schooling came to an end, and he was set to do his share of work— acting, prompting, helping to paint the scenery, and so forth—at the group of theatres which his father was then managing, on what was called the Lincoln circuit. His practical experience of the stage had begun even earlier than this, for at the theatre at Wisbech on the evening of Friday, June 12th, 1834—that is, when he was five years old—he appeared in the play of *Rob Roy* in the character of Hamish, Rob Roy's son, for the benefit of two members of the company, a Mr Shield and a Mrs Danby. Why the fortunes of Mr Shield and Mrs Danby were thus linked I cannot explain. One's imagination is stirred by the circumstance. But the reason may have been prosaic enough; it may have been the custom in those days of 'benefits' to reward a minor performer with only half a benefit, and to polish off two on the same night. Anyhow it has nothing to do with the business in hand, and I mention this performance merely to show that Robertson's own statement that he was 'nursed on rose-pink and cradled in properties' was not without foundation.

On the Lincoln circuit Robertson remained for four years, playing everything, according to his son's Memoir, from Hamlet to the low-comedy part in the farce of *Did you ever send your Wife to Camberwell?*; and then, the popularity of the circuit having dwindled, and the

company being disbanded, he broke away from his family
and went to London. There he accepted any employment
he could obtain in connexion with the theatre, usually,
as he told his son, at that class of theatre where the performance was advertized to take place at an hour which,
however often the hour was changed, the public evidently
found to be an inconvenient one. He had not been long
in London when he wrote his first piece, a little drama
called *A Night's Adventure.* After persistent efforts to get
his play produced, he contrived to win the sympathy of
William Farren, the elder, then manager of the Olympic,
and Farren put the piece upon the stage. It failed utterly,
running—or, rather, staggering—for four nights only.
This was in 1851, when Robertson was twenty-two.

It was about this time that he met, and formed a
friendship with, Henry James Byron—a friendship which
lasted till Robertson's death. Byron, slightly Robertson's
junior, was also an actor and an aspiring playwright. I
shall have a good deal to say about Byron as an author
later on. Meanwhile it is enough to record that these two
young men acted together in various companies, half-
starved together, and lived to see each other popular and
prosperous. Byron was the first of the two to succeed,
and then, as I shall show, he did not forget his friend.
They lived in a foolish, sentimental age.

Among the tribulations which Byron and Robertson
suffered jointly was one arising out of the hiring of a
public room in London for the performance of an entertainment they had written in collaboration—an entertainment so artfully constructed that while Byron was on the
stage in the first part Robertson could fill the office of
moneytaker, and while Robertson occupied the stage,
prior to their appearance in a duologue which finished the
programme, Byron could take control of the pay-box.
A kind patron paid the first week's rent in advance and

contributed towards the printing and general expenses, the idea being that the entertainment would grow into a permanent attraction; but notwithstanding this, when the opening night arrived, Robertson and Byron had spent their last farthing upon the preparations for the important event. At the time announced for the commencement of the performance not a soul had turned up. A few minutes later an elderly gentleman in a glow of perspiration bustled up to Robertson, who was at his station in the box-office, and said, 'Are there any seats left?' 'Oh, yes,' said Robertson, 'right *and* left.' The gentleman entered the empty hall but, nobody coming to join him, his money was returned and the enterprise came to an end.

Up to 1854 there is no record of the production of a further play from Robertson's pen, though a copy of an Assignment found among his papers gives evidence that he was still pegging away at dramatic writing. Let me quote the document in full, as showing his market value as a dramatist at that date. It is headed 'City Theatre'— the City Theatre was at Norton Folgate, in the Shoreditch district:

I hereby assign all rights of my drama, entitled 'Castles in the Air,' to Messrs. Johnson and Nelson Lee, making it their sole property for town or country, on consideration of receiving the sum of £3.

Thomas W. Robertson.

March 29th, 1854.

'Castles in the Air'! A significant title.

It was in the course of this year—1854—that he was engaged by Charles Mathews and Madame Vestris, who had succeeded Farren in the management of the Olympic Theatre, to fill the post of prompter. His salary was £3 a week. £3 seems to have been an obstinate figure with Robertson in those days. Inconsiderable as was the

amount, 'it was', says Robertson, 'a salary of loose and
irregular habits', the management being always in
pecuniary straits. At last, in desperation, he and Byron
determined to enlist in the Horse Guards. Robertson
was rejected, failing to satisfy the regimental doctor, and
Byron refused to enlist without him. So back they both
went to the old drudgery of acting in the minor theatres,
doubtless with many a laugh and joke. And it was
shortly afterwards that Robertson began to do hackwork for Thomas Hailes Lacy, a prominent theatrical
agent and publisher, in the way of adapting plays from
the French. This, it seems to me, was the first, faint
streak of dawn.

It will surprise nobody who has studied the theatrical
temperament to learn that in the following year Robertson married. Rehearsing at a poky little theatre in
Tottenham Street, Tottenham Court Road, he met and
fell in love with a Miss Elizabeth Burton, a young actress
playing the line of parts then known as 'walking ladies'—
perhaps because such characters did more walking than
talking. With a precipitancy not unusual, I believe,
in the theatrical profession, they were married after a
short engagement on the 27th August, 1856, at Christ
Church, Marylebone. It is worthy of remark that that
little theatre in Tottenham Street, then called the Queen's
Theatre—or more frequently, from its state of dirt and
decay, the 'Dusthole'—was afterwards furbished up and
re-named the Prince of Wales's, and was the scene of
Robertson's greatest dramatic triumphs. Soon after his
marriage he set out with his wife for the provinces, and
they acted together, she promoted to the position of
'leading lady', in Dublin, Belfast, Dundalk, Plymouth,
and Rochester. Returning home, they appeared at the
Surrey Theatre and the Marylebone Theatre, and—a
little farther afield—at the theatres rather magnilo-

quently styled the Theatre Royal Woolwich and the Theatre Royal Windsor. It was while he was at Windsor that he had the misfortune to lose a little daughter; whereupon, sorely stricken—for he was a man of deep affections—he resolved to leave the stage and devote himself wholly to writing, his wife continuing to act whenever the chance presented itself. Lacy was still employing him as an adaptor, and, in addition, he was picking up small sums by doing sketches and articles for the lighter magazines and journals. In 1863 he wrote a piece called *David Garrick*, founded upon a French play, *Sullivan*. Rescuing it from the clutches of Lacy, he was lucky enough to get it acted by a famous comedian— Edward Askew Sothern, the creator of the now forgotten Lord Dundreary. The piece is a flashy bit of theatricality, but one offering golden opportunities to a 'star' actor, and it holds the stage to this day. And then, heartened by the success of *David Garrick*, he wrote an original comedy which he called *Society*, dealing with fashionable and Bohemian life; and there we have the first glimpse of the real Robertson.

The circumstances attending the production of *Society* in London are interesting. Marie Wilton, a fascinating and ambitious young actress who had won fame at the theatres in the Strand, had taken the old 'Dusthole' for a term, scoured and tidied it, given it, as I have said, a new name, and started upon a career of management. Trouble befell her quickly. She had entered into a sort of partnership with Byron, who had now come to the front as a playwright, under which he was to supply her with burlesques, the kind of play she was chiefly associated with, and short pieces of the class known as 'domestic drama'. Her opening programme was not long in exhausting its attractiveness, and she turned to Byron for fresh material. But Byron at the moment was com-

mitted elsewhere. What was to be done? A happy
thought occurred to Byron: here was an opportunity of
serving Tom! *Society*, written with an eye to the Haymarket Theatre, where Sothern was acting, had been
refused contemptuously by the manager—Buckstone—
who pronounced it 'rubbish'. It had then been offered
to various other London managers, with the same result.
Truth to tell, it *was* a queer, out-of-the-way thing, almost
monstrous in its disregard of the conventions. However,
owing to the instrumentality of the faithful Byron, it had
been tried for a week or two in Liverpool and had been
favourably received there; and needs must when the devil
drives—in the shape of empty benches. So *Society* was
produced at the little Prince of Wales's Theatre, Tottenham Street, Tottenham Court Road, on the night of
November 11th, 1865; and that night a new form of
drama took root—teacup-and-saucer drama some people
called it. Anyhow, Robertson had the gratification of
sending Buckstone a box for the hundredth performance
of the play, reminding him—good-humouredly I am sure—
of the opinion he had expressed with such curtness. To
cut the story short, *Society* was followed in due course by
Ours; *Ours* by *Caste*; *Caste* by *Play*; *Play* by *School*;
School by *M.P.* *M.P.* was the last of the comedies
Robertson wrote for the Prince of Wales's. It was produced on April 23rd, 1870; and on February 3rd, 1871,
at the age of forty-two, Robertson died. That regimental
doctor was not far out in his diagnosis.

And this brings us to the 'seventies. But before treating
of the 'seventies let us inquire what the condition of the
stage was when Robertson began his series of comedies at
the Prince of Wales's, and what precisely were the nature
and substance of those comedies. First, as to the state to
which our theatre had fallen at the time of the production
of *Society*. It was a theatre, so far as the higher aims of

the drama were concerned, of faded, outworn tradition. Shakespeare was acted pretty regularly in a plodding, uninspired way; but for modern poetic drama audiences were still asked to listen to the jog-trot rhetoric of James Sheridan Knowles and to the clap-trap of Edward Bulwer Lytton. For the rest, the staple fare at our playhouses consisted mainly of pirated versions of pieces of foreign origin and the works of Dion Boucicault, Byron, and a few others of smaller talent. The cribs from the French and German were lurid melodramas, comedies unfolding intricate plots with a stilted verbosity of dialogue, and farces emasculated in the process of translation till nothing remained but humour of a boisterous and elementary kind. Boucicault's vast output was for the most part frankly of the ultra-sensational school, while Byron and his compeers contented themselves with rapidly turning out burlesques and extravaganzas, which were found amusing in proportion to the number of puns they contained, and those domestic dramas which had no more semblance to life than in stature a flea has to an elephant. Some exception perhaps ought to be made in favour of Tom Taylor, a man of culture whose career embraced successively the Professorship of English Literature at University College, the practice of a barrister on the northern circuit, the secretaryship of the Board of Health and, later, of the Local Government Board, and finally the editorship of *Punch*. It affords us a notion of Taylor's industry to read that from 1846 onwards he contributed to the stage no fewer than a hundred pieces. It also throws a light on the amount of leisure enjoyed by a Government servant. But, up to the 'seventies, Taylor, if not always avowedly, was an adaptor, though he possessed the skill, which his fellow literary tinkers lacked, or did not care to exercise, to give his dramas a home-brewed flavour.

This, then, was the position of affairs at the moment
of the advent of *Society*. Now, I am not going to try to
tell you the plot of *Society*, nor the plot of any of the
subsequent comedies written by Robertson for the Prince
of Wales's Theatre. Their plots are the merest everyday
stories—stories of the joys and sorrows of ordinary, un-
romantic people, stories of youth and age, love, parting,
and reunion, of quarrels and reconciliation, of modest
acts of chivalry and self-sacrifice, the whole stippled with
a thousand humorous and pathetic touches, yet narrated
in language devoid of ornament and set in surroundings
of the most commonplace description. A critic, whom
I cannot identify, writing after the first performance of
Caste, said:

'Society' and 'Ours' prepared the way for a complete reformation of the modern drama and until the curtain fell on Saturday
night it remained a question whether Mr Robertson would be able
to hold the great reputation which these pieces conferred upon
him. The production of 'Caste' has thrown aside all doubt. The
reformation is complete and Mr Robertson stands pre-eminent as
the dramatist of this generation. The scene-painter, the carpenter,
and the *costumier* no longer usurp the place of the author and
actor. With the aid of two simple scenes—a boudoir in Mayfair
and a humble lodging in Lambeth—Mr Robertson has succeeded
in concentrating an accumulation of incident and satire more
interesting and more poignant than may be found in all the
sensational dramas of the last half century. The whole secret of
his success is—truth!

There you have an instance of contemporary opinion, and
you have only to consult the journals of the time to find
that that opinion was generally held. To-day very likely
many, reading these half-dozen comedies of Robertson's
maturity, would be inclined to smile at the criticism I
have just quoted; they would declare that Robertson's
best work is thin, wishy-washy, superficial; but in dealing
with the stage you must judge an author's work in relation to the age in which he wrote, the obstacles he had

to grapple with in the shape of ancient prejudices and seemingly impassable barriers, and so judged it can scarcely be denied that Robertson was a man of vision and courage. Consider, too, how strange it was that such work should emanate from one who from boyhood had been steeped to his ears in the common devices and convention-alities of the stage, who had himself wrought some of the poorest of dramatic stuff. Here was a nature that was not 'subdu'd to what it works in, like the dyer's hand'. At what period of his life schemes for departing from the beaten track had entered his brain it is impossible even to guess; probably he had nursed the idea for years, conforming to the conditions imposed upon him by his poverty, but waiting, yearning, for the opportunity of asserting himself. In an old play of mine—*Trelawny of the 'Wells'*—I made Robertson my hero. I disguised him under the name of Tom Wrench and placed him at Sadler's Wells Theatre as an actor of small parts. '*Some-body* must play the bad parts in this world, on and off the stage', says his landlady, consoling him for his having been jeered at on the previous night by a disrespectful gallery. May I read you a few lines of this play, to give you my conception of Robertson's character? A smart West-end actress—Miss Imogen Parrott—herself formerly of the 'Wells', is visiting the mean house in which Tom Wrench is lodging and is listening rather superciliously to his half-serious, half-comical recital of his woes. 'What about your plays,' she asks; 'aren't you trying to write any plays just now?'

TOM

Trying! I am doing more than trying to write plays. I am writing plays. I have written plays.

IMOGEN

Well?

TOM

My cupboard upstairs is choked with 'em.

IMOGEN

Won't anybody take a fancy—?

TOM

Not a sufficiently violent fancy.

IMOGEN

You know, the speeches were so short, and had such ordinary words in them, in the plays you used to read to me—no big opportunity for the leading lady, Wrench.

TOM

M'yes. I strive to make my people talk and behave like live people, don't I—?

IMOGEN

I suppose you do.

TOM

To fashion heroes out of actual, dull, every-day men—the sort of men you see smoking cheroots in the club windows in St James's Street; and heroines from simple maidens in muslin frocks. Naturally, the managers won't stand that.

IMOGEN

Why, of course not.

TOM

If *they* did, the public wouldn't.

IMOGEN

Is it likely?

TOM

Is it likely? I wonder!

IMOGEN

Wonder—what?

TOM

Whether they would.

IMOGEN

The public!

TOM

The public. Jenny, I wonder about it sometimes so hard that that little bedroom of mine becomes a banqueting hall and this lodging house a castle.

In a later scene I show how Tom Wrench is aiming at strict fidelity in the mounting of his plays—a realism eventually achieved by Robertson. On a rainy night, in the company of some of his humble associates, Wrench finds himself by an odd combination of circumstances in the drawing-room of a mansion in Cavendish Square. Speaking to Avonia Bunn, a tawdry little soubrette, he says, looking about him, 'This is the kind of chamber I want for the first act of my comedy—'

AVONIA

Oh, lor', your head's continually running on your comedy. Half this blessed evening—

TOM

I tell you I won't have doors stuck here, there, and everywhere; no, nor windows in all sorts of impossible places!

AVONIA

Oh, really! Well, when you do get your play accepted, mind you see that Mr Manager gives you exactly what you ask for—won't you?

TOM

You needn't be satirical, if you *are* wet. Yes, I will! Windows on the one side, doors on the other—just where they should be, architecturally. And locks on the doors, *real* locks, to work; and handles—to turn! Ha, ha! You wait—wait—!

Well, whether or not I take too romantic a view of Robertson, there can be no question as to his having as a craftsman created a renewal of interest in purely native-born comedy. With the success of his plays at the Prince of Wales's came a demand for goods of home manufacture. The managers sat up and rubbed their eyes, and began to think seriously of reframing their policy. The first author to respond to the impetus given by Robertson was his old friend and colleague Byron. But I will put Byron aside for the moment and turn to more important persons—more important in an artistic sense. Of these the most important was William Schwenck Gilbert; and this brings me once more, after too long a prelude, to the 'seventies.

W. S. Gilbert, in later life Sir William Gilbert, re-
nowned for his share, with Arthur Sullivan, in what are
known as the Savoy operas, was born in 1836 and was
therefore younger than Robertson by seven years. He
took the degree of Bachelor of Arts at London University,
was a clerk in the Privy-council office from 1857 to 1862,
and in 1864 was called to the bar. He turned his legal
experience to good account subsequently by writing a
little masterpiece, for which Sullivan composed the music,
called *Trial by Jury*. Waiting for the growth of a practice
—a quest he soon abandoned—he contributed to the
magazines, and was on the staff of *Fun*, a comic journal
in whose columns his *Bab Ballads* were first published.
These ballads had been offered to *Punch* and had been
refused—a slight which Gilbert never forgave. Gilbert,
though a generous man, if tackled in the right way, was
not perhaps of the most forgiving disposition. An old
story tells us that long after the rejection of the earlier
Bab Ballads by *Punch* he was one of a dinner-party which
included Francis Cowley Burnand, then Mr Punch's editor.
'All the good things are sent to *Punch*,' remarked Burnand,
in the course of conversation at table. 'Then why don't
they appear?' snapped Gilbert. A peculiarity of Gilbert's,
exquisite humorist as he was, was that he was apt to be
exceedingly tetchy, even over trifles, in matters affecting
his personal dignity. He once complained to me in
querulous tones of the rudeness of a barber who came to
his house to cut his hair. 'What do you think the im-
pertinent fellow dared to ask me', said Gilbert, whose
voice rose to a treble in anger, '"when are we to expect
anything further, Mr Gilbert, from your fluent pen?"'
'What do you mean, sir,' said Gilbert to the well-in-
tentioned but unfortunate barber—'what do you mean
by "fluent pen"? There is no such thing as a fluent pen.
A pen is an insensible object. And, at any rate, I don't

presume to inquire into your private affairs; you will please observe the same reticence with regard to mine.' On another occasion he was accosted in the foyer of a theatre by a well-known amateur actor, a Mr H. Such Granville. 'Excuse me, Mr Gilbert,' said that gentleman— 'excuse me for speaking to you without an introduction. You may have heard of me; my name is Such, but I act as Granville.' 'Oh, do you,' retorted Gilbert, resenting the liberty, 'then I wish your name was Granville and you acted as such.' This encounter took place at the Garrick Theatre. Gilbert built the Garrick Theatre as a speculation, and leased it to his friend John Hare. To the dismay of everybody concerned, when the digging for the foundation had reached a certain depth a copious spring was discovered, and for a while it was feared that the building could not be proceeded with. 'Well,' said Gilbert, with more philosophy than he usually displayed, 'at least we shall be able to let the fishing.'

Gilbert's first essay in dramatic writing was a piece called *Dulcamara*, a burlesque of the *Elisir d'Amore* of Donizetti and Romani. This was produced by Miss Herbert, the lessee of the St James's Theatre in 1868. Miss Herbert had invited Robertson to furnish her with a Christmas entertainment, but his hands were too full to allow of his accepting the job, so he begged her to entrust the commission to Gilbert, in whom he had a firm belief. Miss Herbert acted on Robertson's advice, and thus it came to pass that what Byron did for Robertson, Robertson was able to do for Gilbert. In neither case, as the younger Robertson observes in his *Recollections* of his father, was judgment at fault. But, with Robertson to the fore at the Prince of Wales's as the author of original work, Gilbert was not content to follow up the success of *Dulcamara* with pieces of the same order; and in 1870 the first of his fairy comedies—*The Palace of*

Truth—was produced by Buckstone at the Haymarket Theatre. It is evident that by that time Buckstone, most conservative of managers, was in a chastened mood and had become thoroughly alive to the direction in which, owing to Robertson's ascendancy, the wind was blowing. *The Palace of Truth* was succeeded at the Haymarket, in 1871, by *Pygmalion and Galatea*, and *Pygmalion and Galatea*, in 1873, by *The Wicked World*. These three plays are full of charm, notwithstanding their decided savour of cynicism, and possess a literary quality which, without any loss of theatrical effect, makes them eminently readable. Another fairy play of Gilbert—*Broken Hearts*—was produced at the Court Theatre in 1876, and among his less fanciful pieces belonging to the 'seventies are his pathetic *Sweethearts*, his austere *Charity*, both done in 1874, his whimsical *Engaged*, and a version of the Faust legend called *Gretchen*. *Gretchen* failed to attract. One evening at the Beefsteak Club Gilbert was induced by a little group of admirers to explain in detail his treatment of the Faust story. A too-eager listener broke in with the question, 'And how did it end?' 'Oh, it ended in a fortnight,' said Gilbert, annoyed by the interruption.

It is not within my task to pursue the history of this writer beyond the 'seventies. Suffice it that he proved eventually that the bent of his genius lay in pure fantasy rather than in transcripts of the actualities of life. While the plots of his straightforward comedies are skilfully managed, his dialogue is without Robertson's natural touch; his characters talk in a manner that is stiff, formal, too carefully contrived. He found his *métier* ultimately in his association with Sullivan, and by that association, it is safe to prophesy, he will live. I trust I have not, by any unhappy suggestion, given an unfair picture of Gilbert. He was a brilliant creature, and he added a new word to the English language—'Gilbertian'.

Whose name, in connexion with the 'seventies, ranks next to Gilbert's in importance? Undoubtedly, Albery's. James Albery, author of *Two Roses, Apple Blossoms, Two Thorns, Forgiven*, and a few other comedies was born in 1838, and died, disappointed and embittered, in 1889. His original profession was that of an architect; but joining an Amateur Dramatic Society when quite a young man, he took to writing up the parts allotted to him, with the result that he developed a taste for dramatic author- ship, and in the end threw everything aside for it. That there was a moment when he questioned the wisdom of this proceeding is evinced by the fact that out of the royalties accruing to him from his first successful play— *Two Roses*—he invested a considerable sum of money in a business owned by his family and known as the 'Rope Walk'. The rope business came to grief, I believe from mismanagement, not from any lull in the infliction of capital punishment. This was a sad mischance to befall a man of Albery's desultory habits and want of the power of concentration. I think it was Gilbert who said that anybody can write a first act of a play. Certain it is that Albery left behind him a great many first acts of plays never to be completed; and that supplies the keynote of his character. He could begin, but he could seldom finish. He could write with ease; it was the planning— the spade-work—that was irksome. His initial success was his undoing; self-indulgence led to the gradual loss of such will power as he possessed, and the attractions of Bohemia did the rest.

Two Roses was produced at the Vaudeville Theatre on June 4th, 1870. In it, making a distinct mark in the serio-comic part of Digby Grant, appeared a zealous young actor who was shortly to take the town by storm at a neighbouring house, and whose ashes are interred in Westminster Abbey. *Two Roses* filled the Vaudeville

Theatre till September in the following year, when it was
displaced by *Apple Blossoms*, a delightful but weaker
piece. These two plays were Albery's outstanding successes. In his other original plays there was the sparkling,
promising first act; and then came the slackening of grip
and the signs of infirmity of purpose. Yet there was none
of them that did not reveal a keen insight into life, and
often a vein of genuine poetry. The late William Archer,
that fine critic and honest man—held Albery as a dramatist in high esteem. In an obituary notice, Archer wrote:
'If Mr Albery had fulfilled the promise of the *Two Roses*
and the little group of comedies that followed close upon
it, how deep would have been our mourning to-day!...
Beside Albery at his best, T. W. Robertson at his best is
as appollinaris to champagne, and H. J. Byron—well,
shall we say lemonade?' Yes, dear Archer, but Robertson
was a pioneer, Albery a disciple—in every sense of the
word, a follower. Archer proceeds:

> I may possibly overestimate Albery's powers; for our detestable
> habit of leaving the drama to moulder in dog-eared prompt-books
> renders it impossible for me to check my somewhat remote im-
> pressions. All I know is that some scenes in *Two Roses* and
> especially in *Forgiven*, have caused me as vivid pleasure as
> anything I ever saw in a theatre. It is a mistake to suppose that
> Albery's best work is in *Two Roses*. That may be his best play
> as a whole (his least bad play would be a more correct form of
> expression), but I am much mistaken if several passages in *For-
> given* do not show to much greater perfection his wealth of
> imaginative wit. His fancy, indeed, was too luxuriant to be kept
> within bounds by his rather deficient sense of dramatic propriety.
> But he could certainly have cultivated that sense, as well as the
> other faculties of the serious dramatist, had he so chosen. To a
> man with his eye for character and his delightful gift of dialogue
> nothing should have been impossible, had he only taken the trouble
> to master his craft.

Archer continues: 'My one personal recollection of
Albery is seeing him standing white with rage, before the

Vaudeville curtain, denouncing the "organized opposition" which had damned *Jacks and Jills*—though if ever
there was a foredoomed play, that was it.' I remember
the melancholy incident. That rash act of Albery's closed
his career as a writer of original plays. Thenceforward,
soured and sullen, and apprehensive perhaps of the
attitude of an outraged public, he felt himself driven to
restrict himself to adaptations. Some of those adaptations were excellent—improvements on the originals; but
even in his hackwork he was frequently behindhand and
undependable. In happier days, half in jest, he composed
an epitaph on himself, which showed that he was not
blind to his shortcomings. This is it:

> He revelled 'neath the Moon,
> He slept beneath the Sun,
> He lived a life of going to do,
> And died with nothing done.

Alas, poor Albery!

The name of William Gorman Wills is next on my list
of notable playwrights of the 'seventies. Wills, who was
born in Kilkenny County in 1828, studied at Trinity
College, Dublin, and was a pupil in the art school of the
Royal Irish Academy. He painted many portraits and
subject pictures, but as an artist was a man of mediocre
ability. What led him to the theatre I don't know. A
play of his called *The Man o' Airlie* was produced in 1866
and won him some consideration, but it was not until the
production of his *Charles I* that he became really prominent. This was the first of a series of dramas which
included *Eugene Aram, Jane Shore, Olivia*—founded on
The Vicar of Wakefield—Nell Gwynne, Sedgemoor, and
Claudian—all of great merit. Wills was a charming, if
not very profound writer, but was deficient in dramatic
invention. Given a strong situation to handle, he could
treat it with skill, but he needed guiding. He could hang

his hat on a peg with a fine flourish; but if there was no peg upon the wall, he was at a loss.

Charles I was produced at the Lyceum Theatre in 1872. That theatre was then under the management of H. L. Bateman, an American, and a showman of the Barnum type. A stroke of good fortune had happened to Bateman who, not many months before, had been at the end of his tether. He had started management at the Lyceum to exploit his daughter Isabel, but his early ventures fell flat, and he was on the eve of closing the theatre doors when an actor in his company—one Henry Irving, to whom I have already alluded—pressed upon him a play called *The Bells*, a version of *Le Juif Polonais* of Erckmann-Chatrian, done by a down-at-heel solicitor of the name of Leopold Lewis. Bateman shrugged his shoulders and yielded to Irving's persuasion; it was the desperate manager's last throw. *The Bells* was hurriedly rehearsed and cheaply put upon the stage; and on the morning after its first performance Irving awoke—if he had been asleep, which is doubtful—to find himself famous, and Leopold Lewis, puffed with pride, for ever after posed as the actual author of a play that was hardly more than a bald translation, and accepted grants from Irving, and drinks from all and sundry, till the end of his days. Wills's *Charles I* came immediately after *The Bells*, Irving's noble presentation of the 'martyr king' forming a striking contrast to his tragic, guilt-haunted burgomaster in the previous play. That Wills's piece owed much to Irving's wonderful acting is undeniable, but *Charles I*, in spite of its being disfigured by a shocking travesty of history in the drawing of Cromwell, is a spirited and moving drama. There may be some here who can recall the pitiful final scene, so tenderly written by Wills—the interview between Charles and Queen Henrietta Maria just before Charles is led out to execution.

> Ah, my loved solace on my thorny road,
> Sweet clue in all my labyrinth of sorrow,

says Charles to his weeping wife, 'What shall I leave to thee?'

> To thee I do consign my memory...
> Oh, keep my place in it for ever green,
> All hung with the immortelles of thy love!
> That sweet abiding in thine inmost thought
> I long for more than sculptured monument
> Or proudest record 'mongst the tombs of kings.

I have spoken of Wills's lack of inventiveness. An instance of it occurred in connexion with this very play. He was perplexed as to what to do for a fourth, and concluding, act, his mind continually reverting to the spectacle of the scaffold, the soldiery surrounding it, and Charles emerging from the window at Whitehall to utter his solemn injunction, 'Remember!'—little more than a tableau. Many were the consultations between Bateman, Irving and Wills upon this knotty point, Irving in particular protesting against such an exhibition of crude realism. One night, in a discussion over the supper table, Bateman suddenly snapped his fingers and cried, 'I've got it! The parting of William and Susan in *Black-eyed Susan*!' Thus it came about that from that affecting episode in Douglas Jerrold's old drama—a Jack Tar's farewell to a humble lass—sprang an equally affecting scene of farewell between a monarch and his consort.

And now at long last I come to H. J. Byron. I pass over Watts Phillips—who more properly belongs to the 'sixties—and Burnand, and Charles Reade, and Robert Reece, and other second and third-rate playwrights. These men were industrious enough, but they were never really in the movement started, as I claim, by Robertson. It is true that the indefatigable Tom Taylor, spurred by Robertson's example, came forward in the 'seventies with a couple of ambitious plays described as original—*'Twixt Axe and Crown* and *Joan of Arc*. I have not read these plays—produced as a vehicle for the talent of a lady known as 'the beautiful Mrs Rousby'—but I saw them both; and I recollect that I could never make out whether I was listening to prose which sounded like verse or verse which sounded like prose. At any rate, after I had contemplated the beauty of Mrs Rousby for five minutes, *'Twixt Axe and Crown* and *Joan of Arc* became, to my boyish taste, exceedingly tedious.

Why have I left Byron to the last; why did I put him aside a little while ago, reserving him till I have almost reached the end of this Paper? My explanation that other persons, from an artistic point of view, were entitled to priority was the merest excuse. Having said that he was the first to respond to the impetus given by Robertson, I seem deliberately to have cold-shouldered him. How deceptive are appearances! Like the child who pushes some dainty scrap of food to the edge of his plate—a plum, a morsel of jam, or what not—keeping the tit-bit to the end of his meal, so I, cunningly, for my own enjoyment, have kept back Byron. I confess I have a sneaking fondness for that good-natured, easy-going, handsome man, and I wish I could defend him whole-heartedly from the charges brought against him that he was in his comedies the mere joker that he was in his burlesques, that his plots were poor and stagey, that his characterization was conventional to a degree, his dialogue, though often clever and amusing, overladen with strained repartee and outrageous puns; that, in short, in the guise of a serious dramatist and a critic of life, he was nothing but a purveyor of cockney vulgarity of the most extravagant kind. I fear much of this is well-founded, but I think the dispraise is excessive. I admit that Byron was too often ready to sacrifice probability and appropriateness for the sake of getting a laugh from his audiences. He could even descend to that lowest of theatrical expedients—providing his personages with names that he could make fun of. In one of his later comedies—I forget which—he gave a character, for a reason which is painfully obvious, the name of Drinkwater. I must apologize to an honoured professor of this Society, who has raised that name to distinction, for this illustration of Byron's obliquity. It is hardly necessary to say that there was a moment in the play when that character appeared in what was called in those days a state of inebriety. 'Drinkwater,' said another character on the stage, eyeing the tipsy man sternly—'Drinkwater, *drink water.*' There we have Byron almost, if not quite, at his worst.

And yet, while wilfully committing these atrocities, Byron occasionally writhed under the critical attacks made upon him. It was in such a frame of mind that, incited by Robertson's triumphs at the Prince of Wales's, he wrote *Cyril's Success*. *Cyril's Success* was produced at the Globe Theatre in November, 1868. In a dedicatory preface to the published book of this comedy, addressed to Shirley Brooks, Byron says: 'I have endeavoured in *Cyril's Success* to write a play that would be effective in performance, and not altogether unworthy perusal'. After some further remarks, he goes on: 'And now you naturally ask—Why write and print this? Simply because I am tired of being termed a "droll", a "punster", and so on; and as a mere piece of self-justification—self-assertion it may be termed—beg to remind anyone who may care to recollect the fact, that *Cyril's Success* is original, and a comedy...in five acts! *There!*' What special virtue resides in five acts that cannot exist in three or four may not be clear to us to-day; but five acts are in accord with classic form, and Byron's mood would be satisfied with no fewer. At any rate, I have lately re-

read *Cyril's Success*, and the impression left upon me is
that it has so many faults that it would not be possible
for a smaller number of acts to contain them. The story
concerns a successful young dramatic author—Cyril
Cuthbert—his estrangement from his wife as a consequence of his popularity, and their ultimate reconciliation.
There is a villain in the piece who, detected in paying
illicit attentions to Mrs Cuthbert, fights a duel with Cyril
and, having been wounded to the point of death, on his
recovery duly repents and, in his own words, becomes
another and a better man. And there are many other
characters of the regulation stock pattern, including a
scion of the aristocracy—the Honourable Frederick
Titeboy—described as 'a dapper youth, dressed in the
best taste', which character was acted, as was the custom
of the time, by an extremely shapely young lady. Now,
many a worse story than this has made a good play; but
let me give you, very briefly, a specimen of Byron's
method of telling it. At the rise of the curtain on the
first act, Pepper, a manservant—Cyril's success has been
so great that he has already set up a manservant—Pepper
is discovered alone, seated in his master's armchair. He
reads aloud, for the instruction of the audience, a report in
a newspaper chronicling Cyril's latest achievement. 'By
Jove,' says Pepper, 'master's a-going it—another success
—nothing but success—well, he deserves it—I'm proud
of him—he's a gentleman. No meanness about *him*—no
niggardly ways, or prying into parties' perquisites or in-
terfering with his servants. Let's read the article once
more.' Presently he is joined by Perkins, Mrs Cuthbert's
maid, and together they discuss, for the further enlighten-
ment of the audience, their employers' affairs. Mrs
Cuthbert then enters, the servants withdraw—Pepper
exclaiming 'Missus!'—and the wife indulges in a soliloquy
a page-and-a-half long in which she obligingly informs

the audience of Cyril's neglect of her. She is interrupted by the entrance of her husband who overhears her reading a letter, uncomplimentary to himself, from her old schoolmistress; whereupon Mrs Cuthbert starts to her feet, crumples up the letter, and says, 'Oh, Cyril! I didn't mean you to hear it'—surely a lesson to wives not to read letters, when alone, at the top of their voices. So much for Byron's method of writing a play which he deemed not unworthy of perusal. The piece, with its comic, and communicative, servants, its lengthy soliloquies and preposterous 'asides', was a success, if not quite equal to Cyril's; but it is to be noted that Byron never again essayed a five-act comedy, nor challenged the critics on the score of calling him a 'droll'. Compared with Byron's most successful plays, *Cyril's Success* was flat and dull. Its composition evidently weighed upon the author and restrained his high spirits—those high spirits which, after all, were his most valuable asset.

Byron's most successful play was *Our Boys*. *Our Boys* was produced at the Vaudeville Theatre in January, 1875, and ran until April, 1879—a period of four years and three months. It must be remembered, of course, that in the 'seventies the rents of theatres, the salaries of actors and actresses, and a playwright's royalties were considerably lower than they are to-day. The salary of a leading actor or actress in the 'seventies was seldom more than £20 a week. Nowadays that salary is paid to a subordinate actor for speaking only twenty lines, while £100 a week will hardly keep a leading actor in golf clubs. As for the playwrights, £3 a performance was the usual fee in the 'seventies, as it had been in the 'sixties. That is the payment Robertson received for his comedies at the Prince of Wales's, Albery at the Vaudeville for *Two Roses*, and Byron for *Our Boys* at the same theatre. Since then, I understand, dramatists have become more exacting. But allowing for the different economic conditions which obtained in the 'seventies, there is no gainsaying the enormous success of *Our Boys*. In it are to be found the exaggerations common to Byron's other works; but the characters are consistently drawn, the construction is direct and well balanced, the story cumulative and full of human interest. I think it may be laid down with tolerable certainty that no play, however much it may be sneered at by superior persons, can get such a hold on the public as did *Our Boys* without possessing qualities that are essentially valid. The public does not analyse—how else could it have tolerated that exit of Perkyn Middlewick, the vulgar old father, when, after his angry scene with his son over the latter's love affair, he bounces out of the room shouting, 'And that's my ultipomatum!'?— the public, I repeat, does not analyse, but it *feels*; and the feelings of the people are, in the main, to be trusted.

Our Boys was followed by another play of Byron's— *The Girls*. Who can wonder that, after the phenomenal success of the piece that preceded it, *The Girls* proved rather a damp squib? But it had its amusing passages. Let me, in taking leave of Byron, cite one of them as a sample of his observant wit. A young married woman is giving her cook the morning orders. At the end of the interview the cook shows a disposition to linger. 'Well?' says the mistress. 'Please, m'm,' says the cook, 'the beer.' Those were the days, recollect, when it was the custom for the brewer to deliver at pretty regular intervals a small cask of ale for consumption in the basement. 'Beer!' says the lady, 'We had a new cask in less than a fortnight ago. You don't mean to tell me it's empty!' 'No, m'm,' says the cook, uncomfortably, 'it ain't exactly empty—but *it's tilted*.'

Byron did not long outlive the success of *Our Boys*. He died in the month of April, 1884, at the age of fifty.

Genial, warm-hearted, light-hearted Byron! We could have better spared a better dramatist.

I have left myself little time or space to deal with the acting in the 'seventies. I can give it only the merest glance. In 1870 there was no actor of commanding position and, except for Marie Wilton, who had married and become Mrs Bancroft, no actress. Phelps was sixty-six and past the height of his powers. Mathews, Buckstone and Webster, too, were old men and in their decline. A school of natural acting—the teacup-and-saucer school —had been created by the Robertson comedies at the Prince of Wales's and its novelty was overshadowing the rank and file elsewhere. That the influence of this school was wholly for good can hardly be maintained, though the artists who appeared originally in the Robertsonian plays did not make the mistake committed by most of those who followed them in the revivals of Robertson's pieces. The seasoned and experienced actors and actresses who originally interpreted Robertson at the Prince of Wales's recognized that acting is an imitation of life, not a reproduction; and so at the beginning the teacups-and-saucers were handled in such a way as to be entertaining to the occupants of the back row of the gallery. But already, in 1870, there were signs of an acquisition of strength behind the footlights. At the Haymarket Theatre, infusing new blood into an ageing troupe, there was appearing a young actress who for many years was to be the embodiment on the stage of fresh, glowing womanhood—Madge Robertson, a sister of the dramatist, still with us as Dame Madge Kendal. And as the 'seventies advanced, a young man with ascetic features and a beautiful voice made his *début* at the now vanished Princess's Theatre in Oxford Street, showing promise that has been richly fulfilled—a young man of the name of Forbes-Robertson. That diverting low-comedian in petticoats—Mrs John Wood—also came to the front in the 'seventies; and marching slowly forward was another young man who was to stamp his name indelibly on stage history—Charles Wyndham. I could give a score of other names pertaining to the 'seventies, but I forbear. I must, however, again speak of Henry Irving who, after electrifying audiences in 1871 as Mathias in *The Bells*, rose higher and higher in public esteem—an esteem which culminated in a wide expression of sorrow when he fell, exhausted, at Bradford in 1905. It has been urged against this extraordinary man that he did nothing for the modern drama; and it must be confessed that his ambition was centred in himself. He aimed at being acknowledged as the greatest actor of the age, and to be hailed as the legitimate successor of Garrick and of Kean; and he was content to achieve that aim, adding lustre to his calling in the process. But it was said of him, I think with truth, that, such were his inherent gifts, his determination, and his infinite patience, there was no walk in life in which he could not have succeeded. He was the most dignified figure in any assembly, no matter how eminent; and, breaking through a personality that was somewhat awe-inspiring, he had a smile that almost brings tears to one's eyes in the recollection. Finally, in 1875, after an apprenticeship in the provinces and a few fugitive and inconspicuous appearances in London, there came definitely upon the scene that lovely lady, Ellen Terry, later to be Irving's associate at the Lyceum. In April of that year she acted Portia in a revival at the Prince of Wales's of *The Merchant of Venice*, under the celebrated Bancroft management; and in the familiar words of Burke, spoken of a less fortunate woman, 'surely never lighted on this orb, which she hardly seemed to touch, a more delightful vision'. Continuing the quotation, I can say, 'I saw her just above the horizon...glittering like the morning star, full of life and splendour and joy.' An undimmed memory!

To sum up, the theatre in the 'seventies was a simpler theatre than the theatre of to-day. It was a place of charm and mystery. Though its drama had a smaller relation to facts than our drama now has, it was less pretentious; and as it had less freedom, its practitioners made less clamour. And it was as healthy and clean as the veriest fairy-tale. One recalls the warning given by Hippolyte Taine to Anatole France after the publication of *Sylvestre Bonnard*. 'Remain where you are,' said Taine, 'and compensate us for so much contemporary talent which has gone astray and, under pretext of presenting us with the truth, causes us to be disgusted with life and with literature.' It was not possible—luckily, you doubtless think—for the Drama to remain what it was in the 'seventies; but for the rest of Taine's advice, perhaps it would be well for some of us to ponder those words at the present time.

§ 8

Tennyson, Swinburne, Meredith— and the Theatre

By HARLEY GRANVILLE-BARKER

THE 'seventies saw Tennyson's first play acted and Swinburne's *Bothwell* published, and they heard Meredith lecture—a selected gathering at the London Institution heard him—upon Comedy and the Comic Spirit. Drama is a strong lure to creative minds; the theatre—outlandish little world that it must seem, perverse, self-conscious!—as often finally repels them, and is, for its own part, content with easier company. Throughout the nineteenth century such alliance as there was between the English theatre and English letters, was spasmodic, uneasy, unprofitable. Neither, it seemed, had much to bring the other. Keats tried his juvenile hand at a play; Shelley completed one, but he could hardly have looked for its acting. Byron wrote tremendous dramas, sublimated blood-and-thunder; his name's magic rather than their own gave them a short, galvanic life. Scott's influence bore dramatic fruit abroad, but our Victor Hugos were Bulwer Lytton and Sheridan Knowles. There were faults on both sides. Macready's diaries are instructive reading. He was passionate for the credit of his calling. Shakespeare was his stand-by, but he received new authors gladly and wrestled with them for their salvation —a painful process, for both parties, it would seem to have been. Nor did he need a reputation to set him on the track of talent; he saluted Browning as a poet of great account upon a first reading of *Paracelsus*. But (his own touchy temper apart) we see his theatre as a poor school for a renascent drama, too set in its methods, uninspiring, the actor and his egoisms in firm possession; he himself, poor man, plagued on all sides, and self-plagued. The main fault, however, may have been in the national disposition of the time towards a certain moral contentment, new-found creature comfort and the fire side. Great drama with its emotional stirrings and the irony of comedy, are enemies to content; and it is not the theatre's business to be at odds with its public, as its public will soon make plain.

Not till Meredith was dead did anyone know—though, knowing him, it might have been guessed—that the *Essay on Comedy* was but the critical shadow of a creative impulse; not till the fragments of three or four plays were found among other work laid aside. He had liked in his old age to talk of plays that he might have written, might still write (though he was then writing no more), had liked to scheme them at length; elaborate fantastic comedies. But these fragments he never fetched out. Well, he had done enough not to be troubled by the thought of what he might have done. It is for us to sigh over them a little —more than a little.

Swinburne had kept his earliest plays within the theatre's compass, whether with an eye to their acting or no. *Bothwell* must be about 15,000 lines long, and would outlast a winter's night; but *The Queen Mother, Rosamund, Chastelard*, are physically actable at least[1]. We can hardly see him happy, though, in the theatre, amenable to its discipline, content with its compromisings or tolerant of its small follies. Because he saw Fechter give

[1] For the benefit of those to whom such measurements mean nothing, Shakespeare's *Antony and Cleopatra* is a little over three thousand lines long.

a stupid twist to a famous passage in *Othello* he vowed he would never see a play of Shakespeare's acted again. Ah! if men of letters were to be finally judged by their worst rather than their best, by their slips of syntax and errors of taste, by the stuff that second thoughts send to the waste-paper basket! We conspire to forget a great writer's worst work. But second thoughts in the theatre are apt to come too late, and best and worst must stand in the moment's limelight together.

By 1873, at any rate, we have Swinburne writing to John Morley:

> If ever accomplished this drama will certainly be a great work in one sense, for, except that translation from the Spanish of an improperly named comedy in 25 acts published in 1631, it will be the biggest (I fear) in the language. But having made a careful analysis of the historical events from the day of Rizzio's murder to that of Mary's flight into England, I find that to cast into dramatic mould the events of those eighteen months it is necessary to omit no detail, drop no link in the chain, if the work is to be either dramatically coherent or historically intelligible....

And the completed mass of *Bothwell* stands defiant.

What there is to be said in favour of closet-drama—of a work of art done in deliberate neglect of its proper medium—I really do not know. To a novelist or epic poet the exchange of freedom of narrative for the constraint of dialogue is in itself, surely, unprofitable, though there be some gain in actuality and in directness of attack. But a play's life lies in its amenity to acting. It may be suited to one sort of stage or another; but it must be committed to human expression, and the possibilities of its artistry, however various, are yet dependent upon this, even as a human body's beauty dwells in its common uses. About five-sixths of *Bothwell*—say five ordinary plays' lengths— is dramatically inert. The speeches flow sonorously on. They are lengthy in themselves, but that need not condemn them. If John Knox preaches us a sermon 370 lines long—well, he was a man of many more words than this! But if the material is dramatic, the product is not. The trouble is that Swinburne seldom, if ever, sets his characters free. He conceives them, brings them to a sort of a birth; but he still speaks through them, they are megaphones at his mouth. With freedom they would do as all human beings do, contest, come to cross-purposes, give way, refuse to say the things they should say, stand altogether dumb, and be a dreadful nuisance to their author, doubtless. How to round them in again and face them towards their destiny? In that lies the art of the playwright. They can be brought within conventions as formal as Racine's; but they must at some time have been free. In the theatre this freedom, as the actor inherits it, is a part of the natural order of things, is indeed its fount. The closet-dramatist can with difficulty imagine or allow for it.

Tennyson's case was quite other. He was sixty-five when he wrote *Queen Mary*, and people thought—to quote his son's biography—that to begin publishing plays at his age was a hazardous experiment. But, encouraged by Spedding, George Eliot and Lewes, he persevered. He had always liked the theatre, had been a constant playgoer in early and middle life and 'regarded the drama as one of the most humanising of influences...always hoped that the State, or the Municipalities...would produce our great English historical plays, so that they might form part of the Englishman's ordinary educational curriculum'. (For how much longer is that hope to be deferred!) 'For himself', we are further told, 'he was aware that he wanted intimate knowledge of the mechanical details necessary for the modern stage.... His dramas were written with the intention that actors should edit them for the stage, keeping them at the high poetic level'.

A great man's simplicities are endearing. *Queen Mary*, produced at the Lyceum on the 16th of April, 1876, was edited indeed. Twenty-seven characters were cut out altogether. Still, the Poet Laureate had but to write his first play and London's best theatre would stage it, London's best actor, fresh from the glories of Hamlet and Othello, content himself with the shadowy Philip of Spain. Irving made Philip, however—he could hardly help it—the most notable thing in the play, and Whistler has made the figure of him memorable. The portrait is in the Metropolitan Museum in New York. Will an English National Theatre ever buy it back again? Irving's biographer insists that Tennyson himself did the editing; but if so, no doubt he took expert advice—Irving's own, possibly. It was good advice on the whole. Cranmer's spiritual conflicts, which went by the board, are tame drama: and the rewritten 'theatrical' ending (to be found in the Biography) is as legitimate, and better of its kind, than the spun-out allusiveness of the published play; with Elizabeth, Cecil and the rest forecasting history, while Mary does her dying 'off' as a classic heroine should.

There were obvious flaws in Tennyson's modest approach to playwriting; even, perhaps, in its modesty. He speaks—or his son speaks for him—of drama and the theatre as a sort of House of Lords and House of Commons, with the play as a Bill sent down to be pulled about a bit, rewritten a little and at last turned out as an effective Act. Such practical politics make for poor art. He thinks of the theatre, apparently, as a place of mechanical craftsmanship, more or less, in which an absolute art of drama is adulterated and turned to account. This is just true enough to be dangerously misleading; but one sees where the error is bred. What mangling and botching has not the absolute drama of

Shakespeare survived? Tennyson went to school to Shakespeare; no English poet turning playwright but by instinct does that! The trouble with him was that he never quite grasped what he had to learn, nor the significance of what he did learn there. There is much that is fine in *Queen Mary*. Tennyson is a poet, and he can frame character and see history in terms of drama. There is even, at moments, something of the absolute dramatist in him, for he can project a scene, fully significant only in its action, conceived so, evidently, not plotted out on paper. Had he trusted to his native dramatic instinct, whatever its worth, it would finally have been better for his play. There is, of course, no such arbitrary division between drama and the theatre as it suited him to assume. Why do English men of letters find it so hard to approach the theatre unselfconsciously? Some native dramatic instinct we all have. Acting, singing and dancing are, fundamentally, as nearly instinctive as art can be. The laws of the theatre, about which he was so graciously diffident! There are none. There are none, at least, that the true dramatist cannot remake to his purpose as he goes along. The theatre is an element. We ought all to feel at home in it; but, whether or no, we must plunge into it, to sink or swim, as one takes a plunge into the sea. Learn a few strokes by all means; but if we are never to be beyond the need of swimming bladders, we are not in our element, and there's an end. The best brains are not needed to make a swimmer. We can cry out as we sink that swimming is a very vulgar art. But all that need be learnt of the laws of the theatre is soon learnt, and then the sooner it is forgotten the better, even as we cease to use an alphabet when we know how to read. The truly great dramatists, who have made old things new in drama, gained this unconscious mastery betimes. Shakespeare did, so did Molière, and Ibsen.

Then they made laws and broke them, remade them and broke them again, and probably gave not much thought to the matter at all. Drama was their language; they spoke it and did not hesitate. But two centuries and a half of vain repetition (such as the Heathen use) have, not unnaturally, turned Shakespeare's dramatic dialect largely to gibberish.

Blank verse is still the chief pillar of the superstition, an accepted vestment for serious drama, the silk hat of respectability. Poets almost inevitably turn to it; and, with no pretentions to being a poet, one can string out ten-syllable lines by the yard—they will pass for poetry. Ridicule has glanced from its tough sides; superstitions are seldom killed by ridicule. *The Critic* could not laugh it from the theatre; the audience would make merry over Tilburina and Whiskerandos and weep the next night at heroics little less absurd. Sheridan himself wrote *Pizarro*. For nearly another century the thing flourished in full turgidity. It had its phases, its turns of fashion. By 1870 the orotund school of acting was in decline, and such altiloquence as Sheridan Knowles and Bulwer Lytton had purveyed to it was consequently in less demand. Westland Marston plied a tamer pen; W. S. Gilbert—at so uncongenial a task—a very dull one. Tom Taylor was writing a series of conscientious, mild, historical tragedies. His *Anne Boleyn* was staged at the Haymarket Theatre in March 1875. Here is the end of it. Anne, on her way to execution, is saying farewell to her attendants:

> I have not much to give, but I've had ordered
> Some little books of high and holy thoughts
> For thee and Madge and Ann here and the rest.
> See that they have them. I ask Heaven's forgiveness
> For all unkind deeds or words or thoughts
> Done, said or thought by me to anyone.
> Chief I pray pardon of the Lady Mary
> For aught she may have suffered at my hands

> Or for my cause. And, that done, there is nothing
> But thanks and still thanks for your loving-kindness
> In this my sore strait and my doleful prison.
> 'Twas hence I set out for my coronation.
> All is as it was then. Only a Queen
> Who goes to take a higher crown than England's.

Harmless, lullaby stuff! Tom Taylor, it is true, was not taken very seriously as a poet. But his plays ranked high in theatrical respectability; they show the furnishing of the arena into which Tennyson was to step a year later.

We do not look for such colourless, ambling, 'right butter-woman's rank to market' writing from him. And, to be fair, at a climax we shall not find it. Tennyson is Tennyson, and can rise in some sort to an occasion. But open the play at random. Here is Gardner at Pole's reception.

> We, the Lords spiritual and Temporal
> And Commons here in Parliament assembled,
> Presenting the whole body of this nation
> Of England, and dominions of the same,
> Do make most humble suit unto your Majesties
> In our own name and that of all the State,
> That by your gracious means and intercession
> Our supplication be exhibited
> To the Lord Cardinal Pole....

But he is reading a petition. The passage must probably be a dull one, anyway. Turn a few pages, though. Mary is now rating the Lord Chancellor:

> I come for counsel and ye give me feuds,
> Like dogs that set to watch their master's gate,
> Fall, when the thief is ev'n within the walls,
> To worrying one another. My Lord Chancellor,
> You have an old trick of offending us;
> And but that you are art and part with us
> In purging heresy, well we might, for this
> Your violence and much roughness to the Legate
> Have shut you from our counsels....

Now she is excusing herself to Philip:

> Alas, the Council will not hear of war.
> They say your wars are not the wars of England.
> They will not lay more taxes on a land
> So hunger-nipt and wretched; and you know
> The crown is poor. We have given the church-lands back;
> The nobles would not; nay, they clapt their hands
> Upon their swords when ask'd; and therefore God
> Is hard upon the people. What's to be done?
> Sir, I will move them in your cause again,
> And we will raise us loans and subsidies
> Among the merchants; and Sir Thomas Gresham
> Will aid us. There is Antwerp and the Jews.

And so on and so forth.

Why blank verse, or any sort of verse at all for the stage? Dryden raised the question; but, after that, it was generally assumed to be the right sort of thing. Its aesthetic merits apart, the Elizabethan dramatists had sound practical reasons for clinging to it. It is easy stuff to write, as we have said; and they had no time to waste. It is easy to learn too; and the actors had less. Besides, as what is too stupid to be said can be sung, so will sounding blank verse cover a mighty lot of nonsense. But the grand dramatic merit of verse, of course, is that it is in itself an emotional thing; and the appeal of drama will be first or last—first and last, very often—to the emotions. Verse is hypnotic; the mere rhythm of it can fascinate and hold the hearer. It can often be too hypnotic so spoken; one has seen audiences saved from sleep only by the extreme discomfort of the stalls they were wedged in—not always saved, moreover. The scientific side of the matter may be found broached in a most interesting pamphlet written for the English Association by Sir Philip Hartog, *On the Relation of Poetry to Verse*. He quotes the psychologists, speaks of the central attention which we consciously offer to a subject, and of the uncontrolled 'marginal' attention which wanders. The function of rhythm and rhyme is to absorb this marginal attention so that we may be wholly surrendered to the spell of the poet. He quotes Bergson:

> The object of art is to lull to sleep the active, or rather the resisting powers of our personality, and thus to bring us to a state of perfect docility, in which we realise the idea suggested to us, and sympathise with the sentiment expressed (to us).

And very appositely, Mr Middleton Murry:

> Rhythm and metre...have the power of throwing the reader into a state of heightened susceptibility to emotional suggestion... the recurrence of a regular rhythmical beat has an almost hypnotic effect; it completely detaches our attention from the world of every day...and if it is regular and monotonous enough, actually sends us to sleep....The poet's business is to take advantage of the tendency, and instead of letting it reach its logical physical conclusion, by an infinite rhythmical variation of the metrical basis, to keep us intensely aware. There is a background of metrical sameness separating us like a curtain from the practical world; there is a richness of the rhythmical variation to make the world in which we are worthy of our most delighted attention.

Yet, strangely enough, he does not cite poetic drama and the common experience of the theatre as the most patent possible evidence in his favour[1]. Moreover, in the suggestion (but Sir Philip dissents from this) that it is rhythmical variation which keeps us intensely aware and provokes our 'delighted attention' lies one of the chief, though more recondite, secrets of the writing of dramatic verse; and ignorance of these simple, fundamental facts of the art of speech and command of attention (the ABC of the theatre) is a chief cause of the literary dramatist's failure.

What is wrong, from a dramatic point of view, with this verse of Tennyson's? It is not, presumably, bad verse in itself (I do not pretend to know what good verse, in the abstract, is, or if there be any such thing. But I

[1] Perhaps Mr Middleton Murry does; I cannot refer to his book as I write.

do know better than to depreciate Tennyson lightly), and if it were, it could certainly be matched by passages from Shakespeare himself, who could, on occasion, write as crudely, flatly, consciencelessly, as you please. But Shakespeare, at his worst, could not be more than momentarily undramatic. He writes as by instinct to be spoken, not to be read. His verse is naturally rhetorical; and it is always more or less charged with emotion; for nobody, speaking to a crowd (and the actor is speaking to the audience as well as to his fellow-actors) will keep to cut and dried thought alone. It has something about it, then, that Sir Philip Hartog's rhyme and rhythm alone cannot give; it has an added carrying power.

This was the point from which Shakespeare and his followers started. They had to capture and hold an unruly audience, and their chief means to do it was rhetorical emotional verse. Shakespeare's own progress as an artist can well be studied (and should be, by any poet anxious to turn dramatist) by tracing the development of his verse-making, from its early lyric fervour—which is sometimes monotonous and dramatically ineffective[1]— and from the commanding, but unyielding rhetoric of the Histories, to the masterly breadth and delicacy and variety, to the subtle suggestiveness of character and mood to be found in the later plays. But we are too apt to admire these mature elaborations (one suspects that they chiefly influenced Tennyson) and forget the fundamental strength of simple emotional rhetoric still underlying them. Shakespeare never forgot that first need. In the greater plays the emotional tension is high throughout. But should he feel the strength of a scene and its carrying power slackening he is ready enough with a piece of pure

---

[1] This is one good reason for supposing that such plays as *Love's Labour's Lost* and *A Midsummer Night's Dream* may have been written rather for special audiences than for the public theatre.

rhetoric; and he never comes to despise even the conventional claptrap of the rhymed couplet, for the effective whipping up of a scene's end.

Tennyson's verse was, almost inevitably, of another cast. He had written all his life to be read rather than spoken. He wrote reflectively, analytically. This might not have mattered—it never mattered with Shakespeare—had there been the primary emotion beneath; but there so seldom is. His verse does not vibrate. He wrote now pathetically, now fancifully; and he could never fail in dignity.

Cranmer's confession of faith:

> Good people, every man at time of death
> Would fain set forth some saying that may live
> After his death and better humankind;
> For death gives life's last word the power to live,
> And, like the stone cut epitaph, remain
> After the vanished voice, and speak to men....

(One remembers Buckingham's farewell. Fletcher's work is it—which is also as apt to lack underlying passion? Tennyson suffers not at all by comparison here.)

The tale of his burning:

> Then Cranmer lifted his left hand to heaven
> And thrust his right into the bitter flame;
> And crying in his deep voice more than once,
> 'This hath offended—this unworthy hand!'
> So held it till it all was burned, before
> The flame had reached his body; I stood near—
> Mark'd him—he never uttered moan of pain:
> He never stirr'd or writhed, but, like a statue
> Unmoving in the greatness of the flame,
> Gave up the ghost....

(How fine! But it is narrative, and not immediately dramatic. He outruns the allowance of narrative proper to a play, for it is a very small one. A temptation, this, to most practised writers turning dramatist!)

Then there is the pretty fancy—as she hears the milk-maid singing—of Elizabeth's

> I would I were a milkmaid,
> To sing, love, marry, churn, brew, bake and die.
> Then have my simple headstone by the church,
> And all things lived and ended honestly.
> I could not if I would. I am Harry's daughter....

This is authentic Tennyson, and holds its own for a due moment.

Philip is written somewhat flatly—his main business is to be bored and yet more bored by England and his queen —but with true economy and admirable irony. And who, that ever heard him, cannot hear Irving saying

> By St James I do protest,
> Upon the faith and honour of a Spaniard,
> I am vastly grieved to leave your Majesty.
> Simon, is supper ready?

But Mary herself has, as she should have, the best of the play; and Tennyson is, at the crucial moments, spontaneously at his best in the writing of her. The calculated effectiveness of the second act's ending with its echoed

> My foes are at my feet and I am Queen.

could be carpentered up by any one, and the slashing of Philip's picture is commonplace. But her lonely thrilling to the hope of the unborn child:

> He hath awaked! He hath awaked!
> He stirs within the darkness!...
> The second Prince of Peace—
> The great unborn defender of the Faith,
> Who will avenge me of mine enemies—
> He comes, and my star rises.
> The stormy Wyatts and Northumberlands,
> The proud ambitions of Elizabeth,
> And all her fiercest partisans—are pale
> Before my star!

> The light of this new learning wanes and dies:
> The ghost of Luther and Zuinglius fade
> Into the deathless hell which is their doom
> Before my star!

This is the real thing, and its feeling, as if spontaneously, moulds its form. The miserable forsaken figure of the last act is, in itself, well pictured. The acclaimed gesture of

Alice Your Grace hath a low voice.
Mary   How dare you say it?
       Even for that he hates me. A low voice
       Lost in a wilderness where none can hear!
       A voice of shipwreck on a shoreless sea!
       A low voice from the dust and from the grave.
(sitting on   There, am I low enough now?
the ground)

is legitimate and fine. But, as we see, these good moments are reflective, analytic moments. And the action as a whole is too often irrelevant, loose-knit and slack. Its pulse beats feebly.

Incidental virtues will not make a play. Tennyson devises characters, incidents, pretty effects by the dozen that are significant and interesting in themselves; yet they do not cohere into drama. He turned instinctively to Elizabethan form; its freedom invited him, but he never saw where its inner life lay. Emotional rhetoric, which is at the very heart of it, which sustains and suffices it at its simplest, was, as we argued, alien to his temper. But, this apart, he was for an elaboration of action that it would have taxed Shakespeare's maturest skill to contrive, articulate, keep proportioned, each part of it seeming to go its own pace, diversity yet yielding to the unity of the whole. The freedom of the form—once a plain tale is departed from—makes almost infinite variation possible; so many combinations, contrasts of scene with scene, this sort of character with that, the tragic, the comic, verse set against prose, this sort of verse against that. A most delicate mechanism, which, then, like all mechanism, must be put to the test; either it will go, will act, gain a keener life in the actor's hands, or it will not. And the mainspring that sets it going? Each art has its master-secret; and here is the theatre's; hidden from the wise often, and made plain to the foolish.

We need not suppose that the Elizabethan dramatist sat down to calculate his play's construction to a nicety, or thought of aesthetic laws. He had mastered this instrument of the theatre, in its crudity, in its delicacies; and, upon it, given his theme, he improvised. That is nearer the truth, if not quite true. We, after the event, with but a groping knowledge of the instrument, must analyse the scant evidence of the printed play, re-create the actors and their acting and their audience too, in our imagination. This is work for the critic and historian, and for actors also to re-interpret, if they can, this yesterday in terms of to-day. But what writer, intent on creative expression, will cumber himself with machinery that he cannot set going, that, set going somehow, will go its own way, not his. Yet this, in effect, is what the playwright does who writes a play in Elizabethan form, knowing nothing of the Elizabethan theatre. This is what Tennyson did.

Search behind form and method to find his intention there, and what good quality we find! Take such a scene as that short one in the fifth act, before the Palace:

A light burning within. Voices of the night passing.

in which form and method are as much his own as the matter, and matter and method are at one, and how alive it is! But in the main the play is a machine that, set upon its road, will not go; it has to be pushed.

Swinburne, rejecting the theatre, is yet far more the dramatist than Tennyson. He is, to begin with, the natural rhetorician; he speaks and sings, rather than

writes, and whatever else he may lack, it will not be
emotion. His determination in *Bothwell* to leave nothing
unsaid, cannot result in that most selective of literary
forms, a play; but it is amazing how much emotional
pressure he can sustain behind the hundred-line, two-
hundred, three-hundred-line speeches from which he
pours history. When the work was in the doing he would
visit his friends, an act or two under his arm, and amaze
them by 'shrieking, thundering, whispering, fluting'
through scene after scene of it, far into the night. They
were left stunned or sleeping, one supposes; incapable,
certainly, of any such thing as 'delighted attention'
after an hour or more's buffeting by the charged monotonous verse. One gratefully borrows Mr Middleton
Murry's phrase and, reading the play now, only wishes
that Swinburne could have profited by his dictum.

Again, open the book almost at random:

> Tell him, night and day
> And fear and hope are grown one thing to me
> Save for his sake: and say mine hours and thoughts
> Are as one fire devouring grain by grain
> This pile of tares and drift of crumbling brands
> That shrivels up in the slow breath of time
> The part of life that keeps me far from him.
> The heap of dusty days that sunder us
> I would I could burn all at once away
> And our lips meet across the wild red flame
> Thence unconsumed, being made a keener fire
> Than any burns on earth. Say that mine eyes
> Ache with my heart and thirst with all my veins,
> Requiring him they have not. Say my life
> Is but as sleep and my sleep very life
> That dreams upon him...

and so on for a hundred and ninety lines more. It is
Mary's message to Bothwell. The thing soon becomes intolerable. As the old country saying has it: 'Tisn't the
hunting nor the hurdles that makes the holes in the
horses' hoofs, 'tis the hammer, hammer, hammer, on the

hard high road'. Not a fence, not a ditch, nor a check and a little detour will Swinburne allow us. Nevertheless, if not drama, it is the true stuff of drama. It has authentic impulse, it is not the mere filling out of an Elizabethan pattern. The play is not made for acting, there is no give and take about it, Swinburne is its only actor. He is the audience too, the hypnotiser and the hypnotised. It has its story but hardly a plan, and no complexity of structure at all. It has no preparation, nor intrigue, variety, surprise, relief—neither the arts nor the artifices of the dramatist are called on. It is at a constant climax; as unhealthy a condition in a play as fever in a human being, for when climax is due, there will be no strength left. Yet Swinburne too can rise to an occasion. Time and again great moments occur. If they rested upon ample foundation, we should have great drama.

The scene of Rizzio's murder is a fine thing. Its ending:

Queen.	What have ye made my servant?
Ruthven.	A dead dog.
	His turn is done of service.
Darnley.	Yea, stark dead?
Ruthven.	They stabbed him through and through with edge on edge
	Till all their points met in him; there he lies
	Cast forth in the outer lodge, a piteous knave
	And poor enough to look on.
Queen.	I am content.
	Now must I study how to be revenged.
Darnley.	Nay, think not that way; make it not so much:
	Be warned, and wiser.
Queen.	Must I not, my lord?
	You have taught me worthier wisdom than of words;
	And I will lay it up against my heart.

—pregnant, sure and tuned like a bell. The compassing of Darnley's death at Kirk o' Field is true drama, if too long drawn out. Mary with Bothwell and Jane Gordon at Dunbar; when he leaves her; at Lochleven; at Langside—there is enough dramatic passion in these scenes

alone to furnish half-a-dozen plays. The last scene of all
is the finest. It starts subduedly. Herries is pleading
with the Queen, even now, when she stands on the shore
at Solway, even at this last moment to stay.

> Go not hence:
> You shall find no man's faith or love on earth
> Like theirs that here cleave to you.

So he ends, and she answers

> I have found
> And think to find no hate of men on earth
> Like theirs that here beats on me.

Quotation is unfair: the scene is an entity and the very
simple form of it helps to give it beauty and power. Mary's
sombre wrath rolls up like a wave, sentence crowning
sentence, to its first height. Then it subsides to the soft-
ness of

> Come, friends,
> I think the fisher's boat hath hoised up sail
> That is to bear none but one friend and me:
> Here must my true men and their queen take leave,
> And each keep thought of other. My fair page,
> Before the man's change darken on your chin
> I may come back to ride with you at rein
> To a more fortunate field: howe'er that be,
> Ride you right on with better hap, and live
> As true to one of merrier days than mine
> As on that night to Mary once your queen.
> Douglas, I have not won a word of you:
> What would you do to have me tarry?

George Douglas.   Die.

Douglas speaks no other word throughout the scene. The
still figure standing there, passionate in silence, made
eloquent by one word! Who shall say that Swinburne
had not the stuff of the dramatist in him?

But the boy's devotion only stings her now:

> I lack not love it seems then at my last.
> That word was bitter; yet I blame it not,

Who would not have sweet words upon my lips
Nor in mine ears at parting. I should go
And stand not here as on a stage to play
My last part out in Scotland; I have been
Too long a queen too little...

And so she passes to the quite magnificent apostrophe
that ends the play:—

Methinks the sand yet cleaving to my foot
Should not with no more words be shaken off,
Nor this my country from my parting eyes
Pass unsaluted; for who knows what year
May see us greet hereafter? Yet take heed,
Ye that have ears, and hear me; and take note,
Ye that have eyes, and see with what last looks
Mine own take leave of Scotland; seven years since
Did I take leave of my fair land of France,
My joyous mother, mother of my joy,
Weeping; and now with many a woe between
And space of seven years' darkness, I depart
From this distempered and unnatural earth
That casts me out unmothered, and go forth
On this grey sterile bitter gleaming sea
With neither tears nor laughter, but a heart
That from the softest temper of its blood
Is turned to fire and iron. If I live,
If God pluck not all hope out of my hand,
If aught of all mine prosper, I that go
Shall come back to men's ruin, as a flame
The wind bears down, that grows against the wind,
And grasps it with great hands, and wins its way,
And wins its will, and triumphs; so shall I
Let loose the fire of all my heart to feed
On these that would have quenched it. I will make
From sea to sea one furnace of the land
Whereon the wind of war shall beat its wings
Till they wax faint with hopeless hope of rest,
And with one rain of men's rebellious blood
Extinguish the red embers. I will leave
No living soul of their blaspheming faith
Who war with monarchs; God shall see me reign
As he shall reign beside me, and his foes
Lie at my foot with mine; kingdoms and kings
Shall from my heart take spirit, and at my soul

Their souls be kindled to devour for prey
　The people that would make its prey of them
And leave God's altar stripped of sacrament
As all kings' heads of sovereignty, and make
Bare as their thrones his temples; I will set
The old things of his holiness on high
That are brought low, and break beneath my feet
These new things of men's fashion; I will sit
And see tears flow from eyes that saw me weep
And dust and ashes and the shadow of death
Cast from the block beneath the axe that falls
On heads that saw me humbled; I will do it,
Or bow mine own down to no royal end
And give my blood for theirs if God's will be,
But come back never as I now go forth
With but the hate of men to track my way
And not the face of any friend alive.

Mary Beaton. But I will never leave you till you die.

—ends it, but for Mary Beaton's echoing murmur; wistful, sinister. Swinburne had evidently planned to link up his Trilogy by this strange recurring note of fatidic devotion to the Queen, blent with the patient hunger for vengeance to fall on her for Chastelard's betrayal, a hunger to be sated at last. But in the densities of *Bothwell* the effect is lost.

This last scene is true drama; it will answer to any test. If it seems not to fit the work-a-day theatre, a theatre can be moulded for it. Authentic art has never failed of interpretation yet. Could Swinburne but have disciplined himself, not to the mechanics of a given stage, but to the inevitable rigour of dramatic form; could he have relaxed and lost himself a little in its amenities (Had he not been Swinburne! Yes, it always comes to that), his plays would have won their theatre in the end; and this none too opulent theatre of ours would have won a dramatist and poet as well.

What of Meredith's place in the story? It would seem, by virtue of but a few scattered scraps of dialogue, to be one of no consequence at all. He was that thing least regarded in England, a conscious literary artist; he was self-regardful too, perhaps in excess. He set out to please himself by what he wrote; happy enough no doubt, if he pleased other people as well, but incapable of swerving an inch from his path to make matters easier for them, apt indeed to lead them defiantly a little bit more of a dance. It was not mere wilfulness, rather a sort of religion with him to show the barbarian that art, in its making or liking, must be a spiritually athletic thing.

He was fifty when he wrote the *Essay on Comedy.* It sums up much of his literary faith, and lets us see, incidentally, how far he was—and he knew it—from anything like popularity.

'There are plain reasons', he says, 'why the Comic poet is not a frequent apparition; and why the great Comic poet remains without a fellow. A society of cultivated men and women is required, wherein ideas are current and the perceptions quick, that he may be supplied with matter and an audience. The semi-barbarism of merely giddy communities, and feverish emotional periods, repel him; and also a state of marked social inequality of the sexes; nor can he whose business is to address the mind be understood where there is not a moderate degree of intellectual activity....

'Moreover, to touch and kindle the mind through laughter, demands more than sprightliness, a most subtle delicacy. That must be a natal gift in the Comic poet....People are ready to surrender themselves to witty thumps on the back, breast and sides; all except the head: and it is there that he aims. He must be subtle to penetrate. A corresponding acuteness must exist to welcome him.'

That is not the attitude, those are not the demands of the popular writer. He talks ostensibly of the theatre only, of Molière, Congreve, Wycherley, admits that since the time when 'our second Charles' set up as patron of a Comedy of Manners

> Our tenacity of national impressions has caused the word
> theatre...to prod the Puritan nervous system like a satanic
> instrument...

and with some cause! He praises Congreve reservedly,
Molière without reserve, and puts *Le Misanthrope* on a
pedestal. He goes further afield, rounds in Menander,
Aristophanes, Goldoni and the Spaniards; it is a feast
of sound criticism, brilliantly served. And the conclusion
of the matter is that

> Our traditions are unfortunate. The public taste is with the idle
> laughers, and still inclines to follow them....
>
> Our bad traditions of comedy affect us not only on the stage,
> but in our literature, and may be tracked into our social life. They
> are the ground of the heavy moralizings by which we are out-
> wearied....

What would such a public make of a Molière, or of such
a play as *Le Misanthrope*?

> The fable is thin. Our pungent contrivers of plots would see no
> indication of life in the outlines. The life of the comedy is in the
> idea. As with the singing of the skylark out of sight, you must
> love the bird to be attentive to the song, so in this highest flight
> of Comic Muse, you must love pure Comedy warmly to understand
> the Misanthrope: you must be receptive of the idea of Comedy.
> And to love Comedy you must know the real world, and know
> men and women well enough not to expect too much of them,
> though you may still hope for good.

Le Misanthrope, truly, was at first a failure in the theatre,
but

> It is one of the French titles to honour that this quintessential
> comedy...was ultimately understood and applauded.

For

> One excellent test of the civilization of a country, as I have
> said, I take to be the flourishing of the Comic idea and Comedy;
> and the test of true Comedy is that it shall awaken thoughtful
> laughter....
>
> A perception of the comic spirit gives high fellowship. You
> become a citizen of the selecter world, the highest we know of in
> connection with our old world, which is not supermundane. Look
> there for your unchallengeable upper class!

If the essay is a window into Meredith's mind, it is also something of a key to his own artistic development; for this may be held to have reached its maturity in *The Egoist*. Now *The Egoist* is pure Comedy in conception and execution; moreover, it is even constructed as a play should be. Certain superfluities allowed for, it falls perfectly into acts and scenes. It is hard to believe that, at some time or other, he did not think of it as a play. And now, or a little later, the fragments of *The Sentimentalists* must have begun to accumulate in his desk. Handwriting does something to date them, but the kinship of the subject to passages in the essay does more. There they are at any rate, his sketches for such a comedy as Molière might have put a hand to. They were found after his death, and (again by the evidence of the handwriting) he had worked over them from time to time in his later years. They are parts, evidently, of a full-length play, they come from the first two acts of it; and the plot of the whole can be guessed at—as slight a plot as is *Le Misanthrope*'s; the comedy in the idea. Some scraps are in prose, some in verse, sometimes the verse had been rewritten into prose. J. M. Barrie took them in hand, put them in sequence, taking little away, adding nothing of his own but a stage direction here and there, and they were staged at the Duke of York's theatre in 1910.

'"The Sentimentalists": an unfinished play by George Meredith'—there was, for the few, a thrill in the very sight of the placard. But public taste had not changed greatly in those thirty years; nor has another twenty changed it, except, in the theatre, somewhat for the worse. It was, and is, still dominated by the 'idle laughers'. *The Sentimentalists*, it may be owned, is not a full, or a fully flavoured, meal of entertainment; the civil 'thank-you' it gained was perhaps all that could be expected. And yet, and yet, one asked—and is still asking!—is there

no interest in the art of the theatre for its own sake? Had
two movements of a Mozart quartet been snatched from
oblivion, how amateurs and critics would have descanted
on them, studying every page, every bar! Yet here was
the one piece of dramatic work done by a great man just
dead, a master of character and wit, of prose and verse,
and it was casually appraised at its mere entertainment
value. Did Meredith's ghost sit sardonically chuckling
in the author's box, asking what the devil one had taken
all the trouble for? Not displeased, though, to see these
figures of his fancy brought to life, and in the glamour of
the footlights! But he had said his say upon the matter
long before. We turn back to the essay:

> In all countries the middle class presents the public which,
> fighting the world, and with a good footing in the fight, knows the
> world best....

> Of this class in England, a large body, neither Puritan nor
> Bacchanalian, have a sentimental objection to face the study of
> the actual world. They take up disdain of it, when its truths appear
> humiliating: when the facts are not immediately forced on them,
> they take up the pride of incredulity. They live in a hazy atmo-
> sphere that they suppose an ideal one....Philosopher and Comic
> poet are of a cousinship in the eye they cast on life: and they are
> equally unpopular with our wilful English of the hazy region and
> the ideal that is not to be disturbed....

> Thus, for want of instruction in the Comic idea, we lose a large
> audience among our cultivated middle class that we should expect
> to support Comedy, the sentimentalist is as averse as the Puritan
> and as the Bacchanalian.

There was the very theme of the comedy he began to
write, there was the reason that he never troubled to
finish it; there, in the theatre for a few nights, thirty
years or so later, sat the cultivated middle class—
respectfully bored, most of them, doubtless.

Our traditions are unfortunate indeed if we cannot
bring some imagination to the making of this morsel of
genius (for it is nothing less) complete enough for enjoyment. Have we not humour enough to see the humour

and an ear for the symphonic prose of the chorus of
Sentimentalists crooning in ecstasy over the eloquence of
Professor Spiral? Or read the scene between Lyra and
Astraea, between the wife pursued by her husband—

> May no woman of my acquaintance marry a man of twenty
> years her senior. She marries a gigantic limpet. At that period of
> his life a man becomes too voraciously constant.

—and the widow, the 'dedicated widow', pursued by
suitor after suitor, boldly, timidly, slyly, most slyly of
all, we surmise, by the great Professor Spiral himself even
while he pledges her to 'sovereign disengagement'. This
promises to be the play's plot, and he to hold a candle
(and a bright one possibly) to Tartufe himself. Read the
scene, read it aloud. It has one parallel at least in English
dramatic literature, the counsellings of Rosalind and
Celia in Arden; and it suffers not at all by the comparison.

> *Lyra.* Oh! Pluriel, ask me of him! I wish I were less sure he
> would not be at the next corner I turn.
> *Astraea.* You speak of your husband strangely, Lyra.
> *Lyra.* My head is out of a sack. I managed my escape from him
> this morning by renouncing bath and breakfast; and what a relief,
> to be in the railway carriage alone!—that is, when the engine
> snorted. And if I set eyes on him within a week, he will hear some
> truths. His idea of marriage is, the taking of the woman into
> custody. My hat is on, and on goes Pluriel's. My foot is on the
> stairs; I hear his foot behind me. In my boudoir I am alone one
> minute, and then the door opens to the inevitable. I pay a visit,
> he is passing the house as I leave it. He will not even affect sur-
> prise. I belong to him—I am cat's mouse. And he will look doting
> on me in public. And when I speak to anybody, he is that fearful
> picture of all smirks. Fling off a kid glove after a round of calls;
> feel your hand—there you have me now that I am out of him for
> my half a day, if for as long.
> *Astraea.* This is one of the world's happy marriages!
> *Lyra.* This is one of the world's choice dishes! and I have it
> planted under my nostrils eternally....
> ...And you are the cunningest of fencers, tongue or foils. You

lead me to talk of myself, and I hate the subject. By the way, you have practised with Mr Arden.

Astraea. A tiresome instructor, who lets you pass his guard to compliment you on a hit.

Lyra. He rather wins me.

Astraea. He does at first.

Lyra. Begins Plurielizing, without the law to back him, does he?

Astraea. The fencing lessons are at an end.

Lyra. The duets with Mr Swithin's violoncello continue?

Astraea. He broke through the melody.

Lyra. There were readings in poetry with Mr Osier, I recollect.

Astraea. His own compositions became obtrusive.

Lyra. No fencing, no music, no poetry! No West Coast of Africa either, I suppose.

Astraea. Very well! I am on my defence. You at least shall not misunderstand me, Lyra. One intense regret I have; that I did not live in the time of the Amazons. They were free from this question of marriage; this babble of love. Why am I so persecuted? He will not take a refusal. There are sacred reasons. I am supported by every woman having the sense of her dignity. I am perverted, burlesqued by the fury of wrath I feel at their incessant pursuit....

Laugh at me, half my time I am laughing at myself. I should regain my pride if I could be resolved on a step. I am strong to resist; I have not strength to move.

Lyra. I see the sphinx of Egypt!

Astraea. And all the while I am a manufactory of gunpowder in this quiet old-world Sabbath circle of dear good souls, with their stereotyped interjections and orchestra of enthusiasms; their tapering delicacies; the rejoicing they have in their common agreement on all created things. To them it is restful. It spurs me to fly from rooms and chairs and beds and houses. I sleep hardly a couple of hours. Then into the early morning air, out with the birds; I know no other pleasure....

Lyra. What does the Dame say?

Astraea. Sighs over me! Just a little maddening to hear.

Lyra. When we feel we have the strength of giants, and are bidden to sit and smile! You should rap out some of our old sweet-innocent garden oaths with her. 'Carnation! Dame!' That used to make her dance on her seat. 'But, dearest Dame, it is as natural an impulse for women to have that relief as for men; and natural will out, begonia! it will!' We ran through the book of botany for devilish objurgations. I do believe our misconduct caused us to be handed to the good man at the altar, as the right corrective. And you were the worst offender.

Astraea. Was I? I could be now, though I am so changed a creature.

Lyra. You enjoy the studies with your Spiral, come!

Astraea. Professor Spiral is the one honest gentleman here. He does homage to my principles. I have never been troubled by him; no silly hints or side-looks—you know, the dog at the forbidden bone.

Lyra. A grand orator.

Astraea. He is. You fix on the smallest of his gifts. He is intellectually and morally superior.

Lyra. Praise of that kind makes me rather incline to prefer his inferiors. He fed gobble-gobble on your puffs of incense. I coughed and scraped the gravel; quite in vain; he tapped for more and more.

Astraea. Professor Spiral is a thinker; he is a sage. He gives women their due.

Lyra. And he is a bachelor too—or consequently.

Astraea. If you like you may be as playful with me as the Lyra of our maiden days used to be. My dear, my dear, how glad I am to have you here! You remind me that I once had a heart. It will beat again with you beside me, and I shall look to you for protection. A novel request from me. From annoyance, I mean. It has entirely altered my character. Sometimes I am afraid to think of what I was, lest I should suddenly romp, and perform pirouettes and cry 'Carnation!' There is the bell. We must not be late when the professor condescends to sit for meals.

Lyra. That rings healthily in the professor.

Astraea. Arm in arm, my Lyra.

Lyra. No Pluriel yet!   (*they enter the house*)

This is about a third of it; and, for all its discursive air, it is, as dramatic dialogue should be, so closely knit as to make extract difficult. It is 'artificial' comedy, of course. Not that the epithet is more than the label of a method as little artificial and as much as any good writing meant to make a particular effect must be. So is Mozart's music artificial. Whatever its method, this is true dramatic dialogue, lucid, dynamic, and as full of melody as Mozart is.

Another scene survives, a night scene in the garden between Astraea and young Arden her suitor (there has been much about him already) who, we may be sure, is destined to win her. It is in verse, and probably from an earlier draft of the play[1]. Here is the start of it.

Scene VI.

Astraea, Arden.

Astraea.	Pardon me if I do not hear you well.
Arden.	I will not even think you barbarous.
Astraea.	I am. I am the object of the chase.
Arden.	The huntsman drags the wood then, and not you.
Astraea.	At any instant I am forced to run,
	Or turn in my defence; how can I be
	Other than barbarous? You are the cause.
Arden.	No: heaven that made you beautiful's the cause.
Astraea.	Say, earth, that gave you instincts. Bring me down
	To instincts! When by chance I speak awhile
	With our professor, you appear in haste,
	Full cry to sight again the missing hare.
	Away ideas! All that's divinest flies!
	I have to bear in mind how young you are.
Arden.	You have only to look up to me four years
	Instead of forty!
Astraea.	Sir![2]
Arden.	There's my misfortune!
	And worse that, young, I love as a young man.
	Could I but quench the fire, I might conceal
	The youthfulness offending you so much.
Astraea.	I wish you would. I wish it earnestly.
Arden.	Impossible. I burn.
Astraea.	You should not burn.
Arden.	'Tis more than I! 'Tis fire. It masters Will.
	You would not say 'Should not' if you knew fire.
	It seizes. It devours.
Astraea.	Dry wood!
Arden.	Cold wit!
	How cold you can be! but be cold, for sweet
	You must be. And your eyes are mine: with them
	I see myself: unworthy to usurp
	The place I hold a moment. While I look
	I have my happiness.
Astraea.	You should look higher.

[1] If my memory serves, it had at some later time been partly redrafted into prose.

[2] She is, we remember here, the widow of 'the venerable Professor Towers.'

Arden.   Through you to the highest. Only through you! Through
                    you
             The mark I may attain is visible,
             And I have strength to dream of winning it.
             You are the bow that speeds the arrow: you
             The glass that brings the distance nigh. My world
             Is luminous through you, pure heavenly,
             But hangs upon the rose's outer leaf,
             Not next her heart. Astraea! my own beloved!
Astraea. We may be excellent friends. And I have faults.
Arden.   Name them: I am hungering for more to love.
Astraea. I waver very constantly; I have
             No fixity of feeling or of sight.
             I have no courage: I can often dream
             Of daring: when I wake I am in dread.
             I am inconstant as a butterfly,
             And shallow as a brook with little fish!
             Strange little fish, that tempt the small boy's net,
             But at a touch straight dive!
             I am anyone's, and no one's! I am vain.
             Praise of my beauty lodges in my ears.
             The lark reels up with it; the nightingale
             Sobs bleeding; the flowers nod; I could believe
             A poet, though he praised me to my face....

Meredith has here forged a verse all his own, and all his
play's own, too. It is light and swift and sparkling, a
vehicle for wit as well as emotion. It is eloquent but
never orotund. It has artifice enough to keep it in key
with the rest of the play, with the Sentimentalists and
their preciosities, never so much as to rob it of romance.
He avoids the tempting error of the rhymed couplet,
which would have seemed too calculated. The scene
is, in fact, as the play is, for all of its incompleteness,
something unique in English Literature.

What Meredith lost in losing this medium of the
theatre is very obvious. He speaks of Molière writing
'purely, in the simplest language, the simplest of French
verse'; of his wit as

like a running brook, with innumerable fresh lights on it at every
turn of the wood, through which its business is to find a way. It

does not run in search of obstructions, to be noisy over them: but where dead leaves and viler substances are heaped along the course, its natural song is heightened. Without effort, and with no dazzling flashes of achievement, it is full of healing; the wit of good breeding, the wit of wisdom.

Strange qualities are they, for the author of *One of our Conquerors* and *Lord Ormont and his Aminta* to admire? There is the point: he did admire them (who does not?) and strove after them (again who does not?) as best he could. The notion that such men as Meredith are wilfully, mischievously obscure is an impertinence. They have much to express and, left with themselves for an audience, the plain thing seems hardly worth saying, for it is known already. But let Meredith the talker start a bright idea, Meredith the listener will set him refining it, and refining again, twisting it this way and that till it is running exhausted in a circle—a vicious circle—and, expressed at last, may drop dead. This is the danger run by all men of teeming minds, driven in on themselves by neglect. The easy popularity of the theatre brings worse dangers, heaven knows! He was little likely to have been caught in these. See how he works and works for his private satisfaction on this fragment that was never to see the light. But the theatre compels a man at least to the virtues of lucidity, of simplicity, of economy. There is the audience of average men and women, and you must make your meaning clear to them as you go along.

And in losing Meredith, what did the theatre lose? No great influence upon its course, perhaps. By the 'seventies the play of artifice had had its day; the ground was fallow and ready for Ibsen and the 'naturalists' when they came. He would have stood in drama as in fiction, brilliantly alone! Very much, probably, as in French drama Rostand stands to-day; and Rostand is a child in artistic force beside him. He would have owned, perhaps, to kinship with Congreve; but not cordially. He allows Sheridan one slighting sentence in the essay, will have none of Wycherley, labels Goldsmith (justly) as farce-writer, and mentions practically no other English dramatist at all. He turns, as to the sun, to Molière; and here is a certain weakness in his position which might have been reflected in his work. Drama is, inevitably, the most national of the arts; for, its writing apart, it must command native interpretation. And if, as Meredith complains, the English have not risen to appreciation of the Comedy of Idea, it may be because ideas as such do not much interest them. A reproach to them, doubtless; but a vain reproach for the would-be dramatist to make, who must not only write for them, but enshrine them as they are in his writing. To poetry and humour, the English will respond: ideas they find inhuman. But the creator ousts the critic, and, as this one fragment of a play shows, Meredith would have found his feet in the theatre, could have made a place of his own there and given us in drama as in fiction a few splendidly refracted pictures of his time. And we might have had to-day half a dozen of his plays, the product of his maturity, of that humorous sane mind, as abiding refreshment to our own.

Tennyson, Swinburne, Meredith, would-be dramatists; and a theatre that could not profit them, nor profit by them. Something was very wrong, surely; and for that matter, still is, perhaps.

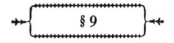

§ 9

Critics and Criticism in the
'Seventies

By Frederick S. Boas

My colleagues in this series of papers have given their attention to creative writers and leading personalities during the 'seventies. It has fallen to me to attempt a more prosaic task, and to say something not about the poets and novelists of the decade, but about those literary camp-followers, the critics. And even here the field of survey may seem at first very circumscribed. For the period was one in which literary questions had been pushed into the background. *The Origin of Species* had appeared in 1859; a Reform Act had been passed in 1867; the first Education Act followed in 1870. The thoughts of men were occupied with evolution and the 'higher criticism' of the Bible; with political and social movements. They had little time to spare for aesthetic problems. As we shall see, even the greatest personality in English criticism since the Romantic trio, Coleridge, Lamb, and Hazlitt, was tempted away from his true field.

But all was not loss. The arresting ideas and principles generated in the scientific, especially the biological, sphere inevitably had their reaction on critical investigation and judgement in literature. And thus there flourished in the 'seventies some notable writers whose predominant interest was not in aesthetics or in the technique of poetry

or prose but who brought to the task of critical interpretation conceptions, not to say prepossessions, from other
spheres of study.

The preoccupation of the decade with other than purely
literary problems is illustrated by the first important
publication falling within its limits which included work
of fine critical quality. In 1871 Richard Holt Hutton
issued in two volumes his *Essays Theological and Literary.*
He was at this time forty-five years of age. Trained for
the Unitarian Ministry he had come under the influence
of F. W. Robertson and F. D. Maurice and had become a
Churchman of their school. As co-editor with Walter
Bagehot of *The National Review* (1855–64) and with
Meredith Townshend of *The Spectator* from 1861 onwards
he had full opportunity for the exercise of his journalistic
and literary talents, but his interest in religious and
philosophical questions was always predominant. Hence
in his critical papers, even when poets and poetry were
his theme, he was less concerned with aesthetic questions
than with the writers' criticism of life.

With the theological volume we are not here concerned,
though anyone who wishes to appreciate fully Hutton's
standpoint as a literary critic will profit by a knowledge
of such essays as 'Science and Theism', 'Popular Pan-
theism' and 'What is Revelation?'. The literary volume
in its first form included a somewhat miscellaneous
selection of subjects ranging from 'Goethe and his influence' and 'The Poetry of the Old Testament', by way
of some Romantic and Victorian poets, to George Eliot
and Nathaniel Hawthorne. A number of these, though
revised, had appeared in periodicals and do not strictly
belong to our decade. But those on Browning and Clough
deal with publications of 1869, and the enlarged edition
of the essays in 1877 included two additions on the poetry
of Matthew Arnold and Tennyson. This quartette of

papers falls therefore within this survey and they are favourable examples of Hutton's critical art. I doubt indeed if there are better introductions anywhere to the poetry of Clough and Matthew Arnold, and I still remember gratefully the thrill that I got in my Balliol days from these appreciations of the two distinctively Balliol poets. Both of them gave scope for Hutton's intimate psychological analysis. He who had found anchor in a liberal orthodoxy could enter into, and yet stand apart from, their doubts and questionings. Here is part of his vivid mental portrait of Clough:

So eager was his craving for reality and perfect sincerity, so morbid his dislike even for the unreal conventional forms of life that a mind quite unique in simplicity and truthfulness represents itself in his poems as

'Seeking in vain, in all my store,
One feeling based on truth.'

Indeed he wanted to reach some guarantee for simplicity deeper than simplicity itself....

This almost morbid craving for a firm base on the absolute realities of life was very wearying to a mind so self-conscious as Clough's, and tended to paralyse the expression of a certainly great genius. As a rule, his lyrical poems fall short of complete success in delineating the mood which they are really meant to delineate, owing to this chronic state of introspective criticism on himself in which he is apt to write, and which, characteristic as it is, necessarily diminishes the linearity and directness of the feeling expressed, refracting it, as it were, through media of very variable density.

His description later of Clough as 'a modern and intellectualised Chaucer', suggested by the tales in *In Mari Magno*, strikes one as somewhat of a *tour de force*, and the quotations given in support scarcely prove the case. Nor is anything said of Clough's metrical technique, as in his use of the hexameter in *The Bothie* and elsewhere. But the essay is a permanent memorial of the impact of Clough's complete output in verse and prose, published posthumously, on one of the most sensitive minds of his age.

The essay on the poetry of Matthew Arnold is more fully worked out and in it, as I think, Hutton reaches his critical high-water mark. In his perspective of the influences on Arnold, Goethe and Wordsworth are somewhat unduly stressed as compared with the Greeks, but his interpretation of the poet's distinctive position among his contemporaries shows piercing insight:

Mr Arnold's poems are one long variation on a single theme, the divorce between the soul and the intellect, and the depth of spiritual regret and yearning which that divorce produces. Yet there is a didactic keenness with the languor, an eagerness of purpose with the despondency, which give half the individual flavour to his lyrics. A note of confidence lends authority to his scepticism; the tone of his sadness is self-contained, sure, and even imperious, instead of showing the ordinary relaxation of loss.

From such relaxation Arnold is preserved in large part by the fortifying influence of Nature. There is nothing better in the essay than the subtle discrimination between Arnold's attitude to Nature and that of Wordsworth, Shelley, Byron and Tennyson, and the more unlooked for comparison with Gray:

He paints Nature, like the author of *The Elegy in a Country Churchyard*, with the cool, liquid, rather weary tone of one who comes to the scenery to take a heart from it, instead of giving the heart to it; but he does it with infinitely more of the modern tenderness and insight for Nature than Gray possessed, and with far more flowing and continuous descriptive power.

But with all Hutton's insight into Arnold's high poetic achievement, he lays his finger on his fundamental limitation:

When I come to ask what Mr Arnold's poetry has done for this generation, the answer must be that no one has expressed more powerfully and poetically its spiritual weaknesses, its craving for a passion that it cannot feel, its admiration for a self-mastery that it cannot achieve, its desire for a creed that it fails to accept, its sympathy with a faith that it will not share, its aspiration for a peace that it does not know. But Mr Arnold does all this from the intellectual side—sincerely and delicately, but from the surface and never from the centre....The sign of this limitation, of this exclusion of this externality of touch is the tinge of conscious intellectual majesty rearing its head above the storm with the 'Quos ego' of Virgil's god, that never forsakes these poems of Mr Arnold's even when their 'lyrical cry' is most pathetic. It is this which identifies him with the sceptics, which renders his poems, pathetic as they often are, no adequate expression of the passionate craving of the soul for faith. There is always a tincture of pride in his confessed inability to believe—a self-congratulation that he is too clear-eyed to yield to the temptations of the heart.

And there follows in illustration Hutton's masterly analysis and discussion of the splendid stanzas in *Obermann Once More* describing the victory of the infant Church over the majestic materialism of Rome—a victory that in Arnold's eyes, but not in Hutton's, was based upon a dream.

In the essay on 'Mr Browning', Hutton, as might be expected, is predominantly interested in the poet's 'various delineations of the worldly force of ecclesiastical dignities struggling with, or flavouring, the Catholic faith'. At a time when Browning's genius was imperfectly appreciated, and before the propaganda work of the Browning Societies, Hutton's interpretation of such poems as *The Soliloquy of the Spanish Cloister, The Bishop orders his Tomb, The Epistle,* and the speeches of the ecclesiastics in *The Ring and the Book* was valuable to readers bewildered by the strangeness of the themes or their treatment. The critic was an expert guide into what was for many at the time an intellectual labyrinth. But he was less to be trusted in metrical matters, as when he declares that Browning's 'versification is almost always best when it is nearest to prose, where, as in the dramas, the metre is blank verse without rhyme'. It is surprising that a critic of Hutton's quality should lend countenance to the 'vulgar error' that blank verse is more akin to

prose than rhymed metres. And though he singles out
for eulogy the apostrophe 'O lyric love! half angel and
half bird' he does not seem to have an ear for the subtle
and haunting cadences in the speeches of Caponsacchi
or Pompilia—not to speak of the dactylic rhythms
of *The Lost Leader* and *Abt Vogler* or the anapaests of
Saul.

Perhaps this would be too much to expect from a
critic whose essay on Tennyson is a long-drawn paean of
praise. Anyone who wishes to relish again the full flavour
of mid-Victorian adoration of the Laureate, in its con-
summate expression, should read or re-read this fine
essay—and then turn to the iconoclastic lecture by Professor Oliver Elton, or to Mr Harold Nicolson's mordant
critical study, and afterwards (to strike a balance) to
Dr A. C. Bradley's English Association Pamphlet, *The
Reaction against Tennyson*. There are only two features of
Hutton's essay to which I will now refer. It was written
soon after the publication of Tennyson's first play, *Queen
Mary*, which is dealt with in the preceding paper by Mr
Granville-Barker. Hutton makes what seems to me an
inept comparison between it and *Henry VIII*, stating that
he would 'be surprised to hear that any true critic would
rate *Queen Mary*, whether in dramatic force or in general
power, below *Henry VIII*'. The latter is of course not in
the organic sense a play, but it contains dialogue (whether
by Shakespeare or Fletcher does not here matter) of a
poignancy and liquid beauty that are quite beyond the
pale of Tennyson's dramatic art. And with regard to *The
Idylls of the King*, Hutton, as I think, confutes beyond
a peradventure Swinburne's contention that Tennyson
should have traced the ruin of the Round Table to
Arthur's youthful sin with his half-sister, Bellicent. But
he fails to recognise that the poet attempts the impossible
when he makes Arthur fill the double rôle of spiritual hero

and accusing husband. Yet when all discount has been made I feel that these essays of Hutton on the great Victorian poets deserve the epithets that he applied to Arnold's poems—'stately and fascinating'.

The shorter pieces of criticism that he reprinted from *The Spectator* in *Contemporary Thought and Thinkers*, of which those on Poe, Dickens and others fall within our decade, are of less moment, and I merely mention them. He also edited in 1879 two volumes of *Literary Studies* by his former colleague, Walter Bagehot, reprinted from *The National Review*. As these had originally appeared in the 'fifties, they are outside our present survey, but they contain a number of notable essays, 'Shakespeare the Man', 'Sterne and Thackeray', 'The Waverley Novels' and others.

Hutton had moved from a Unitarian to an Anglican position; Stopford Brooke had reversed the process. The one had theology in attendance at the right hand of his editorial chair; the other brought poetry inside the sanctuary. On Sunday afternoons in St James's Chapel during the season of 1872 Brooke delivered a series of lectures on 'Theology in the English Poets', which were published in 1874. Apart from the merits of the lectures the experiment is memorable in itself. The course, after a preliminary survey from Pope onwards, included Cowper, Coleridge, Wordsworth and Burns. Brooke, as he explains at the outset, was not attempting to expound their personal convictions:

It is plain that in ordinary life their intellect would work consciously on the subject, and their prejudices come into play. But in their poetry, their imagination worked unconsciously on the subject. Their theology was not produced as a matter of intellectual co-ordination of truths, but as a matter of truths which were true because they were felt—Cowper's theology in his poetry soars beyond the narrow sect to which he belonged into an infinitely wider universe.

Thus in one of the most effective sections of the volume, Brooke shows that while Cowper's personal theology 'fixed its talons in his heart' and drove him to madness, his poetical theology saw God as the deliverer and avenger of the oppressed, and contributed distinctly new elements to our poetry, 'above all new in their tremendous power of awakening and maintaining the human emotions which most create a human poetry'.

But the major part of the book, nine out of the sixteen lectures, is devoted to Wordsworth. His spiritual conception of Nature, his poetic realisation of the divine immanence in the universe were in conformity with Brooke's own attitude. His exposition of the central elements of Wordsworth's poetic creed is remarkably lucid and sympathetic, and went far to gain for the book its immediate popularity and its place as a standard work. The editor of the Everyman reprint of the lectures goes so far as to say that 'a nobler appreciation of Wordsworth is not to be found anywhere'. This is a high claim to which I am not prepared to subscribe without reserve. Brooke has not the arresting pregnancy of phrase of Hutton, nor does he flash sudden illumination like F. W. H. Myers and Walter Raleigh in their monographs on Wordsworth. M. Legouis in his *La Jeunesse de Wordsworth* and Professor de Selincourt in his textual edition of *The Prelude* have opened vistas unknown to Brooke. But he would have rejoiced to know that Wordsworth's poetic theology, of which he was the ardent interpreter, was even more explicit in the original manuscripts than in the printed version of 1850, where it had been in part accommodated to current orthodoxy.

Stopford Brooke's gifts of popular exposition found a still wider appeal in 1876 in his *Primer of English Literature*. In some 200 pages he gave a masterly bird's-eye view of the poetry and prose of what he calls the

'noble company, which has been teaching and delighting
the world for more than 1000 years' These words give
the key to the spirit in which the little book is written.
It deservedly ran through more than a dozen editions
before it was enlarged in 1896, and we can scarcely blame
Brooke if it was perverted from its true purpose by school-
boys who learnt pages of it by rote for the benefit of
examiners. It has recently been re-issued with an
additional chapter on literature since 1832 by Mr George
Sampson, and has thus entered on a new lease of life.

The year of the publication of Brooke's *Theology in the
English Poets*, 1874, was marked also by the appearance
of the first collection of critical essays by a writer of a
very different school of thought. Leslie Stephen had
already given proof of his versatile powers in his satirical
Sketches from Cambridge (1865), his essays on mountain-
eering entitled *The Playground of Europe* (1871), and the
Essays on Free Thinking and Plain Speaking (1873) in
which he anticipated the attitude of *An Agnostic's
Apology* in a later year. In 1871 he had become editor of
the *Cornhill Magazine* to which he contributed a series
of literary essays called 'Hours in a Library', and this
title he retained for the three volumes (1874–9) in which he
republished them and kindred pieces. Stephen's affinities
were predominantly with the rationalistic elements in
eighteenth-century thought of which he was at this time
writing the history, and his sober-coloured style and
method of analytical dissection are seen to advantage in
the articles on the novelists and poets of that century.

Thus in the essay on 'De Foe's Novels' he characteristically repudiates any romantic associations with the
position of a solitary like Alexander Selkirk marooned for
years on an island:

We may infer, what is probable from other cases, that a man
living fifteen years by himself, like Crusoe, would either go mad or

sink into the semi-savage state. De Foe really describes a man in prison, not in solitary confinement....He cannot tire us with details, for all the details of such a story are interesting; it is made up of petty incidents, as much as the life of a prisoner reduced to taming flies, or making saws out of penknives. The island does as well as the Bastille for making trifles valuable to the sufferer and to us....It is one of the exceptional cases in which the poetical aspect of a position is brought out best by the most prosaic accuracy of detail; and we imagine that Robinson Crusoe's island, with all his small household torments, will always be more impressive than the more gorgeously coloured island of Enoch Arden.

That last touch is very characteristic of Stephen, whose motto later, as first editor of the *Dictionary of National Biography*, was 'No flowers by request'. In lighter vein is his exposition of the results of Richardson's epistolary method, as illustrated by the ninety-six pages of letters written by Miss Byron, the object of Sir Charles Grandison's affections, in three days:

We discover what was Sir Charles Grandison's relation at a particular time to a certain Italian lady, Clementina. We are told exactly what view he took of his own position; what view Clementina took of it; what Miss Byron had to say to Sir Charles on the subject, and what advice her relations bestowed upon Miss Byron. Then we have all the sentiments of Sir Charles Grandison's sisters, and of his brothers-in-law, and of his reverend old tutor; and the sentiments of all the lady Clementina's family, and the incidental remarks of a number of subordinate actors. In short we see the characters all round, in all their relations to each other, in every possible variation and permutation.

But in spite of such sedate banter, Stephen shows a whole-hearted appreciation of Richardson's greatness as a novelist, though his admiration for Clarissa may seem a trifle tepid to those who like myself have a love for her just this side of idolatry. But in speaking of the 'infusion of feminine character' in Richardson's personality Stephen makes a prophecy which has been curiously falsified:

A novelist should have the delicate perception, the sensibility to emotion, and the interest in small details, which women exhibit in perfection. Indeed this is so true that there seems to be at present some probability that the art of novel-writing will pass altogether into feminine hands. It may be long before the advocates of woman's rights will conquer other provinces of labour; but they have already monopolised to a great extent the immense novel manufacturing industry of Great Britain.

Had Stephen lived till our day he would have seen that the advocates of woman's rights (how out of date the phrase sounds!) had secured their position in nearly every province of labour, not to speak of their triumph in the political sphere. But in spite of this, perhaps partly on account of it, there seems less prospect than ever of their monopolising the realm of fiction. We have very distinguished women novelists in this generation—some of them are among the most eminent Fellows of this Society—but (to say the least) they have not played Mr Wells, Mr Galsworthy and Mr Arnold Bennett off the stage. And these are only a few of the masculine names that will occur to everyone. Here at least is one anticipation by a singularly cool-headed critic in the 'seventies of which Time has made a laughing stock.[1]

But it may seem surprising that I have got so far without mentioning, except as a poet, the most famous and influential of mid-Victorian critics, Matthew Arnold. The reason is that the decade of the 'seventies is, in a remarkable way, a watershed between the two streams, the earlier and the later, of Arnold's literary criticism. During his ten years' occupancy, 1857–67, of the Oxford Chair of Poetry, he had published his *Lectures on Translating Homer* (1861–2), the first series of *Essays in Criticism* (1865), and the *Lectures on the Study of Celtic Literature* (1867). Needless to say that each of these is in its own way a classic, even the last, though Arnold knew no Celtic tongue. *Essays in Criticism* is one of the books to which the hackneyed epithet of 'epoch-making' may be truly applied in its own sphere. The second series of

[1] Stephen himself seems to have afterwards modified his view for the passage is omitted in the 1892 revised edition.

Essays in Criticism appeared in 1881, and in 1880 Arnold contributed his Introduction to T. H. Ward's *Selections from the English Poets*, in which is found his famous, and inadequate, definition of poetry as a criticism of life. But in the intervening period he was almost entirely occupied with treatises on theological and social questions, including *Culture and Anarchy* (1869), *Friendship's Garland* (1871), *Literature and Dogma* (1873) and *Last Essays on Church and Religion* (1877). Anything that Arnold wrote was bound to contain striking phrases, and these tracts for the times had a wider and more immediate vogue than the critical essays. But he had neither the temperament nor the technical qualifications for controversy in such fields and we are moved to address him in his own words:

> Not here, O Apollo!
> Are haunts meet for thee,
> But, where Helicon breaks down
> In cliff to the sea.

And fortunately, in the very last year of our decade, 1879, Arnold did have his hour on Helicon and brought back his Introduction to his Selection from the poems of Wordsworth. Within its short range it is one of his most masterly achievements. He was out to save the poet from his friends—the Wordsworthians who 'are apt to praise him for the wrong things, and to lay far too much stress upon what they call his philosophy'—though he afterwards confesses that he is a Wordsworthian himself. Wordsworth's philosophy, if interpreted in the right way and in the light of what he originally wrote, is of greater significance than Arnold was inclined to allow. But he was right in putting in the forefront his pure poetic power which he interpreted in words of noble, and exquisitely apt, simplicity:

Wordsworth's poetry, when he is at his best, is inevitable, as inevitable as Nature herself. It might seem that Nature not only

gave him the matter for his poem, but wrote his poem for him.
He has no style...Nature herself seems, I say, to take the pen out
of his hand, and to write for him with her own bare, sheer penetrating power.

Wordsworth had figured prominently in *The Golden
Treasury of English Songs and Lyrics* (1861) edited by
F. T. Palgrave, who, like Arnold, was an education
official, and who was later one of his successors in the
Oxford Chair of Poetry.

In 1877 Palgrave paid tribute to an earlier pastoral poet
in the graceful preface to his Selections from Herrick—a
gathering of some of the choicest of the golden apples
from the garden of the Hesperides.

But it was a younger Oxford man than Arnold or
Palgrave who stirred most deeply the waters of the
'seventies. In 1873 Walter Pater, Fellow of Brasenose,
published his *Studies in the History of the Renaissance*.
The book, by the novel charm of its style and its uncon-
ventional attitude, caused something of the same excitement (though the subjects are poles asunder) as Mr
Lytton Strachey's *Eminent Victorians* in our own day.
With a prelude on the French tale of Aucassin and
Nicolette and an epilogue on Goethe's Hellenist master,
Winckelmann, the studies were mainly of Italian artists
in the fifteenth century, including the famous essay on
Leonardo da Vinci. These particular studies lie outside of
our present subject and my own competence (though
not my interest). But what was of most significance was
the challenge thrown out in the opening and closing
pages. Pater urged that little store was to be set on
attempts

to define beauty in the abstract...to find a universal formula for
it. These attempts help us very little to enjoy what has been well
done in art or poetry....To define beauty not in the most abstract,
but in the most concrete forms possible, not to find a universal

formula for it, but the formula which expresses most adequately this or that special manifestation of it, is the aim of the true student of aesthetics.

And not only must beauty be sought in this or that particular manifestation, but the criterion of it, Pater declared, must be purely that of the individual who experiences it:

What is this song or picture, this engaging personality presented in life or in a book to *me*? What effect does it really produce on me? Does it give me pleasure? and, if so, what sort or degree of pleasure?...The answers to these questions are the original facts with which the aesthetic critic has to do...one must realise such primary data for oneself or not at all.

And even these primary data are based on nothing substantial. It was significant that as the headline of his 'Conclusion' Pater quoted the Greek verse:

λέγει που Ἡράκλειτος ὅτι πάντα χωρεῖ καὶ οὐδὲν μένει.

Experience is analysed into a group of impressions 'unstable, flickering, inconsistent' and 'ringed round for each one of us by that thick wall of personality through which no real voice has ever pierced on its way to us, or from us to that which we can only conjecture to be without'. The highest service of religion, philosophy, or culture to the human spirit is accordingly 'to startle it into a sharp and eager observation'. Hence it follows that the aim of life is to have as many sensations as we may at their finest and their fullest:

A counted number of pulses only is given to us of a variegated, dramatic life. How may we see in them all that is to be seen in them by the finest senses? How can we pass most swiftly from point to point, and be present always at the focus where the greatest number of vital forces unite in their purest energy? To burn always with this hard gem-like flame, to maintain this ecstasy, is success in life. Failure is to form habits; for habit is relative to a stereotyped world.

In a rhythm of stately, pensive beauty the gospel of *carpe diem* in its transfigured form of the cherishing of art for art's sake reaches its close:

> We have an interval and then our place knows us no more. Some spend this interval in listlessness, some in high passions, the wisest in art and song. For our one chance is in expanding that interval, in getting as many pulsations as possible into the given time.... Of this wisdom, the poetic passion, the desire for beauty, the love of art for art's sake has most; for art comes to you professing frankly to give nothing but the highest quality to your moments as they pass, and simply for those moments' sake.

Such doctrine from an Oxford cloister might well startle the dovecotes, and when the second edition of the volume appeared in 1877, the Conclusion was omitted lest, as Pater stated, it might possibly mislead some of the young men into whose hands it might fall. But fortunately it was reinserted, with slight changes, in later editions. Whatever one may think of the validity of Pater's 'criticism of life' in the 'seventies either on philosophical or ethical grounds, we have it here in its quintessential form. What a descent from the haunting cadences of this grave *apologia* for 'sensationalism' to the freaks and follies of the 'aesthetic' movement, not to speak of the abyss of the sensual sty! It was in many ways a different Pater who spoke in *Marius the Epicurean* and other later works, but from the first there was a hard intellectual fibre beneath the decorative surface of his writing. The two occasions on which I heard him speak were, in a way, symbolic of his two sides. The first, in the early 'eighties, when in his own rooms at Brasenose he read a paper to a small society of intellectuals; the second, some ten years later, when he lectured to a crowded University Extension audience in the Oxford Examination Schools.

The year, 1873, that saw the publication of Pater's studies in the Italian Renaissance marks something of a new stage in the study of our own greatest Renaissance figure, Shakespeare. For it was in 1873 that F. J. Furnivall founded 'The New Shakspere Society' with a wide programme but with a special interest in the employment of verse tests to determine the authorship of disputed plays and the chronological succession of plays within the Shakespearean canon. F. G. Fleay was the chief apostle of this method, which won Furnivall's enthusiastic support. The opening paper in the Society's first volume of *Transactions* was by Fleay on 'Metrical Tests as applied to Dramatic Poetry', and in other contributions he applied this criterion. An article by James Spedding on the shares of Shakespeare and Fletcher in *King Henry VIII* was also based largely on Fletcher's distinctive use of 'double-endings'; and in the 'weak-endings' of Shakespeare J. K. Ingram developed another aspect of metrical investigation.

Though the Society did other valuable work, it became peculiarly identified with this line of research, and A. C. Swinburne who was at the time engaged on his *Study of Shakespeare* became incensed with what he thought was an attempt to judge the dramatist's work by mechanical rules. He opened fire with an attack in *The Examiner* (April, 1876) on 'The newest Shakespeare Society'. Furnivall replied with equal asperity, and a long, unedifying controversy followed. But the 'metrical tests' method, though it may be perversely or unintelligently applied, has proved to be a permanent instrument of Shakespearean research, and the Society's publications are still of first-rate value to Elizabethan students.

The influence of Fleay's and Furnivall's investigations was acknowledged by Edward Dowden when in 1877 he published *Shakspere: His Mind and Art*, which has throughout a chronological basis. In this volume he attempted 'to connect the study of Shakspere's works with an inquiry after the personality of the writer, and to observe, as far as is possible, in its several stages the growth of his intellect and character from youth to full maturity'. It is well known how Dowden developed his thesis, not identifying the dramatist with any one of his creations, but finding in Romeo and Hamlet and Prospero successive phases of Shakespeare's own personality. Recent criticism has in the main turned against this 'subjective' treatment of the plays, but the permanent worth of Dowden's book is not, in my opinion, thereby invalidated. His speculations rest on a base of wide and accurate scholarship; as he said himself, 'Shakspere is not to be approached on any side through dilettantism'. And he has that charm of style which is the birthright of the Anglo-Irish, and which made him a worthy interpreter of literature in the university of Congreve and Swift, and (as we are bound especially to remember at present) of Goldsmith and Burke.

There are other names not unworthy to be held in memory, such as the two Scottish Professors, J. C. Shairp and William Minto, who after other meritorious critical work, were amongst the earliest contributors to 'The English Men of Letters Series', which began its long career in 1878, under the editorship of John Morley, and is now having a renewal of youth under the aegis of a Fellow of this Society, and a member of its Academic Committee, Mr J. C. Squire. The *Spenser* of Dean Church and the *Johnson* of Leslie Stephen, to name two of the most distinguished of the early volumes, stretch across the gulf of half a century fraternal (or should I say, paternal?) hands to the *Swinburne* of Mr Harold Nicolson and the *Walt Whitman* of Mr John Bailey.

The old-established Reviews, quarterly, monthly and weekly, continued their supply of critical matter, the best of which generally found its way later into book form. But one important new enterprise in the magazine world

which took shape on the very eve of the 'seventies needs
special mention. On the 9th of October, 1869, appeared
the first number of *The Academy,* 'a monthly record of
Literature, Learning, Science, and Art'. *The Athenaeum,*
the chief existing journal devoted entirely to the humani-
ties, represented general literary culture, and its reviews
of books were anonymous. *The Academy,* as its name
implies, was to have a closer connection with academic
scholarship, and its articles were to be signed. Its first
number contained an imposing list of contributors; in
literature Matthew Arnold, in aesthetics Sidney Colvin,
in theology Lightfoot and Cheyne, in science Huxley and
Lubbock, in classical scholarship Mark Pattison, Coning-
ton, and Robinson Ellis. But the magazine, started under
such brilliant auspices, had a chequered career and finally,
after a transformation in which nothing but the name was
retained, it died suddenly on the 11th of September, 1915,
one of the victims of the World War.

But in the 'seventies no one dreamt of the iron time
to come. I was myself a schoolboy, and my first acquaintance with the works of the writers who figure in this
survey was either in my salad days at Clifton or in
the next decade at Oxford. They are thus to me as old
family friends, and if this gives anything of a bias to my
judgment, I can at least claim to speak from long
familiarity and early appreciation. Some, no doubt,
would have preferred the verdicts of *un jeune féroce*
'defaming and defacing'. But I venture to think that
a decade that has to its credit Pater's *Renaissance*; the
best critical work of R. H. Hutton, Stopford Brooke,
Leslie Stephen and Edward Dowden, and Matthew
Arnold's *Wordsworth*; and which saw the birth of the
New Shakspere Society and the 'English Men of Letters
Series', will be able to hold up its head and look any
future in the face.

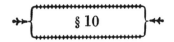

§ 10

Oxford in the 'Seventies

By R. W. Macan

I. THE COMMEMORATION OF 1870

THE Old Order was not quite a thing of the past in Oxford at the dawn of the fourth decade of the Victorian age. Mr Gladstone, elected in 1847 one of the Parliamentary Burgesses of the University and 'rusticated', so to speak, in 1865, for his latent Liberalism, had travelled via West Lancashire and Greenwich to Downing Street by November, 1868, to rule and reign for five sessions of highly contentious legislation. Reform was the order of the day. All the world was on the move. The depression of the first decade of the Queen's widowhood was beginning to lift. Schleswig Holstein (1864), Sadowa (1866), and in this very year of grace, 1870, Sedan and Versailles had exalted Prussia to German, and Germany to continental, primacy. But that was hardly a triumph for Liberalism, though it was a good advertisement for German culture and science. England was not quite happy about it. Oxford was not quite happy about it, or about herself, even though in that very summer the University had been celebrating a specially brilliant Commemoration of Founders and Benefactors, with its new Chancellor, Lord Salisbury in the chair, two dainty pages, little Lords Cranborne and William Cecil, to uphold his black and gold train, and a crowd of eminent recipients of degrees, *honoris causa*, among them the President of the Royal Academy to represent Art, and Mr Matthew Arnold of Oriel College, to personify Letters, all duly 'presented' by the Regius Professor of Civil Law, one James Bryce; the gala including an Ode, by the Professor of Poetry, Sir Francis Doyle, set to music by the Professor of that ilk, Sir Frederick Gore Ouseley, and concluding with the recitation of the Newdigate Prize Poem, by its stripling author, a fair-haired fresh-complexioned Scholar of Corpus, whose golden appearance and sonorous eloquence were not unworthy the occasion. Yes! Things were beginning to look brighter, even in Oxford; but *l'ancien régime* had still nine-tenths of the law under its caps and gowns.

II. A SERMON IN STONES

The very stones of the place had a tale to tell. The streets were still paved with cobbles, and men moved with difficulty in and out and about the City. Unless you were wealthy and kept a horse, you trusted mainly to your own legs for locomotion. Pedestrianism was still the joy of the reading man in the Oxford of the 'seventies. But then, he still had the unravished country of the Scholar Gipsy to wander over, with or without a companion. High bicycles were rare and alarming engines. The world had still years to wait for the geared safety machine, simple and obvious as it looks. But when did mankind ever arrive at the simple and obvious straight away? There were a few old hansom cabs and four-wheelers about, but little trade with them, save at beginning and end of term, for conveyance to and from the railway station: the railway had insisted, despite the Dons, on coming to Oxford, even by a roundabout route, and on a broad gauge, which it was soon to discover could not be maintained. In the summer term we still drove out, on mighty chars-à-bancs, to the old Magdalen Ground and the Cowley Marsh for Cricket: Christ Church and Merton were the only Colleges then blest with playing-fields within the precincts. Oxford was still a duodecimo City in those days. The country began just beyond the bridges, south and east and west, and soon after passing St Giles his church, if you went north towards Woodstock or Banbury. Before the 'seventies slipped away, the City Fathers were pushing afield, and had discovered need for a water reservoir atop Headington Hill, and a sewage farm out of sight, beyond Littlemore. But within the old line of Walls the City still wore its early Victorian aspect. Carfax was as yet unimproved. The cobbled High Street from Carfax to Eastgate was still its dear old self. St Martin's Church at the upper end, and the narrow bridge, just wide enough for two carriages to pass, at the lower end, were still in being. The deplorable King Edward Street was still but a project in the Oriel brain. The famous Angel Inn had not as yet made way for the New Schools. Shops, piled with books or drugs or clothing, occupied the positions now filled by the new fronts of Brasenose and Oriel. The St Swithin's Buildings of Magdalen, had they existed, would have been hidden by the umbrageous trees, which then masked the School Room and the College out-houses. On a summer's morning, looking betimes from your window on the High —if you were so lucky as to be lodged thereabouts—you might observe the archaic method of laying the dust. A copious tap turned on at Carfax, sent water down the street in two streams, one in each gutter. On either side a municipal *Aquarius*, armed with large wooden shovel and encased in long boots, advanced down street, and with a tarpaulin contraption every thirty or forty yards dammed the stream into a pool, and with his shovel flung the water half-way across the street, careful to avoid drenching his *vis-à-vis*, diagonally and similarly engaged. The progressive 'eighties supervened to spoil all that, with their one-horsed tramcars, and sets, and macadam,

and so forth. And though all this too is now in turn as
dead as Queen Philippa or Queen Anne, a great expansion
of Oxford came on with the 'eighties—not only extending
the area but reconstructing the core and corpus of City
and University. Never was there, of course, a decade in
the history of Oxford when some building was not toward.
The 'sixties—not to go back beyond living memory—had
witnessed the erection of gaunt Veneto-Gothic buildings
in 'The Parks' for the Sciences, and in 'The Meadows'
for lucky denizens of 'The House', from plans illuminated
—as was whispered—by *The Seven Lamps of Architecture*.
But since the erection of the Martyrs' Memorial in 1841
the leading mediaevalist in Oxford's architectural experiments had been the first Sir Gilbert Scott, whose
rather heavy digit may be traced in the Libraries of
University and Exeter, and in the Broad Street and
Holywell fronts of Exeter and New College respectively.
Scott also inaugurated the restorations in Christ Church
during the early 'seventies, some features of which provoked the whimsical wit of 'Lewis Carroll'—that merry
mathematician—into printed sallies of now bibliopolist
rarity. But no architect, in the living legend of Oxford
building, has had so free a hand and so full a favour as
Sir Thomas Jackson, whose victorious career was sealed
by the commission for the New Schools, the discussion
over which bulked large throughout the 'seventies. The
most important Collegiate building of the decade was
Butterfield's variegated elevation of Keble College in
brick, which marked a new departure for College ideals
in more than an architectural sense. The rebuilding of
Balliol in stone (by Waterhouse) at least conformed to
local tradition, even if economy dictated the addition of
an extra storey (as previously at Exeter and at New
College)—an example which once set and copied,
threatens to darken the streets of Oxford with collegiate

and commercial sky-scrapers. The clouds hang so low
betimes in Thames valley.

III. EPOCHS OF HISTORY: THE THREE
COMMISSIONS

But even this sermon in stones—which is far from
exhausting the text—proves the untowardness of rigid
time-limits, in dealing with movables, such as life and
letters, which do not arrange themselves in neat packets
of ten years for our convenience. But roughly the
'seventies serve to date the fourth decade of the Victorian
Age, the latter half of the Mid-Victorian Epoch, and
cover the phenomena of that dim and difficult period of
transition between the crescendo and collapse of the
Early Victorians (1837–61) and the crescendo and finale
fortissimo of the Late Victorians (1881–1900). Now,
during the last quarter of the nineteenth century and the
first quarter of the twentieth, Oxford has been rebuilt,
reconstituted, nationalised, imperialised, popularised, or
at least prepared for popularity; so that, in contrast with
the present day, the Oxford of the 'seventies looks barely
distinguishable from the Oxford of the 'sixties, or even of
the 'fifties—once the 'fifties were fairly under way. Yet
the 'seventies brought matters to a crisis. Indeed, three
great crises in the history of the Oxford of living memory
are marked by three statutable Commissions which,
within a lifetime, have visited the University and its
Colleges, to investigate and to reform them, or to sanction
their self-reformation. Oxford has ever been a mirror of
England's life and culture, and its three recent crises have
been organic to larger moments in the nation's history.
The Oxford Commission of 1854 and its work were fore-
ordained in the Reform Act of 1832. It broke up the
Elizabethan and Caroline constitution of University and
Colleges, not indeed completely but sufficiently to set the

ball rolling. It initiated the emancipation of the University from the College dominium. It taxed the Colleges for the benefit of the Professoriate; it provided a cheaper adit to University education by establishing non-collegiate students. It destroyed the old local liens on College endowments, and substituted—in accordance with ruling ideas of the day—Open Examinations and Competition for patronage and privilege in the award of Scholarships and Fellowships. In short, it enlarged the University to the classes which had been enfranchised by the Act of 1832, subject to certain reservations. In especial, it left the resident University still predominantly a clerical and celibate society; and Oxford, with its endowments, was still to be restricted to members of the Church of England, except that Matriculation and the Baccalaureate were relieved of Tests by the Act of 1854. But, before the 'sixties were over, these survivals of Laudian Oxford had become intolerable. Changes effected by the first Commission, which had seemed revolutionary at the time, left resident Oxford unsatisfied and conspiring for more radical measures. The newly invented 'Prize-Fellow', a non-resident who applied his stipend to better his start in life outside Oxford, was bracketed with the 'Idle Fellow', as an abuse of College endowments. The lack of permanent provision for lay teachers, competent and willing to undertake Higher Education as their life's work, was pronounced anomalous and absurd. The endowment of Research, in lieu of cram and competition, became the *mot d'ordre* of the advanced reformers. Already in 1870 the Queen's Speech at the opening of the Session commended to Parliament a legislative settlement of religious tests in the Universities and Colleges of Oxford and Cambridge: and although Lord Salisbury contrived the postponement of the Bill, a measure to that effect was enacted in the session of 1871.

But, albeit 'Reform from within' had been proceeding slowly meanwhile, the demand for a fresh Commission, to extend, co-ordinate and accelerate the process was too urgent to be much longer resisted. The Universities Commission of 1877, emanating from a Conservative Government, was the welcome result. The demand for further University reforms had accumulated, by no mere accident, an irresistible force within ten years of the Reform Act of 1867; and no one thought of describing the Universities Bill of 1877 as 'a leap in the dark'. The Oxford Commission accomplished its proper task by the close of 1882, and made way again for the normal and statutable process of 'reform from within'; which sufficed down to the late Lord Curzon's famous 'Red Letter' of 1908, and on to the third Commission of 1923, clearly relative to the Reform Acts of 1918 and 1927, which have added 5,000,000 souls—or suffragists—to the Electorate, making things pleasant for the Proletariate. The third wave should by rights be the most overwhelming. But our third Commission, though summoned by Moab and Philistia to curse, has ended (they tell me) in blessing the academic Israel altogether. In fact the Commission, perhaps, effected, in consultation with University and Colleges, little ·which the University and Colleges were not prepared to do of their own motion. The effects, however, have been more uniform and rapid. Further results are of course in the future. We know what and where we are, but we know not what we shall be; nor what shall be the condition of Art and Letters, of Science and Religion, in the Oxford of the 'seventies, forty years ahead, which some of us may live to see. However that may be, within now living memory Oxford has undergone a series of inner changes and developments, in view of which the former 'seventies may fairly be described as a purely transitional section: preserving much, in matter and in

spirit, of the Oxford anterior to the first Commission, yet
already palpitating with the promise of the Oxford of the
'nineties, or even of the present century to date; but
lacking, perhaps, a clear and eminent character of its own
—a period of disappointment, unsatisfied demands, apparent reaction, yet with a touch of spring in the air; a
time of latent push and now visible importance, though
anything but 'the perfect star, we saw not, when we
moved therein'.

IV. OXFORD AND LITERATURE

What has all that to say to Literature? Much every
way! But we must discriminate between life and letters,
between literature and literature. The relations between
Universities and Literatures are manifold and compli-
cated, direct and indirect, local and ecumenical. Oxford
University is at any given moment a large association,
with a still ampler penumbra: the city of Oxford contains
but the headquarters and nucleus of the brotherhood.
The majority of its members, past and present, arc dis-
tributed throughout the country, the dominions, the wide
world. As men, and women, of culture and education,
they owe these advantages, in greater or less part, to
Oxford. If literature means anything to them—and it
not seldom means at least bread and butter—Oxford has
helped them to that meaning, and has, perhaps, spread
the butter a little thicker on the bread. Those of them for
whom literature has a purely cultural value, would not
disown a debt to Oxford. But what critic would be bold
enough to attempt, from this point of view, an estimate
of the service of Oxford to literature? The learned Professions, the Civil Services of the empire, other Universities, Schools of all grades, Churches of all denomina-
tions, are staffed by men and women, who—no doubt
with varying consciousness and results—are what they

are and do what they do thanks to their trivium or quadrivium in Oxford. But this theme is so obvious, so vast, so intangible, that we must here be content to take note of it, and pass on. Let us concentrate attention upon the domestic activities of the University during the period prescribed by our title. In the 'seventies, as always, and primarily, the University was a High School, which offered a literary and scientific training, and prided itself especially on its paedagogic values for practical life, 'that there might never be wanting a succession of fit persons for the service of God in Church and State': an ideal, which is in part a bequest of the clerical tradition, and more especially a product of the College *régime*. Oxford's aim has always been to educate our masters, that is, the class—or the mass—which governs the country, and decides its destinies. It is so now: it was so, *mutatis mutandis*, in the 'seventies. But this great purpose is not in itself a direct gain to Letters and Science, but rather a discomfort for them, however well it may sort with other elements in the life of the place: sports, clubs, social intercourse and friendships, for which Oxford affords unsurpassed opportunities. So it comes about that Oxford's primary relations with Literature are indirect, critical, propaedeutic. The University exists rather for the conservation and study than for the production of literature. It appreciates and imparts the power to appreciate literature, which it does not itself produce. It devotes itself to teaching and learning, more than to poetic increment. It practises original research rather than original invention. If it displays some literary activity, its output is apt to be a contribution to knowledge rather than a gift to *Belles Lettres*. Its most impressive results in print will generally be aids to science or learning: word-books, text-books, commentaries, introductions, prolegomena, manuals—in short, not literature, but the implements of literary production, not the thing itself, but its technical prerequisites. Universities, as such, are hewers of wood and drawers of water to the true lords of literary creation.

Moreover, a University such as ours, with its serried ranks of Professors, Readers, Demonstrators, Tutors, Lecturers, and 'Coaches', creates a local depression not over-favourable to literary productivities. There are too many clever men on the same ground doing the same thing. Too many cooks spoil the broth. The air is too highly charged with negative criticism. The perpetual study and exposition of classical masterpieces (whatever the languages in which they are preserved) is adverse to the student's originality: the vision of the Best is hostile to the idea of the Good. In this respect younger Universities, less fully equipped, where one or two teachers are at work in each department, may diffuse a less fatal miasma over literary ambitions, and afford a more favourable soil for literary experiments. At Oxford where there are twenty Colleges, or more, and every College insists on secreting its own philosopher, its own historian, its Lector in Greek and its Lector in Latin, its Tutors, its Demonstrators, *et caeteros*, posing as a little University in itself—to say nothing of the phalanx of Professors duplicating and reduplicating the teaching offensive, and raising the dynamic of mutual criticism to infinity—the would-be author of a half-crown handbook in a Clarendon Press series will think once and again before exposing himself to the chilling silence or the tepid appreciation of his *commilitones*, by rushing into print. Doubtless there is a deal of anonymous authorship in periodical literature traceable to academic sources: but 'safety first' is your scholar's watchword. The list of projected but unprinted works in any given decade of the nineteenth century in Oxford might make a tragi-comic tale of the good intentions of that pathetic sub-species, *Homo sapiens academicus*. And again: the advance in the style and standard of tutorial and professorial work, already apparent during the 'seventies, made heavier demands on the time and energies of the teacher, leaving him less happily disposed for literary achievements. But the influence most of all fatal to productivity was, and is, the Examination system, with its power over the methods and conditions of study and teaching, especially the fixed curriculum and the time limit for the Honour Schools. Not merely do such conditions introduce a competitive note or *motif*, into the Examination. Not merely does Examination under such conditions demoralise the examiner even more than the examinee—for the latter soon escapes into the fresh air. The worst of it is that a prescribed curriculum, under a time limit of study, is apt to be eclectic and arbitrary, precluding the student from 'carving the capon by the joints', and from pursuing the topics most attractive or suitable to his idiosyncrasy; while the competitive examination at the close—on which his immediate fortunes may depend—dictates cram and sophistry, and offers a premium to the pen of the too ready writer.

In a sense the system might, indeed, appear to favour literature of a sort rather than learning, to encourage rhetoric, or 'the art of putting things', at the expense of genuine knowledge. And the old Oxford education, which was at its zenith in the 'seventies, was open to some such indictment, at least in the literary Schools: Mathematics and Physical Science (as it was then called) were in their very nature less liable to sophistic corruption. But the other two final Schools—there were but four in all at the beginning of the 'seventies—*Literae Humaniores* and *Law and History* were marvellous exercises in literary camouflage; especially the former, which was generally recognised as the best preparation for the two professions,

whose functions have sometimes been described as being
to make the better case appear the worse, and the worse
case appear the better, to wit, Journalism and the Bar.
Such Schools were certainly nothing, if not literary. The
Classical School included Greek and Latin Literature,
with Philosophy and Ancient History: but the Literature
and History were confined to certain select authors or
books, and the Philosophy to a couple of Greek texts,
plus a hotch-potch of modern authorities, mainly taken
on trust from Lecturer or Coach. The Modern School
drove Law and History in double harness, or tandem, the
general result being that its examinees, at the end of two
years, or so, were neither qualified lawyers, nor competent historians, but had acquired a certain facility in
tackling a question, though the literary results were
admittedly not up to the classical standard. Changes
inaugurated in the 'seventies have in course of time
brought about a vast improvement in Oxford education:
an improvement, which has been described as the substitution of scientific for literary methods and standards
in education, but has really covered an amelioration on
the literary no less than on the scientific side. One co-
efficient in this improvement may be seen in the separa-
tion of Law and History into two Schools, in 1872. Only
while such a *mésalliance* lasted could such a solemn farce
have been staged in Oxford as the millenary celebration,
in 1872, of the foundation of University College by King
Alfred—a pure myth, or rather mare's-nest, though recognised by the Courts from Richard II to George I, and
to that extent the law, if not the history, of the land. The
School of Theology, dating likewise from the early
'seventies, was also from its nature more truly 'scientific'
than *Literae Humaniores* or *Law and History*. The same
observation holds good of the English School, and the
Schools of Modern Languages and Oriental Languages,

for which Oxford had to wait several decades. And so strong has been the old literary tradition of classical 'Greats', that in the present scientific age the University has thought it could do nothing better for the Greekless youth surviving the war than to devise a sort of antitype, or parody, of *Literae Humaniores* in a Final School, embracing Philosophy, History, and Economics, all without tears, that is to say, English for the English. Happily things are different with the late-born Research Degrees (B.Litt., B.Sc., D.Ph., D.Litt., D.Sc.), for which candidates choose their own subjects of study, pursue them at leisure, and obtain academic Honours only on the production of adequate literary results. Such results are more scientific and at the same time more literary than anything procurable in the old-fashioned Schools of the University. Only in justice to *l'ancien régime* be it remembered that the better system was germinating in the University of the 'seventies, under the multiplication of subjects, the increase in the Professoriate, the organisation of combined College Lectures, the adoption by College teachers of academic work as a permanent career, the rising number of students: in short, the growth of those elements and movements in the life of the University, which were germane to the work of the Commission of 1877, and as developed *ab intra* by succeeding generations have made the Oxford of 1928, if juxtaposed with the Oxford of the first half of the nineteenth century, or even of the 'seventies, look really rather like a new academic heaven and earth in little.

Granted that the Schools had merely a paedagogic relation to literature, yet University prizes served as incentives to authorship, especially in the native tongue. Such prizes are generally awarded under conditions hardly felt as hindrances to production; though the subject be prescribed, the composition is voluntary, and

the successful result a work of supererogation, redounding
to the repute and even to the consolation of the winner;
for, although such prizes fall, as a rule, to men whose
names are to be found in the First Class of the Honour
Schools, a University prize not infrequently attests the
merit of a student, who has worked at a disadvantage
under the conditions of the normal examinations. Such
freer exercises obviously leave more scope for special
ability and individual preferences than the prescribed
and congested programmes of the Honour Schools. A
reassuring evidence of the value of such academic pre-
miums for individual study and production may be seen
in the permanent place, which some prize compositions
have taken in contemporary literature. The most notorious
instance, James Bryce's Arnold Essay on *The Holy
Roman Empire*, carries back to 1863. Albert Dicey's *On
the Privy Council*, three years earlier, at least prefigured
his standard works on the English Constitution. John A.
Doyle on the eve of the 'seventies won the same prize
with an Essay on *The English Colonies in America before
the Declaration of Independence*, which afterwards grew
into five volumes, the work of a life-time. The Chancellor's Prize in 1863 for an English Essay on *The
Renaissance* was won by J. A. Symonds, the future
historian of *The Renaissance in Italy*, and author of
several cognate works. In 1871 the Chancellor's Prize
was offered for an Essay on *The Universities of the Middle
Ages*, but the time was not ripe, and the prize was not
awarded. The same subject, when repeated in 1883,
evoked a response from Hastings Rashdall, which re-
appeared, twelve years later, expanded into three volumes,
to become at once the standard authority upon the subject. In 1879 the Arnold Prize was appropriately taken
by a grandson of Dr Arnold's with an essay on *The
Roman System of Provincial Administration*, which, when

published in book form, was recognised as an admirable handbook on an important topic of ancient history, and passed through several editions. But *habent sua fata libelli*. Not every prize essay worthy of a literary apotheosis obtains publication. *The Normans in Italy and Sicily* 1070–1270, the 'Arnold' for 1873, was long destined to appear in enlarged book form. Its author, R. L. Nettleship, for a while had deserted *Literae Humaniores* to invade the mediaeval preserves of the crescent School of *Historia Moderna*, demonstrating thereby not so much the unity of history as the enterprise of philosophers. But first a rumour that Edward Freeman was engaged upon an exhaustive history of Sicily, and then the heavy demands of a Balliol Tutorship, and one thing with another, conspired to check literary possibilities, which perished with that all too gallant soul on Mont Blanc in 1893.

V. UNIVERSITY IDEALS: JOWETT AND PATTISON

Class Lists and Prize Lists of the 'seventies contain not a few names, besides those above mentioned, of men destined in or out of Oxford to make notable contributions to literature—the Sweets, Sonnenscheins, Lodges, Firths, Godleys, Kers, Mackails, Margoliouths and others —who must here make way for the older men of literary distinction and academic prestige, prominent and dominant in the University during that decade. The greatest man of the time and place was Benjamin Jowett, Regius Professor of Greek; and the 'seventies, in the first year of which he succeeded Scott, of lexicographic fame, in the Headship of Balliol College, was the period of his mature vigour, influence, and success, though his Vice-Chancellorship fell into the subsequent decade. Jowett was fifty-three years of age when he became Master of Balliol, and he reigned over Balliol for three and twenty years, being throughout the most conspicuous personality in Oxford and one of the most important intermediaries between the University and the outer world. Devoted as Jowett was to the interests of his College, 'always thinking of the Undergraduates', and with a definite policy for the University as a palaestra for the training of able youths, whether rich or poor, for service, or success, in practical and public life, Jowett was also an eminent man of letters, with high ambition ('Can I ever write as well as Renan?') and immense industry; and his actual literary achievement, though falling far short of his plan and intention, was very considerable. He had suffered in various ways for his anticipations of modernist theology; but, though his opponents had managed to starve him awhile as Professor of Greek, he was invulnerable as Master of Balliol. The 'seventies witnessed the publication of his chief work: the complete translation, with elaborate introductions, of the *Dialogues of Plato*, a work, aptly described in the Inaugural Lecture of his illustrious successor, Ingram Bywater, as 'an English Classic'; and the 'seventies barely closed before his translation of the *History of Thucydides* was published. These two great tasks, the former of which appeared in a second edition within five years, far from exhausting his literary record, were preceded and succeeded by work of hardly less significance in its day. Jowett's English style makes him one of the great authors of the Victorian Age; but it is a style in which the right word and the felicitous sentence count for more than the synthesis of the paragraph or the dialectic of the argument. In academic politics Jowett was the chief exponent of the theory and practice which treat the University as a training station for practical life rather than as a laboratory of science; his heart was in the College, *imprimis* his own College, not in the organisa-

R. W. Macan

tion of Faculties or the endowment of Research. Yet he was zealous for University Institutions such as the Bodleian Library, the Indian Institute—just then on the *tapis*—the Clarendon Press, even the New Museum; and he was one of the pioneers of the University Extension Movement, though not over-cordial to the feminist invasion of Oxford itself. Much of all this was doubtless of service to Literature as well as to Education. Still it must be admitted that younger reformers in Oxford during the 'seventies looked elsewhere for a lead and a programme. They found the programme to hand in Mark Pattison's *Suggestions on Academical Organisation*, published at Edinburgh in 1868. Some of them found it also in their own experience of University life and methods abroad—for a fashion was now beginning, which led serious students in Oxford to frequent continental, and chiefly German, Universities for a year, or more, of intensive study. There lies before me, as I write, the Minute-book of a short-lived Association of young resident members of Convocation, which met twice or thrice a term, during the years 1876 and 1877, and came to a timely end with the appointment of the Commission in the latter year. The two Colleges most largely represented in the membership were Balliol and Christ Church; that is, as some might have said, the College least in need and the College most in need of reform. But from the Association's point of view there was not so very much to choose between them: and Balliol, under its new Master was even, perhaps, the more dangerous of the twain. The object of the Association was six-fold: (1) The support of liberal principles in the University ('liberal' having, of course, in this connection, no political connotation). (2) The abolition of all clerical restrictions. (3) The reform of the constitution of the University. (4) The promotion of learning in the University. (5) The improvement of teaching in the University. (6) The reform of the examination system. The Honorary Secretaries of the Association were two young graduates, who had spent some months together at the Universities of Jena and Zürich. Of the fourteen Masters of Arts who attended the inaugural meeting on the 14th of June, 1876, in Mr Tatton's rooms at Balliol, four survive to-day, and might be forgiven if they had forgotten all about it. Be that as it may, they have seen their programme more than realised during the half-century which has elapsed since that scarce-remembered meeting. The term 'Literature' did not occur in the programme, but it was implied, together with Science, in at least half the items; and various associates, were their names divulged, might rank among the more productive sons of modern Oxford. But to return to Pattison and Jowett: both had been among the alarming Essayists and Reviewers of 1860, together with Frederick Temple, D.D., at that date still Head Master of Rugby School. It was more important, apparently, for the Head of a School than for the Head of a College, to be a Doctor of Divinity—at that time, and until recently, a merely formal and financial distinction in the University—and neither Pattison nor Jowett ever proceeded to the higher degree, which they might have had for the asking, and the fees. Both were Liberals in the academic sense, and each had his own ideal for the University: Jowett's, the more immediate, practical, and insular; Pattison's, the more remote, far-reaching, and continental. But there was much common to the two: *imprimis*, a freer access for all classes of citizens to the University. If it was the Rector of Lincoln who demanded that students should be allowed to live in lodgings, and so cheaply, it was Balliol which first took or obtained leave for such residence, to ease the rebuilding of a large part of the College about the beginning of our period. The institution of non-collegiate students, known in those days as 'Unattached', further helped forward this movement for economy.

VI. PHILOSOPHY AT OXFORD IN THE 'SEVENTIES

It clarified the situation to have the alternative ideals of University progress, Education versus Learning, respectively personified in 'The Master' and 'The Rector', with 'Results' as the supposed watchword of the one, and 'Research' that of the other. Fortunately, as the sequel proved, there was room in Oxford for both. Yet the distinction cut deeper than might appear at first sight. Pattison was above all things a philosopher, and would have had philosophy, in conjunction, perhaps, with theology, recognised as crown of the sciences, and goal of the academic curriculum. But he was no less hostile than Jowett to philosophy, if reduced to merely literary and eclectic study of the metaphysical essays or systems of the past. In his conception philosophy was based upon the scientific investigation of nature, including human nature, and should achieve the progressive synthesis of discovery and knowledge from generation to generation. Jowett's attitude was really more conservative and traditional. As he aged he became more and more mistrustful of metaphysic, without acquiring more than an imperfect sympathy with the growth of the 'Natural Sciences'—a title which first became official in Oxford during the 'seventies—and 'The Master' fell back upon what has been called above the literary in contrast with the scientific position, emphasising the value of University education as a preparation for civil life and labours. He distrusted the development of philosophic speculation, which was a marked feature of our decade; in his own College he virtually reduced Thomas Hill Green, its

chief promoter and exponent at the time, to temporary
silence. Mark Pattison might not have fully endorsed
Green's particular trend in philosophy, which was rather
remote from an attempt to build up a metaphysic from
the sublimation of the natural sciences, such as is now
being evolved before our very eyes; and yet might have
recognised it as a vast improvement on the sensationalist
and materialist doctrine in vogue during the 'sixties.
Green regained independence with his belated election
to the Chair of Moral Philosophy in 1878. The product of
his all too short-lived activities is documented in his
Prolegomena to Ethics (1883) and in the three volumes of
his *Philosophical Works* (1885–8), all posthumous publications but representing substantially the character of
that philosophy which gradually acquired predominance
in Oxford during the 'seventies. The work of his best-
known followers—Herbert Bradley and Bernard Bosanquet—carried the new metaphysic to conclusions which
had no doubt been implicitly contained in it all along;
but neither of these notable writers was enrolled in the
University Professoriate. Bradley lived, indeed, for more
than fifty years in Merton, but never held any teaching
post in College or University. Bosanquet withdrew from
Oxford, after a short spell of College tuition, partly (as
I believe) in disgust with the limitations imposed on any
attempt to philosophise freely under the examinational
reign of terror. Lewis Nettleship's *Philosophical Lectures
and Remains*, two volumes edited by his friend and sometime colleague, Andrew Bradley, and published in 1897,
contain further materials for an estimate of the philosophic teaching current in the Oxford of the 'seventies
and 'eighties; and additional evidence may meet us in
less obvious quarters. Philosophy, in spite of some
losses, was a growing power in the Oxford of that period,
and has been such ever since, even if its colours and

complexion are greatly changed. A brilliant symptom of its vitality in those earlier days was noted, when a young Tutor of Merton, William Wallace—who was destined to succeed to Green's Chair in 1882, and to vacate it by a fatal accident fifteen years later—announced, in 1873, a course of lectures on the Logic of Hegel, which was well attended, chiefly by still younger graduates, and issued in a substantial volume from the Clarendon Press in 1874. Significantly enough Wallace warned his readers that Hegel's work had all been accomplished at a time, nearly half-a-century before, 'when modern science and Inductive Logic had yet to win their laurels, and when the world was in many ways different from what it is now'. A detached mind might surmise that, from such beginnings, philosophy in Oxford would have had an even richer and more rapid harvest, had it been more closely related to the new School of Natural Science, and delivered, if not from its preoccupation with Greek literature, at least from its liaison with Ancient History (Greek and Roman). I confess, as a graduate of the 'seventies in *Literae Humaniores*, that I cannot remember to have heard the name of Darwin, or the term Evolution, in other than an Hegelian sense, from any of the philosophic pundits of the time: though I may add that I returned from Germany to Oxford, half-way through the decade, to find Ray Lankester translating Häckel's *Schöpfungs- geschichte* for the British public, a work, the substance of which I had been hearing and seeing (for Häckel was a masterly draughtsman) in the shape of professorial *Vorträge* in the Museum at Jena. My private conclusion then was that not until philosophers became 'scientists', or scientists became philosophers, should we obtain a world-wisdom quite worthy of the time and place. The notion that Natural Science had any quarrel with Literature, sometimes heard in those days, was as superficial

as the cognate notion that science, as such, was hostile
to religion, and might have been refuted by appeal to
the literary eminence of the leaders of science in Oxford
at the time, such as Acland, Rolleston, Henry Smith,
Vernon Harcourt, Moseley and others. But I see now
that I did less than justice to the philosophers in Oxford,
when I deserted their ranks, under the conviction that
historical methods furnished the safest clue to the riddles
of human existence in every time and place.

VII. HISTORY AT OXFORD IN THE 'SEVENTIES

Certainly in the 'seventies the brightest hope for letters
in Oxford lay with the growth and vigour of the School,
or Faculty, of Modern History, especially after its release
from the *mariage de convenance* with Jurisprudence. Not
that Jurisprudence was not alive at the time, at least in
the Professoriate. Throughout our decade Sir Henry
Maine was delivering his classic lectures on Early Institutions, on Law and Custom, and so forth, all immediately fit for publication. But Maine was a non-
resident Professor—like the Professor of Poetry, or the
Slade Professor of Art—and his true academic home
beckoned from the sister University, to which he of right
belonged. Of course our School of Law, as the sequel has
proved, stood to gain quite as much by an independent
constitution, as did its yoke-fellow; it had, moreover, a
unique advantage among the Faculties of the University
in being based, so to speak, on All Souls College, with its
magnificent Library and endowments. But the *floruit* of
the Oxford Law School falls after our limit, and the new
Modern History School was the proudest edifice of the
'seventies, though its early pillars, so to speak, had been
grounded in *Literae Humaniores*, and were good scholars
before they became great historians. William Stubbs
was Regius Professor, and his *Constitutional History of*

England issued from the Press during the 'seventies to
become at once the bible of the Modern History School.
Stubbs himself enjoyed a wide reputation, fortified by his
Introductions and editions in the Rolls Series; and among
the College teachers were several authors, already, or a
little later, eminent of their kind. Kitchin's *History of
France* and Bright's *History of England* were published
in the 'seventies. Mandell Creighton, the future historian
of the Popes, was lecturing indifferently on Ancient and
on Modern History, still as innocent as his colleagues,
Knox and Jayne and Talbot—all historians in their day—
and as their leader, Stubbs himself, of impending episco-
palian translations. In 1874 out came J. R. Green's
ever-green *Short History*: he no Don, yet the veriest
Oxonian of them all! Among the founders of the Oxford
Historical School Charles Boase of Exeter and Arthur
Johnson of All Souls, though not prolific authors, will
long be remembered with honour. Among their pupils
were the Armstrongs, the Smiths, the Pooles, the Mar-
riotts, Protheros, Buckles, Lodges, Touts, Tippings,
Rounds, Fletchers, Reichels and others, soon to be known
as men of learning and letters within or beyond the
Professorial radius. Nor can we forget the immediate
predecessors and successors of Stubbs in the Regius Chair:
Goldwin Smith, one of the Secretaries of the first Commission and still visible in Oxford about the beginning of
our period, a master of terse nervous English, a paragon
of the higher journalism, not inferior even to George
Brodrick; but a sad Radical withal, who found Great
Britain in the 'seventies too small to contain Mr Disraeli
and himself, and escaped to Toronto, in a vain hope
of converting the Canadas to Little Englandism, and
merging them in the U.S.A. Stubbs' immediate successor,
Edward Freeman, was publishing in the 'seventies his
immense history of the Norman Conquest, and two series

of Historical Essays, which some have preferred to his larger lucubrations. The next of the Diadochi, Anthony Froude, had finished his long excursion on the high seas of Tudor history, and was collecting his *Short Studies on Great Subjects*; among whose delinquencies a too easy literary style was, perhaps, included, as it certainly was not eclipsed, by his predecessor. And this brilliant succession may end for us with York Powell and Sir Charles Firth, both remarkable in this connection as pure products of the Oxford School, as it was in the 'seventies. Powell, indeed, bore witness to the unregenerate system, for, on taking his degree, he started as a Law Lecturer at 'The House', devoting his leisure to the joint-production with Gustav Vigfússon, of the *Corpus Poeticum Boreale* (2 vols. 1883: now out of print); and keeping his friends meanwhile well informed about French literature and Japanese art, before he settled down to inaugurate, with infinite labour, an Historical Series, of which he was editor, with a little volume, a school-book but a pageant in its way—*The History of England to the death of Henry VII*. Surely never a man of such supreme literary culture wrote with more reluctance than did he! Doubtless the Modern History School has by this time left the 'seventies far behind. The most popular and by no means the least scientific of the Faculties, it has been adorned by a succession of sound and even brilliant teachers and writers: but its foundations were well and truly laid in the 'seventies, to which (I presume) it should look back with pride, as it doubtless may look forward with confidence to every fresh crisis: *die Weltgeschichte ist das Weltgericht!*

VIII. THEOLOGY AT OXFORD IN THE 'SEVENTIES

The case of Theology in the 'seventies was much less cheerful. The Faculty was still, as the whole University had been until 1854, strictly Anglican. But after the Universities Tests Act 1871, still more after the Oxford Commission of 1877, to maintain a strictly Anglican Faculty of Theology, in a University open without confessional tests to all comers, promised to be an increasingly difficult proposition. The party in possession was not going to surrender at discretion, but was determined to hold on as long as possible to privilege and endowment. They were, however, in the melancholy position of fighting a losing campaign, even if victorious from time to time in a rear-guard action. Thus, when the Honours School of Theology was instituted in 1869, although no confessional test was imposed on teachers much less on candidates in the School, only Oxford priests of the Church of England could be appointed to examine. This anomaly was emphasised by the fact that examinations in Divinity, obligatory on all members of the University (subject to a conscience-clause), were conducted by the ordinary Public Examiners, whose theological creed and competence were taken on trust. Our Church had some more legitimate advantages secured to her in Oxford during the 'seventies by the 'New Foundation' of Keble and the re-endowment of Hertford College, both institutions being protected from the secular arm of the Commission of 1877 by the fifty years' limit provided in the Act; nor has anyone been heard to murmur, even when they were further secured under the Universities of Oxford and Cambridge Act, 1923, by the substitution of sixty years for fifty in the clause protecting trusts of recent foundation. But just half-a-century before the latter Act a former Professor of Poetry, in 'an Essay towards a better apprehension of the Bible', had been trying to persuade us that Literature and Dogma were incompatibles; and the Vatican Decrees of 1871, with their *reductio ad absurdum* of ecclesiastical authority, had brought some at least among us to see that, while Mr Gladstone's fulminations on the civil and political aspects of Vaticanism might leave us comparatively cold, there was, on Church principles, no logical alternative between Papal infallibility and freedom of thought: and to hope that Anglican loyalties might prove to be reconcilable with philosophic autonomy. But the leaders of the Church party in Oxford at that time were not prepared to agree with the apostle of culture, while they were in the way with him; much less with the champions of science, whose First Principles were certainly still in a rather agnostic, not to say unspiritual, stage of development.

But the leaders were by that time hardly abreast of their followers in the University regarding either Apologetics or Academic policy. Younger men, destined to succeed them, soon showed themselves willing to accept loyally the *fait accompli* in the abolition of tests, to admit the Higher Criticism at least as applied to the Old Testament, and to promote the cause of Natural Science, without undue nervousness, fortified as some of them were by the Idealist philosophy, which Green was bringing home to Oxford to supersede the scepticism of the earlier Tractarians, and to replace the sensationalism of Mill and Bain. So it came about that no department of study and teaching in the University suffered a more complete change of method and spirit than became apparent in the Theological Faculty after the 'seventies. That Nonconformists, on their free admission to the University should, sooner or later, be admitted to the Theological as to the other Faculties was inevitable. What was really surprising was the immense modification in the teaching of the Anglican Professors—the Drivers, Cheynes, Sandays, Hatches, Gores and others. The celebrated volume of essays entitled *Lux Mundi* (1889)—the first clear evidence of the acceptance of Historical Criticism and philosophic

idealism by the younger school of Oxford High Church-
men—dated from Pusey House within eight years of
Dr Pusey's death and published while Dr Liddon was
still with us—was the work of men who had been *in statu
pupillari* during the 'seventies. One of them, Henry
Scott Holland, when he succeeded *longo intervallo* to
Mozley's Chair, initiated a thorough-going proposal to
cancel even the profession of a Christian faith for the
Degrees in Divinity: a project, which went beyond the
practical requirements and the conscience of the times,
but made it easier, perhaps, for his successor to effect the
liberal compromise now in being. But to return to the
'seventies: in that actual decade it was apparently left
for laymen to foreshadow the coming 'liberty of pro-
phesying'. Max Müller's Hibbert Lectures in 1877, and
still more the great series of The Sacred Books of the
East, which he inaugurated two years later with his
translation of the *Veda*, encouraged the employment of
scientific method in a department of Theology, which has
been rather unhappily entitled 'Comparative Religion',
but certainly exhibits a tendency to weaken the appeal
to authoritative Dogmatics. About the same date an
essay on the Resurrection, also published by the Hibbert
Trust, and written, as I am, perhaps, more especially
bound to add, by a young Student and Tutor of Christ
Church, which adopted and developed the Visionary
hypothesis in explanation of the Christophanies recorded
in the New Testament, had a rather chilly reception in
Oxford; though something not very unlike that rationale
of the facts is now to be found in such bulwarks of the
new Apologetic as *Foundations* (1912) and *Essays
Catholic and Critical* (1926)—works which leave the
theological position of a Liddon or a Pusey, and even that
of *Lux Mundi*, far behind. These modern, not to say
Modernist, Apologetics, could they have been anticipated

by fifty or sixty years, might have saved the Robert
Elsmeres of the 'seventies from a deal of worry and mis-
giving; for the hero of Mrs Humphry Ward's first novel
must be regarded as a type, reflecting one side of Oxford
life and letters in that decade. Is the book not, indeed,
notoriously a *roman-à-clef*, with some of those named in
this chapter among the *dramatis personae*; though no one
has succeeded in identifying Mrs Ward's eponymous hero
with any individual Oxonian. He was, presumably, a
composite photograph.

IX. SOCIAL ASPECTS: YOUNGER DONS

Another vision of Oxford in the 'seventies is opened up
by the same writer's *Recollections* (1918), dedicated to her
husband 'in memory of April 6th, 1872', and giving a delightful account of the simple life and social intercourse
in vogue with the young married couples in 'The Parks':
startling novelties just made possible during that decade,
by the removal of the celibate restriction upon Fellowships. No more attractive report on Oxford's domestic
renaissance has anywhere been preserved; to attempt a
duplication of it here could result only in a plagiarism or
a fiasco. Yet I would venture to supplement it by one
personal reminiscence of the informal entertainments at
Fyfield House, on Friday evenings in term, to which a
group of young Dons had standing invitations. If one
were not coming on any given occasion, one was expected
to let the lady of the house know in good time. If you
were busy, or had pupils of a night, you were permitted
to slip away early without offence. What gay and sometimes serious talk we had! What amiable differences!
What cordial sympathies! What innocent ambitions,
what sanguine expectations, for ourselves, for Oxford,
for mankind, over the simple meal, and round the bright
fire! Our hosts were Mr and Mrs Arthur Acland, she the

238 R. W. Macan

sole woman present, and in her beauty and her brightness the jewel in the golden ring: he, a quondam Tutor of Keble College, about to reorganise the commissariat at Christ Church and at Balliol, and to give the University Extension a good start, before being rapt away into politics, and lifted out of our reach into Mr Gladstone's Home Rule Cabinet as Minister of Education (1892). Among the constant *Stammgäste* shall be named Charles Heberden, our chief musician (afterwards Principal of B.N.C.); Warde Fowler, the votary of Mozart, the lover of birds, writing essays with a felicity of style not inferior to Elia: Nathan Bodington, who was to quit Oxford for Birmingham, and by and by to transform the Yorkshire College of Science into the University of Leeds: Lewis Nettleship, our ideal *philosophe*, who never said a foolish thing himself but had a sudden smile for the timely follies of others: Frank Peters, a Balliol scholar at the age of sixteen, and then busy, as a Fellow of University, translating the *Nicomachean Ethics* into intelligible English: Paul Willert, the *beau idéal* of the 'Eton and Oxford' type, gently tolerant of more boisterous ancients in the company: Andrew Bradley, in whom his friends already then foresaw the master of literary criticism, which he has since proved himself to be. Was it indeed to any such address that the Master of Balliol could have directed his scathing indictment of the young Dons of the period?

They want to marry and they have no money. They want to write, and have no originality. They want to be scholars, and have no industry. They want to be fine gentlemen, and are deficient in manners. When they have families, they will be at their wits' end to know how to provide for them. Many of them have the fretfulness of *parvenus*, and will always have this unfortunate temper of mind.

Were we really like that in the Master's eyes? Ah, me! *In perpetuom, fratres, avete atque valete.* The few survivors are older now, if not wiser, than the Master was then.

X. UNDERGRADUATE TYPES

Well, well! However young Dons in the 'seventies may have looked to imperfectly Socratic eyes, what should be remembered of the Ephebi, the passing undergraduates? They were not always on their best behaviour! Thus the Encaenia of 1872 suffered an ignominious closure, when the Vice-Chancellor (Dr Liddell) abruptly quitted the Sheldonian Theatre, in consequence of the turbulence of the Olympians. But a prophylactic for such excesses was found by introducing a bevy of sisters and cousins to sit with the undergraduates aloft, while mothers and aunts were left to the dignity of the Ladies' Circle below. The youths of the 'seventies were of many sorts and conditions, on their ways to the Bar, the Services, the Schools, the Churches, the new openings for academic life throughout the country, and some to be men of letters, and some to be men of business and affairs, with a dwindling residuum of idle rich and idle poor. If the 'seventies was the decade of Oscar Wilde (1874–8) the 'seventies was also the decade of Cecil Rhodes (1874–81). Wilde was indeed typical of one phase, or craze, of the moment. Walter Pater's *Studies in the History of the Renaissance* (1873)— a contribution not to historical science but to aesthetic criticism—had unwittingly set young Oxford, or a part of young Oxford, burning 'with a hard gem-like flame', and trying to undo its 'formed habits'—often very good habits formed at the Public Schools. But the Arts had other votaries. John Ruskin had come back to Oxford, as first Slade Professor, with a more distinctly ethical message; and on Tuesday, the 8th of February, 1870, the Large Lecture Room at the New Museum was not large enough to contain the huge crowd which assembled to hear his Inaugural Lecture, and the intrepid Professor boldly adjourned to the Sheldonian Theatre—perhaps the Vice-Chancellor and Proctors were present and gave leave—followed by his multitudinous audience, reinforced with casual recruits enlisted *en route*, to deliver his eloquent prelection concerning 'Art and Religion'. Ruskin remained in fashion throughout the decade, with rooms in Corpus, and even persuaded a loyal band of his followers to take their afternoon exercise in the guise of navvies at the honest toil of road-making to Ferry Hinksey, till the river foiled them, or their ardours cooled. Arnold Toynbee, whom Jowett attached to Balliol in 1875, started another movement, which has not yet run its course, linking the University teacher and student with the artisan and the labour-world, but all too soon gave his own fragile life away, in an effort to expose the fallacies of Henry George to the British working-man (1883). The champions of women's education and franchise laid siege to Oxford in the 'seventies, and before the decade was out had established two strongholds of potential undergraduettes within the gates, Somerville and Lady Margaret Halls. The Extension movement was born, or copied from Cambridge, and University extension and intension went forward, if not hand in hand, at least concomitantly. Oxford set to work, as already indicated above, to rebuild and to enlarge itself. The numbers of the University were on the rise. Matriculations, which had sunk in the 'fifties below 400 yearly, almost doubled that figure before the 'seventies passed (though that may seem few enough, in view of present-day figures). Increase of the Schools, improvements in teaching, due in part to growing combination between Colleges for lecturing purposes, additional Professorships, all tended to multiply the number of students reading for Honours, and to diminish the contrast

between University and College, Professorial and Tutorial
standards. Nor did athletics and the lighter elements in
life suffer. The 'sixties had been a 'record' for Oxford on
the river: the 'seventies are memorable for a unique
event, the dead-heat with Cambridge in the Boat-race of
1877. The flannelled experts got their Cricket-ground and
Pavilion in The Parks (1879), and the five or six varieties
of football, previously in vogue, settled down, like Oxford
philosophy, to a 'hopeless dualism' between Rugby and
Association, or in the local slang, Rugger and Soccer.
The game of Hockey, too, began to attract attention; and
even Golf, like a shy daisy, raised its head from the
Cowley sod, under the genial husbandry of Horatio
Hutchinson of Corpus and Patrick Henderson of Wad-
ham. Music was on the make in Oxford during the
'seventies. The Musical Club, founded by the Donkins
and Charles Lloyd, was well under way, and the Musical
Union was soon to follow. The mutual education, admiration and criticism of undergraduates had fewer organs
than to-day; but there were literary, social, and political
clubs and coteries in existence: above all, there was the
Union Society, where the present Library—for the new
Debating Hall was not yet in being—resounded on
Thursday nights to the adolescent efforts of the Asquiths,
Brodricks, Curzons, Hortons, Milners and other on-com-
ing politicians and divines, to appraise the public problems
of the day. Strange, how much more successful the
political than the literary debate! The character of
Mr Disraeli, the conduct of Mr Gladstone, provoked the
strongest language, and the largest division: the Game
Laws or Home Rule was sure of a lively discussion: but
the question, whether Mr Tennyson or Mr Browning were
the greater poet, found the House liable to be counted
out. So much easier is it to be a successful party politician
than to be a sound literary critic! Yet one motion of a

B   16

slightly later date (1881), reflecting upon the Oxford of the 'seventies, may here be recorded, *ipsissimis verbis*: 'That this House approves the efforts being made to bring Art and Literature within reach of the masses of Englishmen, but condemns the ridiculous class known as aesthetes'—a resolution triumphantly affirmed by 83 to 54 votes, which in those days would have been a goodly division even on a burning political question. The majority *in statu pupillari* had no doubts on the subject of Bunthorne's virtue! But it was far from being puritanical. The New Theatre had not yet superseded the insanities of the old 'Vic.', and a motion in favour of establishing a permanent home in Oxford for 'the Drama', was always sure of approval. Not that theatrical performances (more or less *sub rosa*) were quite unknown, even before the celebrated representation of the *Agamemnon* of Aeschylus in Balliol Hall (1880, with F. R. Benson as Clytaemnestra, W. Bruce in the title-rôle, and W. L. Courtney as Watch or Sentinel), which paved the way for the establishment of the O.U.D.S. founded by Adderley and Bourchier of Christ Church with Jowett's Vice-cancellarian blessing in 1883.

Oxford of the 'seventies may look mild and modest and mid-Victorian beside the Oxford of to-day, but it was alive and moving: still a rather shy and cloistered creature (specially o' Sundays), but shedding its prejudices apace, not to say compromising its principles. And that after all was the Oxford which captivated the imagination of Cecil Rhodes, an exemplary Pass-man of the period, with an enthusiasm to the end for Aristotle and Gibbon (both, by our creed, Oxford men!). But for Oxford Rhodes might never have founded Rhodesia; and but for Rhodesia he could never have founded the trust, which has made Oxford more than ever a pan-Britannic University. Yes! If the 'seventies came in rather sheepishly, they went out like a lion. The Commission of 1877 had, so to speak, fired a torch, which waxed and brightened till the catastrophe of 1914 emptied Oxford of her best blood, and extinguished life and letters in her groves and colleges, handing them over to the men of war in khaki and in blue. But a renaissance was in store, and has been in evidence: though whether the infant reborn has strangled the snakes in his cradle, and made his choice between Pleasure and Virtue, is not for the mere remembrancer of those old 'seventies to determine. *Exorietur aliquis.* Let some happier historian, fifty or sixty years hence, review this decade's Commission and its results, what time our 'seventies shall indeed have become but Ancient History.

XI. LIBRARIES: THE BODLEIAN

But men of letters and Societies of Literature will still require of me some report on those institutions in Oxford which may be regarded as in a sense the chief patrons and parents of books; to wit, libraries and presses, or at least the Library and the Press, the goodliest appanages of the University. Where in the wide world are more books and manuscripts to the square mile than in Oxford? Every College from Merton to Keble has its library, sometimes on a monumental scale. In the 'seventies freer access was being given to College libraries, or special libraries for undergraduates were being started: and they had a library of their own at the Union not to be despised. The University possessed in the Taylor Institution an admirable treasury of foreign literature, and at the Museum a Natural Science Library, transferred thither in the 'sixties by the Radcliffe Trustees. Above and before all it had the Bodleian. The magnificence and longevity of Bodley reduce any given decade to a mere episode in its history. The 'seventies comprised the second and less exciting moiety in the reign of the Rev. H. O. Coxe as Librarian, early famous for his crushing repulse of the forger, Simonides ('I have here, Mr Coxe, a very ancient MS. which should certainly be in your Library: to what century would you assign it?'—'To the latter half of the nineteenth century, Mr Simonides'). Coxe may be said to have inaugurated, on his appointment in 1860, the modern age of expert administration, since carried to such high degrees of virtuosity. The chief events of his reign fall into the first decade, notably the loan of the Camera by the Radcliffe Trustees, and its adaptation to the use of the Library as a Reading Room, available after dark. The General Catalogue of Printed Books, begun in 1860, was completed in 1878, and is still in daily use. The year last specified was further marked by the first Annual Meeting of the Library Association, which was holden in Oxford under the presidency of Mr Coxe: before the close of the decade the erection of the New Examination Schools on the High Street set free the ground floor of the Old Schools in Bodley's Quadrangle for Library uses. There was, and is, a pleasant custom at the annual Visitation of the Library for a Student of Christ Church to deliver a Latin oration in praise of Bodley and in commemoration of Bodleian events of the year. Let me here insert three lines from an old Diary. 'Thursday, 8 Nov. 1877. At 12 I gave the Latin speech in Bodley, before a small but select audience: The Dean (Liddell), in the chair: Mark Pattison, Stubbs, Coxe, and one or two more present.' This exploit procured for me my only personal interview with Dr Pusey, who was at the time acting Treasurer. It still costs me a pang to remember that the gold bangle, with suitable inscription engraved, for which I exchanged his cheque, was raped by an un-romantic burglar, some ten years later: and though the poor devil went into penal servitude, my (or rather, her)

Bodley bangle was never retrieved. One other memo-
randum may appeal to others as to me. On the 5th of
July, 1879, Ingram Bywater, M.A., Fellow of Exeter
College, was appointed a Sub-Librarian in succession to
the Rev. J. W. Nutt. But within the year Bywater retired, and resumed his full work in Exeter, where he had
for years been accumulating that store of choice editions
of the classics, which has now by his generous legacy
passed into the possession of Bodley. In those old days,
were you a pupil of his, and had you soothed him with
a morsel of pretty good work, you might find yourself
rewarded by sight of his latest acquisition, and initiated,
with an ironical lisp, into the secret of the three stages
of Bibliomania: first, care for the contents of the book;
secondly, appreciation of paper, print, and margin;
thirdly, the climax, pure love of lovely binding!

XII. THE PRESS

Two at least of the printing presses in Oxford during
the 'seventies may have satisfied Bywater in his most
critical humour: the private press of his friend Daniel,
and the University Press, whose proper title immortalises
its obligation to Clarendon's *History*. The Rev. C. H. O.
Daniel, Fellow, Bursar, and finally Provost of Worcester
College, might almost be described as a born printer. At
the age of nine years (in 1845) he worked a hand press at
home in Frome, with his brothers, and produced, in the
course of some eighteen years, eleven small books, and
hundreds of labels and notices. He resumed his hobby
in Oxford, during our decade; and though the majority
of his productions are dated after its limit, he printed
*Notes from a Catalogue of Pamphlets in Worcester College
Library* in 1874, and two years later *A New Sermon of the
Newest Sort* 1642–3, from a manuscript. With his *Erasmi
Colloquia duo* in 1880 and *The Garland of Rachel*, twelve

months later, he inaugurated a succession of dainty
volumes, chiefly containing poems by his friends (Bridges,
Dixon, Gosse, Sir Herbert Warren, Mrs Woods and others)
destined to be the despair of impecunious bibliophiles.
Mr Falconer Madan, Bodley's Librarian emeritus, our
greatest authority on books printed in Oxford, to whom
I owe many of these details, describes the Daniel press
as 'a pioneer of the Victorian renaissance of English
printing'. Happy those, who possess one or more of
these amateur bibelots, printed not for lucre but for love;
thrice happy, who possess a complete set of *Our Memories*,
one of Daniel's latest productions, wherein form and
substance are alike the printer's own.

For the University Press the 'seventies was a time of
growing prosperity under the capable handling of the
Secretary, the Rev. Bartholomew Price, Sedleian Professor of Natural Philosophy, afterwards Master of
Pembroke, and so a Canon of Gloucester. For thirty
years, from 1868, he was life and soul of the Clarendon
Press. He purchased for the Delegates the Wolvercote
Paper Mill in 1870. His financial ability was further
demonstrated by his success in buying out the partners
in the business (of whom Mr Combe was the last), who,
since the great Dr Fell's time, had shared in the policy,
and the profits, of the undertaking. Under Price's
management the whole became again the sole property
of the University, and for years contributed a substantial
sum to the income of the Chest. The Clarendon Press
Series, a large selection of works chiefly of educational
interest, in twelve separate sections, was begun in 1867,
and continued throughout our decade. In 1879 the *New
English Dictionary* was undertaken by the Press, the
greatest of those 'lexicographical enterprises, which were
Oxford's chief contribution to learning in the latter half
of the nineteenth century'. The production of the Caxton

Memorial Bible, printed, bound, and exhibited on one day, the 30th of June, 1877, was described by Mr Gladstone, who opened the Caxton Exhibition on that same day, at 2 p.m., as 'a feat whieh might be called the climax and consummation of printing'. There was certainly a sporting element, the ambition for a 'record', in the achievement. One perennial publication of the Press originated with the 'seventies, that jejune yet indispensable 'weekly', which evoked from the *Lyra frivola* of A. D. Godley, sometime Public Orator, the immortal lines addressed *To an old Friend*, and concluding as follows:

Place me somewhere that is far from the *Standard* and the *Star*,
    From the fever and the literary fret,—
And the harassed spirit's balm be the academic calm
    Of *The Oxford University Gazette*!

It was like the new Secretary to substitute for the endless flying notices of University engagements and affairs this punctual, accurate, compact, well-printed hebdomadal folio! Mr Price was, indeed, one of the big six (or so) in the Oxford of those days. Council, Chest, Press all found in him their courage and their security. A few plain words from him settled many a debate or division in Congregation. He was an authority. The trust reposed in him, even by young men, was immense. He was in his prime during the 'seventies. Years after, at the age of eighty, he retired from his University offices, and his friends, to manifest their appreciation of his character and services, entertained him at a well-attended dinner in the Hall of the Queen's College, of which he was an Honorary Fellow, President Magrath presiding. The Master of Pembroke was no orator; he had even a slight impediment in his speech; and he never taxed the patience, or the emotions, of his audience. But could any who heard him on that occasion ever forget the three points which he made—so simply, with such obvious sincerity—in replying to the toast of his health? You have praised me (he said in effect) for the successes of my pupils: I can assure you that I have learnt far more from them than I taught them (and he gave some particulars). You have thanked me for what I have been enabled to do for the University: I must confess that I could have done very little, but for the advice of colleagues and friends in the University (and he mentioned some by name). 'And now (he said in conclusion) I am an old man, and my course is well-nigh run: but I am content to lay down my burden; for I am convinced that there are many younger men in the University willing to serve it, and as capable as any who have ever been here; and that we may all look forward with hope and confidence to the future of the Oxford we love.'

With these or such words he ended. And now we too will leave it at that.

§ 11

Cambridge in the 'Seventies

By W. E. Heitland

Looking back on Cambridge in the 'seventies of last
century I find myself in face of two disquieting thoughts
—first, that there are now few able to confirm or correct
anything I may say on the subject; secondly, that my
memories, vivid on certain points, are inevitably blurred
on other details not less significant. I began the 'seventies
as an undergraduate. After graduating in 1871 and becoming a Fellow of St John's College in the same year,
I was engaged with private pupils in Term and Long
Vacation until I was appointed a College Lecturer at the
end of 1872. Though deeply interested in the Academic
questions and movements of that stirring time, I could
not find leisure for taking part in many clubs or societies
formed for discussion of miscellaneous topics. Therefore
any knowledge of advanced views then in vogue among
intellectual cliques reached me mainly through the conversation of friends. I have sometimes thought that in
this way I heard enough. Since those days memoirs of
some notable characters have appeared. In particular,
much light is thrown upon the private history of the
University Reform movement in the *Memoir of Henry
Sidgwick*. Leslie Stephen's *Life of Henry Fawcett* re-
counts the Parliamentary struggle over the necessary
legislation, and with opportune truth reminds us that a
Radical in national politics could be intensely conservative at a College meeting. So it was; I have heard
Leonard Courtney scornfully compared to the Bourbons

by a junior Fellow of St John's. Fawcett was not singular in this respect.

The period of the 'seventies may be described as the time of fermentation in which the aspirations of reformers were taking a clear and practical form. This meant that the attention of our resident members was concentrated on our internal problems to an unusual extent. It may fairly be said that this decade was not specially remarkable for literary productivity, whether serious or playful, in Cambridge itself. The work of Munro and W. H. Thompson, perhaps hardly 'literature' in the vulgar acceptation, was of earlier date: so were the wit and humour of Calverley and G. O. Trevelyan, and the *Saint Paul* of F. W. Myers had appeared in 1867. It should be noted that Cambridge was well represented outside, though mainly in Science. Still there was the Poet Laureate at the head; and among many others there were Seeley, whose *Ecce Homo* appeared in 1865, and Samuel Butler, who since 1864 was back from New Zealand and was incubating the subtle ironies of *Erewhon* (1872) and the *Fair Haven* (1873). Our non-residents were meanwhile turning critical eyes on their old University. Barristers, Professors, Schoolmasters, Journalists and School-inspectors took various points of view. Leslie Stephen's *Sketches from Cambridge by a Don* (1865) was a vivid description of Cambridge life with its fashions and foibles, reprinted from a London paper. But most of this criticism did not find its way into print; and yet was not wholly without effect. A clique of Progressive Rugby masters, and a few of the same colour from other schools, were active allies of Sidgwick and other residents. To them the internal academic difficulties, ever real to the men on the spot, seemed trivial, and they were sometimes out of patience with the slow advance of residents. A Rugby master, dining in Hall and hearing talk of some question of the hour, said, 'Oh, has that already got down here?'

But for those who were to play the part of resident reformers patience was the first necessity. If new Statutes with far-reaching changes were to be their aim (and nothing less was of any use) they had to wait on the convenience of statesmen. Meanwhile it was desirable by writing and intercourse to weaken the resident opposition. For the practical working of new Statutes would largely depend on the state of opinion prevalent among those who would have to work them when passed. Now Cambridge had not been asleep. Before 1870 new subjects had been recognised in Triposes leading to Honour Degrees in Moral and Natural Sciences (1851), and some Colleges had even provided Lecturers, St John's, Trinity and Caius in particular. The names of Venn, Michael Foster, Henry Sidgwick, and Alfred Marshall, taken from the *Calendar* for 1873, will show that this new move was a real advance. The old Philistine attitude—one of Shilleto's stray pieces spoke of 'this Natural rot, this Moral bosh'—had lost some of its appeal in the age of Darwin.

And the year 1869 witnessed some events destined to be of signal importance in the time of struggles now at hand. It was then that Sidgwick resigned his Trinity Fellowship, refusing to be bound any longer by the religious Test; an act followed by his pamphlet on the *Ethics of Conformity and Subscription* in 1870. In 1869 J. R. Seeley returned to Cambridge, and with him the movement for the establishment of a real History School began in earnest. But in my judgment as important, if we look forward to the results achieved in the 'eighties, was the appointment of G. F. Browne as Secretary for the Local Examinations. This post offered openings for gaining influence in various ways. By taking over the administration of the Local Lectures in the same office (1873), and by unsparing activity in the despatch of other University business, the new officer quietly attained an unrivalled share in the control of current affairs. The effect of this industry appeared as time went by. As Secretary to the Commissioners of 1877 he was in close touch with the preparation of the 1882 Statutes. In the following period his co-operation was indispensable to all engaged in University reconstruction. And in the season of reaction against the still existing forces of the old clerical domination it was perhaps a good thing that proceedings were watched by so competent an adviser on the part of the Church. Looking back, I am amazed to recall how little there was of bitter conflict in those days of constant new developments. The moral force of Sidgwick could work in harmony with the Divines in the days of Lightfoot, Westcott and Hort. The endless claims of the Natural Sciences, pushed with relentless vigour and undeniably overdue, still left room for those of History and cognate studies. It is fair to credit this happy result partly to what Leslie Stephen calls the Cambridge 'system vigorous if narrow', the sound training of which was 'favourable to a masculine but limited type of understanding'. But the men who saw it through, as agents of a great change, without arousing violent storms of 'masculine' prejudice, surely deserve no little praise.

Enough has been said to show that even after the abolition of Religious Tests internal opposition to serious changes remained strong in Cambridge. Private interests honestly created, and prepossessions generally sincere, were alarmed by the now unmistakable intentions of Parliament. Sulky acquiescence rather than hearty co-operation was therefore the temper of a majority. Against this the energy and self-sacrifice of the resident reformers carried on a long struggle, gradually gaining ground as vacancies in the course of nature or ecclesiastical preferment brought a younger generation on the stage. The spiritual light and leading of the reformers was incarnated in Henry Sidgwick first and foremost. Others supported him ably, but it was in him that the heroic and saintly element needed for inspiring younger men never failed, an influence operating by example as well as precept. His action in 1869–70 brought to a head the Tests question, settled in 1871. This matter, till then shelved by Parliament, was causing some excitement among undergraduates in my time. I remember being enticed to a meeting in a student's rooms and pressed to sign a form of protest against the repeal. I was told that, being a member of the Church of England and not prepared to secede from it, my plain duty was to sign. I did not. This illustrates the sort of thing that was going on in the Colleges. The bigotry of some of our elders was raising the cry of 'Sacrilege' at any attempt to 'pervert' the intentions of 'Pious Founders', and quietly encouraging us youngsters to bleat in unison with their protestations. It must be remembered that Dissenters and Jews had for years past been admitted as students, and some of them had won great distinction in examinations. But they could only take the M.A. as a titular degree, not giving membership of the Senate; and they were shut out from Fellowships by the Test. It was notorious that the 'religious' opposition to their claims simply amounted to a refusal to surrender the monopoly of emoluments and power. In 1870 not a few undergraduates were beginning to think for themselves and to view such doings with contempt.

The narrow-minded attitude I have described was fully in evidence all through the 'seventies, though less and less openly displayed as the inevitable drew near. Opportune preferment now and then thinned the ranks of

stalwarts. A good case is that of a grotesquely demon-
strative cleric, who had been a Dissenter himself in his
youth but had seen the error of his ways. In 1876 an
attractive College living fell vacant and induced him to
retire to parish duties. But such openings came slowly,
and did not meet the case of men not in Orders. And the
lay element in the corporate bodies was steadily growing,
and in it were both Nonconformists and so-called Free-
thinkers of various shades. The old school of College Dons
had succeeded in alienating the sympathies of the rising
generation, and there was no small danger that, when
Reform began in earnest, extreme views might prevail.
That this did not happen, was partly due to the sobering
effect of financial interests, and partly to the mistrust
aroused by the visionary proposals of 'cranks'. It was
most important that Cambridge should not feel conscious
of casting away the heritage of prudent thoroughness in
which she had been used to take an innocent pride.

If I am to give a reasonably fair sketch of the influences
at work in Cambridge during the 'seventies, I must say
something of the young men who were then growing up,
destined some of them to bear leading parts in after years.
In a period of acute public controversies, when Press and
Pulpit resounded with the voices of attack and defence,
there were plenty of gifted youths eager to call most
received traditions in question. In the case of men more
or less isolated in small Colleges, where 'advanced' views
found little sympathy, there was not much opening for
social gatherings and exchanges of opinion. Some little
intercollegiate societies there were in which members
could let off their pet theories in an atmosphere of coffee
and criticism. But I think these safety-valves were few.
The effective centre for propounding and testing new
ideas was and continued to be Trinity, where the size of
the College and the presence just then of an exceptionally
brilliant circle of talented youths made such co-operative

bouts of thinking comparatively easy. This was the time
of the Balfour brothers, F. W. Maitland, and others of
the first order. W. K. Clifford only left for a London
Professorship in 1871, and was still in touch with Cambridge. Most of these died young, and strictly belong to
the 'seventies. Behind these bright young figures stood
that of Henry Sidgwick, a maturer seeker after truth,
writing books on Ethics and already giving thought to
Metaphysics, Political Economy, Political Science, and
many other subjects. The relations between him and the
younger men were for various reasons[1] unusually close;
and it was largely through the impression made by this
intellectual company that Cambridge began to lose some
of its old self-satisfaction.

Meanwhile thoughts and pens were not all engaged in
the warfare of serious controversy. If in light literature
the output of the period hardly rivals that of its predecessor, when Calverley and G. O. Trevelyan flourished,
there was no lack of shortlived[2] publications in which
youthful enterprise found vent. Among these I recall the
armchair papers of the *Cambridge Tatler* in 1871–2, in
which V. H. Stanton and A. J. Mason were concerned,
but I think the most notable contributor was Christopher
Wordsworth. All these three were of Trinity. Of certain
very ephemeral journalistic efforts I can remember one
or two names such as the *Moslem*, and *Momus* in which
E. H. Palmer wrote. But by far the wittiest product of
those days was the *Light Green*, where true genius enlarged the scope of Parody with a skill that lifted it high
in the region of literary art. In it occurred, during a
Littlego-examination scene, two lines still often quoted:

> And, though they wrote it all by rote,
> They did not write it right.

[1] See *H. Sidgwick*, a Memoir, *passim* and especially p. 320.
[2] I would note that the Johnian *Eagle*, started in 1859 by S. Butler
and others, is still in flight.

The author[1] was A. C. Hilton, an undergraduate of St John's, who was the chief contributor to the two numbers that appeared. Both in verse and in prose this is the brightest of such publications within my memory—yes, even though the next period saw the early work of Owen Seaman and A. R. Ropes, and the flashes of H. R. Tottenham, J. K. Stephen and R. H. Forster. Indeed I can hardly refrain from further quotations to illustrate the versatile ingenuity with which contemporary writers and academic foibles are alike subjected to jets of happy and original banter. Venom there is none, and the jibes of irresponsible youth play alike on Carlyle or Swinburne, Tennyson or Bret Harte, the *Cambridge Tatler* or the Proctorial system.

One topic seems to call for a paragraph to itself. In the 'sixties the subject of Dreams, Ghost stories, Spiritualism, and the credibility and explanation of alleged phenomena, began to attract considerable interest. I cannot pass over this topic altogether. For among those to whom such problems appealed were Henry Sidgwick and F. W. Myers, through whom the staid unemotional Cambridge received its share of what was to become a widespread infection. The Society for Psychical Research was founded in 1882. That Cambridge men took no small part in its doings, truly indicates that it was largely the outcome of the interest taken in such things here during the 'seventies, though its proceedings took place mostly in London. I am not going to discuss a matter of which I am not competent to speak. But one fact of curious coincidence seems to me well worth mentioning. It was in the 'seventies that E. H. Palmer was residing in Cambridge. This extraordinary linguist, familiar with Oriental tongues and the Oriental appetite for mystery and for

---

[1] Of whom there is a little *Life*, with his literary remains, by Sir Robert Edgcumbe, Cambridge, 1904.

mystery's antidote (conjuring by sleight of hand, in which he was a master), was from the first a sceptical observer of 'Spiritualistic' doings. He believed that the phenomena on which the Psychical researchers relied were capable of being produced by human agency. He gave now and then performances as a confessed conjurer, baffling detection, and constituting a challenge to those who asserted spiritual co-operation in enterprises of the same kind. Between the two views of what passed for evidence I am not fitted to judge; but the fact of their existing side by side is testimony to the interest taken in the subject at Cambridge. On the part of the Psychical seekers there was an honest search for truth with open mind. In the next period we find them employing the services of Richard Hodgson, who exposed the fraud of Madame Blavatsky. But human curiosity in the matter of human immortality still kept alive interest in the problems discussed, and has left them unsolved to the present hour.

It is hardly possible to refer to this 'spiritual' topic without saying something as to the strictly 'religious' situation in the 'seventies. The old Simeonite movement, still powerful in the 'fifties, but already betraying its insufficiency, was no longer an element of importance in Cambridge life. Here and there its principles survived in small cliques, and at least one College was proud to be an Evangelical centre. What really undermined it was neither indifference nor ridicule, but the encroachments of sound learning. Inconsiderate piety, the descendant of eighteenth-century enthusiasm, was steadily lowering the educational standard of the Low Church clergy. This evil called for a remedy, and the great Divines to whom I have referred above were leaders in the endeavour to find one. They not only encouraged scholarly study by every means in their power; they discouraged narrow-minded aloofness from men of different or deficient creed, and themselves held intercourse on equal terms with freethinking laymen of undoubted sincerity. The little society[1] that used to meet at Trumpington Vicarage in the 'sixties marked a stage in this liberalising movement, which went on all through the 'seventies, and helped to keep Cambridge free from the curse of bitterness. The Professors even arranged for lectures on non-Christian religions. I was present on an occasion of the kind. E. H. Palmer was to discourse on Islam, and his reputation drew a large audience. The Divinity Faculty was represented by Westcott and others. Palmer was not the man to attune his utterances to the orthodox proprieties of the place, and treated his subject freely. Towards the end of his address he remarked that Muhammad in his later days was driven to use a certain amount of imposture; but over this he passed lightly, hinting that such lapse was not peculiar to the Prophet among religious enthusiasts. I noticed a slight shudder in some of the company at this frank avowal. Then the meeting, which had opened with prayer, ended with a few earnest words from Westcott, conveying our joint thanks to Palmer. He told us that he had himself given much study to the chief religions of the world, and had come to the conclusion that Christianity as known to us in our own Church was the best of all. This, coming in all good faith from the Regius Professor of Divinity, may serve to illustrate the innocent sincerity of the speaker. The declaration was quite unexpected and hardly called for, and it was not easy to repress a smile. The fact that a meeting of the kind could be well attended is evidence of the interest then taken by serious students in religious topics. F. D. Maurice, who died in 1872, had been a stimulating leader in many good movements, but in religious matters the indefinite nature

---

[1] See *H. Sidgwick*, a Memoir, pp. 184-7.

of his doctrines was a clog on their influence. It was
significant of the Cambridge dislike for an attitude of
balance and hesitation—a dislike due to intensive culture
of the mathematical mind—that the Professorship
vacated by Maurice was given to a clergyman of Evangelical leanings. Sidgwick in defeat judged the electors
and their choice with full Christian charity. But of the
inner meaning of the episode there could not be much
doubt.

When I say that the old Simeonite movement was no
longer a power in the 'seventies, I feel bound to say also
that about 1873–5 the Revivalist crusade of Moody and
Sankey reached Cambridge. American enthusiasm, ever
ready to 'go one better' than Europe in religion as in
other things, was suddenly turned upon our little student
world. Whether this undertaking had been in any way
inspired by the unfavourable picture of Cambridge morals
in the 'forties drawn by C. A. Bristed (New York, 1851),
I cannot tell. At all events the new evangelists, artists
in emotional procedure, succeeded in luring undergraduates
to their meetings, in convincing them of sin (their own
and their neighbours'), and in inducing not a few to seek
a cure by American methods. So far as I know, no lasting
result was achieved. But I came across temporary manifestations that could not be ignored. A captain of a Boat
Club was so possessed by the spirit of the Revival that
he (so undergraduate critics declared) chose oarsmen by
a mixed standard; and indeed his boat, for whatever
reason, was a failure. Now young men talk, not always
wisely, but a College Boat is a sacred thing, and even the
mere suspicion that any officer is playing fast and loose
with its prospects is enough to condemn him as a 'bad
sportsman'. No Moody and Sankey propaganda could
neutralise so deep-rooted a prejudice. And stories of
grotesque doings passed round, such as that of a man

inviting his gyp to a private prayer-meeting in his gyp-room; an offer declined for lack of leisure. So the campaign accomplished no permanent results in changing habits, and in a few years' time it was completely forgotten.

The movement for promoting the Higher Education of Women, and the steps by which it made its first permanent home at Cambridge, have been described so often and so well that little need be said here. The settlement at Hitchin in 1869, and the removal to Girton, record the approach from outside; the establishment of a new examination designed for women, and the provision of lectures in 1869–70, belong to the scheme devised by Cambridge residents on somewhat different lines. The latter began with lodgings or hire of a house, and the first block of residential buildings known then as Newnham Hall was not occupied till 1875. The enterprise had behind it many of the leading academic Liberals of the time. To mention the names of Adams, Bateson, Maurice, Liveing, Bonney, Peile, Ferrers, Venn, the Fawcetts, and the Kennedys, may give a very imperfect roll of honour. Some (Sidgwick for instance) bore financial risks in the venture, and Mrs Bateson acted as treasurer. Histories of Girton and Newnham Colleges supply the details of a development truly astounding. The point I would press here is that the time and interest of many active graduates were during the 'seventies much engaged in forwarding this movement, which gradually became a regular feature of Cambridge life. The admission of women to Tripos examinations (by courtesy of examiners) was not granted officially until 1881, after a good-humoured struggle. The noted triumphs of Miss Ramsay (1887) and Miss Fawcett (1890) were generally welcomed. There was as yet no sign of a reactionary sentiment somewhat analogous to the jealous attitude of Trade Unions.

Controversies on educational matters are peculiarly apt to call forth strange varieties of opinion. One question on which in the 'seventies divergent views were held was the educative value of experiments. That experimental sciences were destined to fill a much larger place in the Cambridge of the future, was as certain as anything could be. But by some graduates of the old school this prospect was not warmly welcomed. It was urged that for examination purposes (here we meet the idol of the day) they were of little or no value. Endlessly repeated, with results long ascertained, they were no real tests of the candidates' capacity, in short, a waste of time. I have often listened to criticisms of the kind from mathematicians. And Isaac Todhunter in his essay on the *Conflict of Studies* (1873), speaking of the 'value of experiments so called', endorses this view. He holds that a pupil ought to take well-established facts on trust. 'If he does not believe the statements of his tutor—probably a clergyman of mature knowledge, recognised ability, and blameless character—his suspicion is irrational, and manifests a want of the power of appreciating evidence.' Many a reader then smiled at this utterance. It is cited here as truthfully suggesting the quaint and honest opinions that helped to make up the mental atmosphere of those days; that is, the environment in which reformers had to do battle for their ideals. Cambridge had gloried in her Senior Wranglers, and for that glory she was paying a price.

Of all the subjects that were engrossing the attention of Cambridge residents none was more important than the question how to revive the prestige and efficiency of official teaching; that is, to prevent its being more and more thrust into the background by the parasitic growth of private tuition. For many years past reformers at both Oxford and Cambridge had advocated a revival of the

Professorial system. At Oxford the College Tutorial system had been becoming the dominant feature of the teaching arrangements, as I believe it still is. At Cambridge, neither Professors nor College Lecturers could compete successfully with the private 'Coaches'. Rightly or not, the student who sought Honours in a Tripos mistrusted official teaching as a means of securing for him the highest possible place in the list; and on his place in the so-called 'order of merit' much depended. To some it meant the chance of a Fellowship, to many more it made all the difference between a more or less favourable start in a professional career. To the average 'Poll' Man, who sought an Ordinary Degree with the least possible mental exertion, the Poll Coach was recommended by the belief that he would impart to his pupils nothing beyond the bare minimum needed for passing muster; that is, for defeating the examiners. In both cases, Honours or Poll, the supply of teaching followed the demand. The consumer did not ask for teaching as an educational boon, but to secure an official record of performance that carried a certain economic and social value. On the face of it the Coach gave him what he asked. If Hamblin Smith nevertheless did do something to educate his Poll men, that was owing to his skill, and few of them would be conscious of the benefit. Now the order of merit in Honour lists and the low pass standard of the Poll were, as things stood in the 'seventies, main features of our examination system. The first was generally regarded with pride, and the second tolerated as representing possible requirements in view of the present state of education in the country.

So far as Honours were concerned, there was no prospect of any change while 'order of merit' prevailed. But some attempt had been made to improve the Poll course by regulations requiring the candidates for an

Ordinary Degree to have attended the lectures of certain Professors, and to produce certificates of attendance. This plan furnished some Professors with classes; and some people fancied that this was in part its object. But to enforce the rule was not a simple matter, and stories of tricks and evasions were current, exaggerated no doubt, but discrediting this solution of an awkward problem. So it happened that in 1876-7 compulsory attendance at Professorial lectures became a 'live issue' in our academic politics, provoking warm controversy. Reports of syndicates, discussions in the Senate, and a shower of fly-sheets, signalised one of the most animated battles of opinion within my memory. Divinity lectures were not those most directly in question, as the compulsion chiefly came from the Bishops in their conditions of Ordination. Yet Dr Lightfoot put forth a portentous fly-sheet, a pamphlet of twelve octavo pages. Fawcett (for Political Economy was a subject in favour with Poll men as something of a novelty) wrote a characteristically frank letter to his friend James Porter of Peterhouse, deprecating change. This the warm-hearted Porter rashly published to the Senate, and exposed Fawcett and himself to the brisk censure of Blore and others. We young men looked on with amusement. Eventually the compulsion had to be abandoned, and the questions then raised had to be dealt with on other lines. The modern Poll Degree is worthy of a great University, and the abolition of order of merit has restored official teaching to efficiency and vigour.

That this grave matter of educational policy was of sufficient importance to claim a large share of the attention of residents, is hardly to be denied. But we must not overlook the fact that a series of striking events abroad had in recent years aroused a special interest in what I may call the 'professorial question'. A notoriously

Professor-ridden people had proved its superiority to all the nations of Europe in practical qualities. To England, and not least to Cambridge, the result of the wars from 1866 to 1871 was a sharp and much-needed lesson. It was not easy to grasp all at once the truth that an educational system with the Professoriate at its head could be the nurse of such prodigious national efficiency. But old English prepossessions were shaken for good. The Government dealt with army reform and elementary education. Meanwhile the old Cambridge self-satisfaction and pride in present institutions began to give way. German ideas and German experience gained respect at the cost of French, a reaction perhaps at the moment excessive, but effectual in preparing men's minds for a period of academic reform. As a sign of the times it may be noted that in 1870 the subject proposed for an University prize essay called forth a learned response in the form of two works on University Life and Studies in the Eighteenth Century. These books (1874 and 1877), dealing with Oxford as well as Cambridge, were by Christopher Wordsworth of Trinity and Peterhouse. Whether the authorities who provoked this inquiry were beginning to suspect that the existing system (dominated by private tuition) was a recent growth, and entitled to no respect on the ground of antiquity, I cannot tell. At all events the books left an impression to that effect on the minds of some readers.

At the back of all these movements and conflicts of opinion, certain convictions were in process of formation, and were by the middle of the 'seventies tacitly assumed. It was evident that something would be done to provide a regular academic career for teachers in Cambridge itself, in fact to recognise official teaching (and research) as a profession in which men might spend their lives. Also that this implied stipends on a living-wage scale; for in a scheme of permanent employment to require celibacy was impossible. But internal debate had proved to a certainty that without external pressure nothing effectual would be done. For any move to strengthen the University large sums of money would be required. The Statutes of 1860 had empowered Colleges to make voluntary contributions to the University funds, but of this naïve permission the Colleges had not made use, and did not seem likely to do so. Public opinion therefore had to find expression in Parliament if the necessary compulsion was to be applied. It is worth noting that the Inquiry Commission of 1872 was appointed by a Liberal Government, but its Report in 1874 had to be dealt with by a Conservative one. I conjecture that the sagacity of Disraeli knew better than to impair the fortunes of his party by shelving an inevitable reform merely to gratify a few academic Die-hards of doubtful merit and undoubted appetite for preferments. The Executive Commission of 1877 was the result. The Act provided for compulsion. Passive resistance on the part of a College would only involve the imposition of new Statutes framed by the Commissioners without regard to the wishes of the Fellows.

At the end of 1877 we had to set to work discussing our policy; that is, what changes we were ready to propose ourselves, and how we could persuade the Commissioners to be content with so much. On this latter aim a good deal of ingenuity was vainly spent in some Colleges. The Commissioners stood firm, particularly on points of finance, and the scheme for College contributions to the University was not modified in deference to College protests. Nor was due allowance made for a possible fall in College incomes, which was already in sight and had disastrous effects after 1879. But for the moment it was the dreadful waste of time and energy in College meetings that was most deplorable. In these wearisome debates every one present had views, many supported their views by arguments, few were convinced, all had something better to do. The additional strain on mind and body was very trying to men who had regular work to be carried on. The habit of debate even affected the ordinary speech of conversation: men would inadvertently use the *cliché* 'I venture to think'. From this exhausting experience the larger Colleges suffered most; the smaller corporations (at least many of them) offered less opportunities for long debate. In Trinity a wise foresight had reached some degree of preliminary settlement before the Act of 1877 was formally in force. So the later 'seventies left many active workers tired and ready to welcome even unpalatable changes as bringing with them a hope of respite from unprofitable talk.

It may be well to bear in mind that the Cambridge of the 'seventies did not consist exclusively of active partisans busy in promoting or opposing projects of reform. Of the cynically indifferent there is no need to speak, for they were few and of no great importance. But there were savants of distinction who took little or no part in the agitations of the time, whatever their views might individually be. This was the attitude of several Professors, who may have preferred not to appear as advocates of a new system in which the Professoriate was presumably to take a more prominent position. But there were others, not Professors, who avoided public debate; of whom Henry Bradshaw the University Librarian was an illustrious specimen. To his profound learning, and his unfailing readiness to place it at the service of others, a choir of students have borne witness. It was a wholesome and proper thing that such men, upholders of the University's reputation in the world, should not turn their talents to the 'rough-and-tumble' controversies of the passing hour. The names of Sir G. Stokes and Clerk Max-

well may suffice to remind us of the serene continuity of
research that went on unbroken. A curious detail of the
time was the increasing difficulty in persuading the non-
resident Professor of International Law to perform
regularly in person the duties of his office. This eventually
led to the appointment of a deputy, but dissatisfaction
did not cease.

There were also not a few elders, notable in various
ways, who saw the 'seventies in and did not see them out.
Survivors from a state of things now passing away, they
were picturesque or quaint figures, subjects of gossip and
legend. Old Adam Sedgwick died in 1873, B. W. Beatson
in 1874, R. Shilleto in 1876. C. W. King, the collector of
engraved gems, lived till 1888. But these men, whatever
their personal views, can hardly be credited with much
influence on the movements of the period. They have their
place in the setting of the academic scene, but they were
not the active characters. On the literary side of the
University the most shining light was R. C. Jebb, not
destined to become Professor of Greek until 1889, who
proved that high scholarship was compatible with versatile elegance and ease. But in referring to this accomplished scholar I am reminded of the unhappy ineffective-
ness of the Professorships of Greek and Latin. The election
of Dr Kennedy to the Greek chair in 1867 was one of the
last instances of preferment bestowed as a reward for
past service, not as a retaining-fee for services to come.
The retiring Professor Dr W. H. Thompson had given a
special character to his office by devoting his lectures to
work of a high order, above the ordinary range of College
teaching. After thirty-six years as schoolmaster, Dr
Kennedy was no longer in touch with the up-to-date
results of scholarly research, and could not like his predecessor attract small classes of the best students. So
with all his great merits he was not a success as a lecturer.

The Latin Professorship founded in his honour (but in-
sufficiently endowed) was first held by Munro (1869–72).
On Munro's retirement in 1872, John E. B. Mayor was
appointed, and held the office for nearly thirty-nine years
till his death in 1910. At the risk of being tedious, I
venture to devote special paragraphs to an appreciation
of this extraordinary man, whose virtues and failings
were known to me through many years of intimacy, and
of whom I retain an affectionate memory.

John Eyton Bickersteth Mayor, a pupil of Dr Kennedy
at Shrewsbury school, Third Classic in 1848, was a signal
instance of what an insatiable appetite for learning, uncontrolled by a sense of measure and proportion, can and
cannot achieve. Great muscular strength, combined with
an exceptionally sound constitution, left him free from
limitations that have hampered many great scholars.
Able to do without exercise, save for occasional resort to
heavy dumb-bells, his industry soon gained him the
repute of extraordinary learning, deservedly. For three
years 1864–7 he was University Librarian, an office in
which he initiated some changes of system that I have
heard one of his successors describe as 'judicious in
themselves, but he never carried them out'. It was a
pity, for his knowledge of languages ancient and modern
was beyond that of any other resident. After his pre-
mature retirement from this post, he settled down to
College duties as Fellow and Lecturer of St John's, in
which capacity I first knew him. Genial and popular
with the men, his influence as a teacher was very slight.
Acting on the assumption that all students were eager to
learn, and were willing to take the trouble of following
up hints given in lecture by private researches on their
own part, he gained no hold on the average undergraduate. And the better students would have preferred
to receive the fruit of his learning in a more ordered and

coherent form. I believe he never prepared a lecture as a lecture, but turned on his tap of erudition and let it run. This method did not suit men looking forward to a Tripos examination; but for such considerations he had a heavenly contempt. To seek advice from him as to a course of reading (freely given) left you staring in amazement at an ideal plan bearing no relation to the facts of the contemporary world.

The truth was that Mayor's dominating impulse was to learn, not to teach. All the while he was accumulating vast stores of detail on a variety of subjects. I wonder what has become of the enormous commonplace-books of which I had a sight now and then. English History, particularly in the seventeenth century, was one of the topics. He did edit and publish five biographical books of that period, and some were brought out after his death by Dr M. R. James. He made raids on College records and edited Baker's *History of St John's*, but the register of Admissions had to be completed by the present Master. It was the same with classical works. I recall one excellent little book which under great pressure he was driven to complete before publication. But in two other cases a part only was issued and the rest never appeared. I suggested to him that he should hand over his notes to a competent deputy, who would bring out the rest. He replied that he must keep faith with the public, and so the books remain fragments to this day. When made Professor, he gleefully remarked that now he would have leisure to finish his books. But it was again the old story; he added masses of illustrative notes to his already massive Juvenal, but still left three of the Satires untouched, though to my knowledge he had by him a prodigious collection of material ready to hand. And so he passed on to a stage in which one passing enthusiasm speedily gave way to another, and in his latter years he was chiefly known as a champion of the so-called Old-Catholics and a Vegetarian Food-reformer. Thus it befel that a passion for heaping-up and never clearing-up, in uncritical innocence treating all details as of equal value (this was a grave defect in an official examiner), made the Professorship in his hands a nullity. Yet his simple tolerance and his personal charm silenced censure and made him a saintly figure, revered to the last. I need hardly say that he was at the mercy of servants and other subordinates. In two cases his simplicity was exploited by Germans to their own profit. A characteristic episode was the disappearance of a Latin dictionary crammed with manuscript additions, the fruit of years. Such a loss was irreparable, so he offered a reward of £5 for its recovery. It struck his gyp that he (the gyp) had used a large book to prop up the Professor's bed, a leg of which was broken. In the joy of happy restitution the cash reward seemed but a trivial portion of the owner's gratitude. That the experience might conceivably recur, was warmly rejected as the suggestion of unworthy cynicism. One of the fancies of his old age was an impulse to rescue others from oblivion by writing their biographies. With great difficulty he was prevented from publishing a Life of Dr Luard the Registrary. But on Isaac Todhunter he lavished all the resources of research and imagination. Though not an intimate friend of the hero, he spun out a wonderful analysis of his character and motives with naïve indiscretion, distressing to the family. The pamphlet of sixty pages (1884) is a literary curiosity of the first order. Enthusiasm, irrelevant and often grotesque, expressed in English of singular grace and purity, surely never outdid itself with more success. One specimen may well be quoted. Speaking of Todhunter's love of animals, he says, 'For dogs in general he manifested little sympathy, distrusting their self-control'.

And many other passages were equally quaint. Of the world around him he knew less and less as he became more and more visionary in his last years. Only too generous in appreciation of the work of others, he was beloved by all who knew him well, and it is sad to reflect that the immense collections he left behind in notebooks cannot be turned to good account by others. I look upon the story of John Mayor as a warning to anyone who is tempted to follow the same course. That great abilities, industriously employed in a long life, should not bequeath the full results[1] of research to after times, is a lamentable waste. And, though the silent tragedy went on more than thirty years longer, its earlier scenes were a feature of the 'seventies.

That this attempt to describe the influences at work in Cambridge during a brief period is so to speak 'full of omissions', I am painfully aware. Space fails me to dwell on the activities of many men whose initiative in various projects or devotion to responsible duties served to make our society what it then was. James Stuart may stand as representing the University Extension movement. But a group of College Tutors, busy in various ways with improving the management of undergraduates, marked a wholesome development of existing machinery. Methods might and did differ, but modern ideals of the relation of Tutor to pupil surely owe much to the examples of Augustus Austen Leigh, H. Latham, C. E. Searle, John Peile, E. S. Roberts and H. A. Morgan. Behind the controversial foreground of the picture a change for the better was unobtrusively proceeding, without legislation or fuss. To one resident in the 'seventies, and warmly interested in movements of all kinds, this silent better-

---

[1] For a list of the numerous articles and notices published by him on a variety of subjects see the Johnian *Eagle* for March, June and December 1911, with a full obituary notice by several hands.

ment of normal Donhood seems worth recording as an item in an old man's memories. The relation of Guardian and Wards is one that brings the College Tutor in touch with parents of pupils, making him conscious of a body of external opinion that is noiseless but often important. In times of change, when it is desirable to estimate rightly the probable effect of changes on the students generally, it is wise to give a full hearing to the College Tutors. In my opinion the reformers of the 'seventies (Sidgwick included) were occasionally too ready to disregard them.

And here let me end my recollections of a stirring time, in which the course of changes that had so far been almost wholly due to pressure from without was being quickened and smoothed by a responsive movement within. I wish I could remember more and set it forth better. But, if I cannot quite say with Wordsworth that 'in that dawn to be young was very Heaven', I may confess that it was good to be alive. I am sure there were others who felt so too. Weary of worn-out methods of teaching and discipline, administered by worthy seniors on whom the lessons of experience seemed wasted, no wonder many of the younger men indulged in the 'pleasant exercise of hope and joy'—too eagerly, perhaps; but not without excuse. It is a comfort in 1929 to feel as I do that so many eager hopes have so far ended in little disappointment. Surely the men of the somewhat stormy 'seventies did their duty well according to their lights, and deserve kindly recognition from us and from the generations to come.

Index

274 Index

Index

Index

Sterne, Laurence, 23, 198; *Tristram Shandy*, 23
Stevenson, Robert Louis, 22, 35, 110; *Travels with a Donkey*, 23, 48
Steventon, 111
Strachey, Lytton, 204; *Eminent Victorians*, 204
Stretton, Hesba, 53, 54; *The Doctor's Dilemma*, 55
Sullivan, Arthur (*see also* Gilbert, W. S.), 145, 147
Sullivan, French play, 138
Sunderland, Thomas, 3
Sweets, the, 224
Swift, Jonathan, 208
Swinburne, Algernon Charles, 15, 59, 60, 87, 97, 98, 99, 117, 161, 162, 163, 164, 175, 176, 177, 180, 191, 207, 256; *Atalanta in Calydon*, 15, 99; *Bothwell*, 161, 162, 163, 176, 177, 178, 179, 180; *Chastelard*, 162, 180; *Poems and Ballads*, 59, 76, 99; *The Queen Mother*, 162; *Rosamund*, 162; *Study of Shakespeare*, 207
Symonds, John Addington, 103; *The Renaissance*, 223; *The Renaissance in Italy*, 223

Tabb, John Banister, 103
de Tabley, Lord, 106; *Collected Poems*, 106; *Misrepresentation*, 106; *Philoctetes*, 106
Taine, Hippolyte, 160
Talbot, E. S., 232
Tasso, Torquato, 88
Tatton, R. G., 227
Tay Bridge disaster, 48
Taylor, Joseph, 64
Taylor Institution, 243
Taylor, Tom, 140, 152, 167, 168; *Anne Boleyn*, 167; *Joan of Arc*, 153; *'Twixt Axe and Crown*, 153
Temple, Dr Frederick, 227
Temple, Sir William, 112
Tennyson, Alfred, 1, 2, 12, 60, 76, 86, 97, 98, 117, 120, 161, 164, 165, 166, 168, 170, 171, 172, 173, 175, 191, 193, 195, 197, 256; *Idylls of the King*, 197; *In Me-*

moriam, 98; *Poems*, 98; *The Princess*, 98; *Queen Mary*, 164, 165, 166, 197
Terry, Ellen, 159
Thackeray, W. M., 2, 8, 17, 22, 23, 25, 26, 27, 28, 31, 33, 53, 83, 198; *Pendennis*, 24
Thackeray, Anne, 55
Theatres: City, 136; Court, 183; Garrick, 146; Globe, 154; Haymarket, 139, 147, 158, 167; Lyceum, 151, 159, 165; Marylebone, 137; New, 242; Old Vic., 242; Olympic, 136; Prince of Wales's, 137, 139, 141, 144, 146, 154, 156, 158, 159; Princess's, 158; Queen's, 137, 138; Royal Windsor, 138; Royal Woolwich, 138; Sadler's Wells, 142; Savoy, 145; Surrey, 137; Vaudeville, 148, 150, 156
Theocritus, 88
Thiers, Monsieur, speech of, 10
Thirlwall, C., 2
Thompson, Francis, 101, 110
Thompson, W. H., 3, 150, 267
Thomson, James ("B.V."), 97, 105, 108, 109, 117; *City of Dreadful Night*, 105, 108, 109
Times, The, 10, 46
Tippings, the, 232
Tocqueville, A. C. H. C. de, 6
Todhunter, Isaac, 261, 270; *Conflict of Studies*, 261; Life of, 270
Tottenham, A. R., 256
Touts, the, 232
Townley, 76
Townshend, Meredith, 193
Toynbee, Arnold, 240
Traill, Dr H., 83
Trench, R. C., 2
Trevelyan, G. O., 250, 255
Trollope, Anthony, 15, 17, 23, 28, 40, 53; *An Eye for an Eye*, 40; *Ayala's Angel*, 40; 'Barchester' stories, 40; *Prime Minister*, 23, 40; *Vicar of Bullhampton*, 40; *Way we live now, The*, 40
Tucker, Charlotte, 54
Turneur, Cyril, 35
Tutankhamen, 72